THE MOUNTAIN SCHOOL

Greg Alder

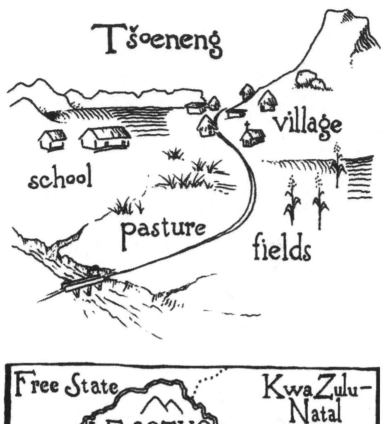

Tšoeneng

village

school

pasture

fields

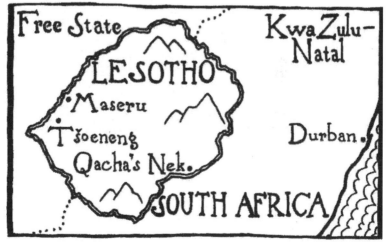

Free State

KwaZulu-Natal

LESOTHO

• Maseru

• Tšoeneng

Qacha's Nek •

Durban •

SOUTH AFRICA

Writing is about getting messages out. Publishing is about controlling the
distribution of those messages. It is therefore beneficial that the writer
also assumes the role of publisher.

Printed in the United States of America

First printing, 2013

Grateful acknowledgement is made to Mark Jenkins for permission to
reprint the excerpt from "Leap Year."

Cover photo by Lerato Thaki
Cover design by Julie Rubtchinsky
Maps by Greg Alder

Title typeface: Ride My Bike
Display typeface: Century Gothic
Text typeface: Garamond

This book is available on Amazon.com, by special order from your local
bookstore, or at www.gregalder.com

ISBN: 978-0-9886822-0-7

To the memory of my father,
Michael Reed Alder,
20 August 1952 – 4 July 2002

And to my mother,
Cynthia Ann Alder

CONTENTS

Author's Note

Acknowledgements
Pronunciation Guide

AUTHOR'S NOTE

THE USE OF TITLES when addressing adults was so deeply inculcated in me while I lived in Lesotho that even now I can't think of people's names separated from their titles. All women get *'me* (*mme*) before their names and all men get *ntate*. If you were to use a man's name without the ntate, it would be like calling him a boy. For me, to even think of ntate Santu as just Santu, for example, makes me afraid he can hear my thoughts. So at the risk of annoying the reader I use such titles throughout the book.

Nevertheless, I tried to make a concession to readability with regard to a few names. I refer to 'me Tsita as Principal Tsita, and instead of ntate Thabo and ntate Santu it's Chief Thabo and Witchdoctor Santu. I know that it can be a challenge to keep track of foreign names, so I hope this helps.

Lastly, I entirely changed one name. The subject matter is sensitive where she falls into my story, and I see no benefit in possibly complicating her life.

GREG ALDER
CALIFORNIA
JANUARY 2013

PART I

To travel is to expect much of the places you visit; to move to one of these places is to expect much of yourself.

- MARK JENKINS

CHAPTER ONE

Breakdown

I ARRIVED IN TŠOENENG when the boys had just come down the mountain from initiation school. They had spent months secluded up there, from spring into summer, being circumcised and learning to fight with sticks: becoming men. When at last it was time to descend from the mountain top and return to the village, they stripped off all their clothes and lay them on the floor of the thatch hut they had built and lived in during their initiation. Then they lit the hut, called a *mophato*, on fire. The burning *mophato* symbolized their youth, going up in flames, turning to smoke and ashes, disappearing. That phase of their life was done. And as the new men walked away from it, they were to never look back.

I knew that I was going to go through my own kind of initiation in Tšoeneng, only I had imagined it would be more straightforward than it turned out to be. Mostly, I thought I would be learning a bunch of new facts. Everything about the place was new. When I first got the news from Peace Corps that they were sending me to live for two years in a country called Lesotho I thought, There's a country called Lesotho? I bought a Lonely Planet guidebook, which lumped it in with South Africa and Swaziland, its nearest neighbors at the bottom of Africa. The guidebook also said the country has a nickname, the Mountain Kingdom, because it's the highest country in the world. Even its lowest valley is more than 4,500 feet above sea level. When I arrived, my first impression confirmed it: Nowhere was flat. Everywhere was a mountain or a valley. I was either looking up or looking down.

I first saw the boys who had freshly returned from initiation—the new men—wrapped in black and red blankets, seated with their bare feet straight out in front of them in a tight group under the shade of a tarp in the middle of the village. There were about twenty of them, and they had smeared their cheeks with red ocher such that their skin matched their blankets. Including their families, who had met them on their way down from the mountain and put the blankets on their naked bodies, over a hundred people were on hand for the ceremony on this day, December 18. The new men were singing with their chins lowered to get their voices as deep and grizzly as possible, to show everyone that they were no longer boys. Together, they sounded like the deep hum of a combustible engine. The only lyrics I could discern were, *"Thola, ngoan'eso"*—Quiet, brother. Though it was my first day in the village, Peace Corps had given me two months of training in the local language, Sesotho, before dropping me off. They literally dropped me off. They drove me out to the village in a white Toyota Land Cruiser and helped me unload my clothes and sleeping bag and some dishes and utensils and there I was. But I couldn't get over the voices of the new men. They were teenagers, yet they were singing below baritone. They sounded like a choir of zombies. There was no way I could get my voice that low. And it occurred to me what that would mean to everyone around me, everyone in the village, everyone who was looking at me right now: this foreigner is not a man. He may look like a man, but he's still a boy.

So I guess it was right that the chief had seated me with the women and children. He had put down a chair for me among them and then called out for them to clear a path so I could watch the new men sing. Along with the women and children, I had a profile view. Only initiated men were allowed to face the new men. But at the moment I was less concerned with my own vantage point than with all of the women and children staring back at me as I looked down the part in their crowd. I felt very self-conscious. I had never felt like such a center of attention. I thought about the expression on my face. How should it look? It should look interested, not bored, but it shouldn't look so interested that it appears judgmental. I wished they would all just turn back around and watch the new men sing like they were supposed to. Then I realized that they had probably seen young men return from the mountains and sing every summer of their lives. Yet this might be the first time they had ever had a visitor like me, so close, sitting right among them. And as far as I knew I was the only foreigner to ever come to live in this village. I only hoped they were staring out of curiosity and not resentment— their countenances betrayed no hint—because not only had the chief given me a chair to sit in, while all of them were standing or sitting on the ground, but he also now gave me an umbrella to block the sun.

Even my sand-colored hair had heated up like asphalt under the scorching rays. How would it feel with black hair? Most villagers were wearing hats, some made of dried grass, some made of cotton and with a full rim in the style of Gilligan. A man carrying a jug circled the group of new men and drizzled water on their heads to keep them cool. The African sun seemed more powerful than any sun I had felt, even in the deserts of Arizona.

One of the new men rose to his feet from among the seated pack. He held up a thick stick and began to speak rapidly over the chorus of the group.

"That one is Sepheche," Principal Tsita whispered to me in English. "He will be one of your students."

I had met Principal Tsita just an hour before, after Peace Corps dropped me off. She was the head of the school where I would be teaching, and she is the one who had brought me to the initiation ceremony. I felt intimidated by the prospect of being the teacher of such a student. Sepheche looked tall and dark and angry. He spoke words I didn't understand, and in a voice that was deeper than mine.

To my right, a man with even darker skin approached the chief and began speaking to him in Sesotho. So much was happening all around me. There was so much to look at. This man speaking to the chief was wearing a red New York Yankees baseball cap. Could he possibly know who the Yankees were? Under the cap, locks of white beads spilled over his forehead. As he spoke to the chief his hands remained still at his sides. He used no gestures. And I couldn't help but stare at this man's fingernails, which were curled over and the yellow color of urine.

Once he walked away, Principal Tsita clued me in. "This is ntate Santu," she said. "He is the witchdoctor. And he also owns the initiation school." I thought it was funny that Principal Tsita called him a witchdoctor, which seemed like a word from a fairytale, or an anthropology textbook, or a travel record written by a 16th century European explorer. "He has invited us into his house."

Principal Tsita and the chief stood up and I followed them.

I began to think of how lucky I was. These were things I had only read about: boys becoming men through initiation school out in the wilderness, African chiefs, witchdoctors. Now I was seeing it all with my own eyes, for real. This was exactly why I had come to Lesotho. I wanted to experience the world firsthand, to see in person the things I had only read about. Unsurprisingly, the firsthand experience didn't align with the stereotypes. The witchdoctor was supposed to wear some kind of feathered headdress, not a Yankees hat.

Soon after we sat down, a young man walked through the door of the witchdoctor's house carrying a metal basin and placed it at our feet. Flies buzzed over the basin, and inside it I saw meat on a large bone. It was the leg of a goat. On the way to the witchdoctor's house we had passed men spreading the hides of goats on the grass and women sorting through innards in tubs. Principal Tsita swiped her hand over the gray meat, and the flies created a rush of noise.

"This is a sign of welcome," she said to me. "You only have to eat a little to show you accept."

I knew everything was going too well. There had to be a catch at some point. During training, the Peace Corps medical staff had warned us repeatedly not to eat food that flies had landed on. Since in Lesotho people keep their livestock right next to their homes, the danger was that the flies feed on animal poop, hop over to land on your food and drop off some of that poop. You eat the food, and with it poop, and you get disease. I stared at the flies, and I saw disease.

The chief handed me a knife and scooted a bag of salt near

my feet. He smiled and I saw that he was missing a front tooth. All the others looked at me and smiled. There was Principal Tsita and Witchdoctor Santu, as well as the chief's wife and the chief's uncle. This was obviously a seminal moment.

I knew how much it mattered what they thought of me. I was alone here. And I had to make sure that they liked me because they were essentially in control of my life. They determined how safe and comfortable the next few years would be. They seemed to welcome me, but if I made a wrong move . . . it was possible that I would never recover their hospitality.

I was sure the flies on that meat would make me sick though. Was sickness worth it? It depended on whether I got standard diarrhea, or some pestilent intestinal worm that ate my insides hollow until they were black and collapsing.

I thought to say no thanks, but then I imagined the witchdoctor's reaction: "I welcome him into my home and offer him my best food and he rebuffs me? Arrogant!" And then my imagination ran wild. The witchdoctor would try to put a curse on me. Or he would command his new men to stop singing and come chase me out of the village immediately. Or maybe even worse, word would get around the village that I had refused to share food with them because I thought I was too good, and then I would spend the next two years being lonely, thousands of miles from home, the only foreigner in a little village in the mountains of Africa.

Just eat the meat. The flies had congregated again densely. I shooed them away and then looked for an area without too much gristle. I carved off a chunk. I took a pinch of salt and sprinkled it over the meat. I took a bite. Everyone watched. I chomped and I chomped and I chomped. It was rubbery. It was also utterly bland. It occurred to me that I'd never eaten plain meat before. In America, meat was always seasoned, or it was marinated, or fried in oil, or covered in sauce, or at least accompanied by side dishes. This was a meal of pure animal flesh. A goat had been slaughtered on the grass, the leg cut off, cooked, and now I was eating it with nothing but a sprinkle of salt. Each bite took minutes to chew and it didn't taste good, but as I chewed I had time to taste the fact that I was not in Lesotho just to see things that I had read about. I would not be increasing the number of facts in my head. I would be, like it or not, part of the action.

ON THE FIRST DAY OF SCHOOL I woke up early, and healthy. The meat hadn't made me sick. I had waited for the onslaught but it never came. After a few days I had to guess that flies didn't always mean disease, which stood to reason, because otherwise how could all of the people in Tšoeneng still be alive if eating food which flies had landed on automatically caused disease?

I had been told that classes started at 8 a.m. so I showed up at Principal Tsita's office at 7:50 a.m., on Wednesday, January 21, in my best collared shirt, a little nervous. When my Peace Corps supervisor first told me I would live and teach at Ngoana Jesu Secondary School in Tšoeneng he also said, "The community there is very excited and supportive. They said they can't wait to get the miracle teacher."

"Oh, ntate Greg, you're early," said Principal Tsita, from behind a cluttered desk, looking surprised to see me. Ten minutes before classes started didn't seem early to me. I felt eager to show her that I was grateful for the warm welcome at the initiation ceremony, and I was ready to do my best to be the "miracle teacher" they were hoping for.

Soon another woman came into Principal Tsita's office. The woman stuck her hand out for me to shake and said, "'Malimpho Ramosoeu. Pleased to meet you, ntate." We shook in the Lesotho way: Right hand outstretched with the left hand on the right elbow. We shook once and then turned our fingers up using our thumbs as pivot points, and then returned to the original shake position, palm in palm. "I am also teaching English," she said.

She took me over to the staffroom and showed me to a desk in the corner—not that the corner was a faraway place; the staffroom was only the size of a small bedroom. She left me there alone. I saw two tables, where dusty books and cardboard boxes and some dishes were stacked. The walls had been painted a bright blue, but they were also dusty, and pocked. There was no ceiling, just rafters holding up a tin roof. Where were the other teachers? Soon, 'me Albertina walked in. I had already met her, actually, because her house was next door to mine there at the school. We shared a wall, in fact. She was sweet, but still she scared me a little after she asked me about my teaching experience. "Where have you taught before?" I crouched and dodged the question. I hadn't taught anywhere before today. I changed the subject. 'Me 'Malimpho came back into the staffroom. After about fifteen minutes one more teacher entered, and this one couldn't go unnoticed, for she was a large woman with a high-pitched and high-volume voice. She let out a loud sigh as soon as she came through the door, as if the walk through the fields to school had been treacherous, and then she started chatting to 'me 'Malimpho and 'me Albertina, and I realized that I was the only male. The three women carried on among themselves, and I felt out of place. This was a hen's den. I tried to follow the conversation, which was about students' results on the previous year's national examinations, I thought, but they were speaking Sesotho. I understood some slow and simple statements in the language but if someone used a contraction I got lost, and my vocabulary was very limited. The ladies could have used English. They all knew it, as they showed when they greeted me. Sesotho, however, came easier for them, and so the only thing I understood about their conversation was that it was about exam results. I heard grades being called out, along with the names of subjects. "B . . . Agriculture." I sat quietly while the women talked, and I began to feel that my desk in the corner was indeed far away.

When were classes going to start? It was well past 8. Finally, I heard Principal Tsita call from her office for a student to ring the hand bell so everyone would assemble. I looked at my watch: 8:45 a.m. The three ladies walked out of the staffroom and I followed them over to a classroom building where students had already lined up. Ngoana Jesu Secondary School consisted of three classroom buildings, plus the building which contained Principal Tsita's office, a kitchen room and our staffroom. That was it. Then down the hill there were the two duplex houses for teachers and one duplex house for students who didn't live in Tšoeneng or a nearby village. There were about fifty students facing the steps of the classroom building and we teachers walked up to the backs of their white and royal blue uniforms. The boys wore slacks and white collared dress shirts. The girls wore crisply ironed blue dresses. All students had shiny black shoes. I hadn't expected them to be dressed so sharply. Their attire contrasted with the bare cement block buildings and fields and mountains.

A couple of students noticed me and stared until a student said, "Our Father," and then everyone recited the Lord's Prayer: "Our Father who art in heaven, hallowed be Thy name . . ." It was in English, but heavily accented. Following the prayer was a Sesotho hymn. The girls and boys sang distinct parts, with the boys singing in the deepest voices they could.

And then Principal Tsita ascended the steps in front of everyone. "You will pay for the classroom windows that have been broken over summer break," she welcomed them, in English. Then she looked my direction. "This is Sir Greg. He is our new teacher and he is from America." The students all looked back. "Do you know which ocean he had to cross to come here?" The students' mouths did not move. Principal Tsita looked embarrassed. She demanded, "Tomorrow at assembly you will tell me which ocean!" She was a very short woman, and with a gentle, round face. My first impression of her had been only that she was sweet. But up on the steps she towered over the student body, and I could now see that she was a ruler.

She continued, "Sir Greg is good for us because he doesn't speak Sesotho, so you will have to speak your English with him." I felt unworthy of the title "Sir," but I knew that Basotho, as the people of Lesotho are called, loved titles and that all of the male teachers were called that way, and all of the female teachers were called "Madam." They did this while in English mode at school, and it seemed to be their translations of the Sesotho titles that they used in everyday life for men and women, *ntate* and *'me*.

And then Principal Tsita gave the students one last command: "You will go to clean your classrooms."

As the students walked off some continued to crane their necks to get additional glances at me. I wondered what it was going to be like teaching them. And when would I find out? When would classes actually start? Then I turned to follow the three ladies back to the staffroom.

I sat down in the corner and they resumed their gossip.

At 10 a.m. I was still sitting and listening, and not under-standing. It was extra discouraging because I hadn't expected language to be an obstacle at school. Peace Corps had told me that English was the medium of instruction at all schools in Lesotho from the fourth grade on, and so I figured I would only need to learn Sesotho to talk to people in the village. Sometimes I thought I heard the teachers say the word *lekhooa*—white person. Sometimes they laughed and looked at me. I laughed too, instinc-tively. But I had no idea what was funny. For all I knew they were laughing at me. I hated not understanding what was going on.

I tried to pretend I didn't care to know what they were talking about and I looked around the room. I counted the desks. Five. Who was the fifth teacher? I tried to read the poster on the bright blue wall, "TIMETABLE" it was titled, and it must have been from last year. I guessed at the abbreviations for each subject: ENG—English, SCI—Science, SES—Sesotho, AGR—Agriculture, D.S.—Development Studies, and REL—Religion. The tin roof was heating up now and beginning to make noise as it expanded under the summer sun. Yet there were also pigeons prancing up there, so I wasn't sure which sounds came from the pigeon feet and which came from the expanding tin. It seemed that I was fated to not understand any of the sounds that were made in the staffroom that day. And the ladies went on talking to each other.

At nearly 11 o'clock Principal Tsita entered through the door of the staffroom. She gave us sheets of paper and announced that we would begin a staff meeting. "Title your notes Work Plan 2004," she told us. "First, students will be fed on Tuesdays, Wednesdays and Thursdays." I jotted that down. I didn't really know why. "And we must have the students do at least one written assignment per week." I took a note of that too. The other teachers then made other suggestions about school assignment quotas, but even though the meeting was being held in English I still had nothing to contribute to the discussion. Eventually it became relevant to me when they divvied up the classes. I would teach English for three grade levels, Forms A, B, and D. They were the equivalent of American grade levels 8, 9, and 11. I wrote down my classes. I heard them say ntate Lemphane would teach agriculture. Ntate? The fifth teacher was a man. Hallelujah! Then the meeting degenerated into gossip about last year's exam results again, which meant nothing to me, and the English was now mixed with Sesotho, sometimes within the same sentence. "'Mapaseka *o feitse*. Just imagine!" I began to tune out once again. It was beyond the lunch hour when Principal Tsita declared, "Let us release the students now if they have finished cleaning and we will all go home."

And I found myself walking back down the dirt path from the staffroom, past the water pump, toward my house and asking myself, Will I teach on the second day of school?

AT MY HOUSE I changed into more comfortable clothes, taking off my shirt with buttons and putting on a simple t-shirt, and then I grabbed my buckets and went up to the water pump. I filled one to use for cooking and the other to use for bathing. My house had no running water, just like the whole village of Tšoeneng had no running water, and neither was my house connected to any power grid. Tšoeneng village, just like most of Lesotho, had no electricity. When the sun went down the world went black.

In my house I only had the light of a candle. I ate dinner and washed my dishes, and then I sat down at my table and it was dark and quiet. It was spooky and isolating to only have a small bubble of illumination, and I did a little reading and writing and quickly got sleepy. But before I turned in for the night I turned on my radio. I found an FM station that was playing pop music in English—Avril Lavigne, I thought. How did I even know that? I had never listened to Avril Lavigne back home. Still, it was nice to understand the lyrics and hear guitars and drums. I felt a comforting connection to the music, a familiar thing popping into this Lesotho world I had entered where everything was unfamiliar.

THE NEXT DAY, Thursday, more students showed up at the morning assembly, probably seventy. I entered a classroom later that morning, and to a standing ovation. When I walked in the door about forty teenagers, in their blue and white uniforms, rose to their feet and said, "Oooohh." They smiled and started clapping. I was totally stunned.

"Good morning," I said.

"GOOD MORNING, SIR," they chorused back. And they remained on their feet.

"You may sit down," said 'me 'Malimpho, who had accompanied me.

She began asking the students English grammar questions, demonstrating to me how she teaches and what the students know. It was her way of introducing me to a class I would be teaching. This was Form B, the ninth grade. Then one girl couldn't answer a question. I stood beside 'me 'Malimpho and felt her displeasure. 'Me 'Malimpho walked over to the girl and the rest of the students sucked air through their teeth. "Hsssss." 'Me 'Malimpho twisted the girl's ear.

And then she left, and I was alone in front of the class. Being a native English speaker, I had thought I was 90 percent of the way toward teaching the language. But now, standing before forty sets of eyes, I was wishing someone would tell me what to do next. I had never stood in front of a class as teacher. This wouldn't have been such a big deal (everyone has to start sometime, somewhere) except that the school expected a miracle teacher. And I felt they deserved it. Why not?

I had only one idea to get things started. "So I can learn your names, let's all tear out a sheet of paper from our notebooks and fold it and make name cards for our desks," I said.

And I waited for the tearing and folding of paper. But there was no movement, no reaction to my words.

"Do you understand?" I asked.

The entire class responded: "YES, SIR."

"OK. Then you can start now," I said.

No movement. Faces were just empty—dull as an urban night sky.

"Take a piece of paper from your notebook and I'll show you how to fold it. OK?"

"YES, SIR."

But still no movement.

"What did I just ask you to do?"

There was a long silence. But they had understood 'me 'Malimpho just fine.

A girl up front finally said: "Sir, we don't hear."

I approached her desk to demonstrate. But when I stepped forward the students made that sound again, sucking air through their teeth: "Hssss." I hesitated. Did they think I was going to twist her ear? I took the girl's notebook and tore a sheet from it. I held it high for all to see and folded it in half, and then said, "Do this."

Gradually, I started to hear the tearing of paper from notebooks. I wrote my name on my folded paper and held it up and said, "Do this, with *your* name."

I couldn't believe how hard it was to get them to do this. Had they really not understood my words? If school was taught in English from the fourth grade on, then that would mean these Form B's had been speaking English for five years.

I walked down an aisle so I could see that everyone was doing the task correctly, and each student I passed leaned away. The students shrunk like plastic held to fire, their heads sunk into their shoulders. And I heard more "Hssss." I picked up a boy's paper to help him fold it in a way that would stand on his desk better, and I noticed that his eyes were transfixed on my hands as they moved in front of him. I wondered if maybe the students weren't only afraid of having their ears twisted, but also just shocked at being so close to someone who looked like me, so entirely different from them.

As I continued to walk around I noticed that the collars on many of the boys' white school shirts were frayed, and some of the girls' blue dresses had been torn and restitched. One girl I passed smelled like she hadn't bathed in a long time. It was an earthy, motor oil kind of smell. My first impression of them at the assembly was that they looked too clean and sharp for the rural and rundown surroundings, but now I thought they did fit the place. They were students at a school in the mountains of Africa.

After some time the name cards all got made and they were propped up on the desks, so I went around the room trying to pronounce them. Many started with m: Mosebatho, Moraba, Morobane, Moliehi, Maleshoane, Maoto, Mahlape, Mpho, Mpoti,

Mpati. Or even two m's: 'Mamaaooa, 'Mantoa, 'Mamahloli, 'Mapaseka. And some were long, like Retšelisitsoe. I butchered the sounds and the students couldn't help but laugh and the mood in the classroom lightened. I cut it off there, on a good note.

Principal Tsita gave me the Form B textbooks and curriculum that afternoon. Written by Lesotho's Ministry of Education, the curriculum stated that by the end of the year these students were supposed to be able to use the simple present, past and future, as well as the present perfect and past perfect verb tenses. They should be able to take a root noun and form it into a verb, adjective and adverb. They should be able to change the active voice into the passive voice and quoted speech into reported speech. They should know how to use polite language and how to answer a telephone. They should be able to construct compound sentences and compose narrative and argumentative essays, as well as business letters. The Form B students should read and comprehend literature books of short stories, a novel, a play, and poems. When reading poems they should be able to identify uses of rhyme, alliteration, simile and metaphor. The curriculum went on and on, getting further and further away from being realistic. It had just taken us an hour to exchange names.

I stayed in the staffroom until five o'clock reading the curriculum over and over, perusing the English textbook and the literature books, racking my brain and laying out plans for how I would attack teaching under these circumstances. I was starting to feel a loss of hope. The situation was starting to seem impossible. The students were supposed to go from English zero to fluency, and they were supposed to get there with my help, the teacher who had no experience. Maybe it should have been comforting to me that I wasn't the only incompetent part of the equation, but I felt nothing like comfort.

I MET THE TWO OTHER CLASSES I would teach on Friday. The Form A's were at about the same level as the B's, but the D's seemed much higher. I would almost say we were able to converse in class. They gave me hope, and I told them, "I'm so happy to teach this class because when I spoke to the Form A's and B's they didn't understand anything I said."

And then I felt lucky to have reached my first weekend. I thought I'd try to set thoughts of teaching aside and not let any apprehension ruin Saturday and Sunday. On Saturday morning I heard clinks coming from the water pump up the hill and I looked out my window to see that a bunch of students were gathered, washing their clothes. There were about thirty students who lived at school, and they did everything themselves, from cooking to cleaning. Hostelers, they were called, and the building they lived in, the hostel. I had dirty clothes too. It happened very fast since nothing was paved and all day you walked on dirt. So I decided to join the students. Up at the pump it was a scene of colorful plastic tubs, sloshing water, white shirts hung on barbed-wire fence, and teenage Africans chatting and laughing. I set my green tub of laundry beneath the pump's spout. The metal pump lever clinked as I worked it up and down, drawing water out of the ground through the bore hole. The students looked up from their wash— sudsy clothes in hand—and watched. I opened a box of Surf and poured the detergent into the tub. My thought was to mimic a washing machine, so I swirled the clothes around. I squished them together and then swirled some more. The students had yet to resume their washing; they were dazzled by mine.

This seemed to be the difference between traveling through a foreign country and going there to stay. While a tourist you goggle at the local people as they do what they do, but the tables are turned when you're there to live—you become the one on stage.

"Sir, you know how to wash?" a girl asked. I knew her name was Nthabiseng from the name card she had made in my Form B class.

"Yes," I said.

"Sir, you don't know."

I wasn't surprised Nthabiseng was so bold. I was sure she was related to Principal Tsita somehow. I thought she might be Principal Tsita's daughter because on the first day of school she arrived in Principal Tsita's Volkswagen, and she was also small and chubby-cheeked, with small teeth just like the principal. Nthabiseng came over to my tub and bent at the waist to lift a pair of socks from the water. "Like this," she said, as she squished them down her left forearm and onto the butt of her palm. She repeated that, dipped the socks into the water, and then went through the motions again. Next, she took a sock in each hand—with thumb and forefinger—and rubbed the toe and heel areas against each other.

I was ready to try, but instead of letting me Nthabiseng proceeded to wash one of my shirts. The other students continued to watch. After a minute she asked, "Sir, do you use the machine in America?"

Like I was supposed to be ashamed of it. "Yes," I said.

"Oh, so you only know how to push buttons." She pretended to push buttons in the air, and the other hostelers snickered.

I had looked forward to interacting with the students outside of class, in an informal situation like at the pump, because I'd thought I wouldn't be such a center of attention and I wouldn't need to perform. I was wrong. I was on stage at the initiation ceremony, as a teacher, and any other time I was outside of my house.

I TOOK A LONG RUN through the fields on Monday morning before school. I went so early that no one was around to see me except a few shepherds and farmers, but I mostly ran in order to calm myself. I had woken up nervous about teaching.

Even though it was summer, the elevation of Lesotho made the dawn air crisp enough to chill my knuckles and make my nose drip as I jogged away from my house. I passed between fields of young corn and sorghum and beans. There were trails going in every direction. I took one to the north, and it was lined with tall grasses and it went across a gully, crested a hill, and then passed through many more fields until it came to a stream. The stream bed was wide and sandy. Some willows and poplar trees grew along its banks. Across the stream to the north was a plateau called Qeme which separated the Tšoeneng area from the capital city, Maseru. Qeme plateau was both a topographical and technological boundary. On the other side was city and electricity; on this side was country and candles. To my left, to the west, was another boundary: the one that separated the Kingdom of

Lesotho from the Republic of South Africa. This boundary was also physical in addition to being political. It was a river. Called the Mohokare by people in Lesotho, and called the Caledon by people in South Africa, the river was not visible to me at this moment standing at the stream, for it was on the other side of a low ridge of mountains called Thupa-li-Kaka.

I had run hard to the north, but then I finished even harder on my way back south. I could see Tšoeneng Mountain, the conical peak under which the village lay. And straight ahead to the south was Kolo Mountain, an even bigger volcano-looking summit under which the village Kolo lay. It was icing to get out of my house and see the country, but the real point of my run was to exhaust myself. I aimed to arrive home with no energy left, and along with my sweat, my teaching anxieties seeped out and evaporated. At least for a few hours directly after the morning run I felt nothing.

I MADE LITTLE DISCOVERIES that day and throughout the second week that helped me teach my classes. When I asked the students in Form A to write a letter, they first acted like they had never heard the word. Until I wrote it on the chalkboard: l-e-t-t-e-r. And then it was like the heavens opened up. "LETTUH!" they all shouted. Pronunciation was the problem. I said *ledder*, they said *lettuh*. It was similar to a British accent. I should have guessed. On the other hand, every day I also came upon new little challenges, something else that further complicated my job. Again with Form A, I learned that they had no books, zero. This class was part of a new government program where the students would rent books (usually, students bought the textbooks for each of their classes). Except that the government had yet to provide any books for the Form A students to rent. So I had to write lessons on the chalkboard. The school had no alternative textbooks, no library, no photocopy machine. It was me and the chalkboard. After every forty minute Form A lesson my right forearm was pumped and my clothes were dusted with chalk.

One morning in that second week of school rain began to fall. I was in the staffroom when it started coming down. At first I thought the patter on the roof was just expansion noise from the heated tin, then maybe pigeon feet, but as it grew louder I looked out the door and saw wet spots. It was raining hard when it came time for me to teach the Form B's, and I stood up, grabbed a piece of chalk and marched toward the door. 'Me 'Malimpho asked, "Where are you going, ntate?"

"It's third period. I have the Form B's for English." The students stay in the classrooms all day while the teachers move from room to room. I opened the door and ran from the staffroom, hopping puddles on the dirt path until I reached the classroom and knocked on the Form B door. The students had closed it to keep the rain out, and the handle was broken on the outside, but eventually they heard me knocking and let me in. I greeted them, but the raindrops made so much noise on the tin roof that nothing could be heard. The occasional roar of thunder didn't help that. So I wrote an assignment on the chalkboard from their textbook and I sat down at the teacher's table to wait for them to finish. They brought their notebooks up one by one for me to correct, and when the period was over I ran back through the rain toward the staffroom, bursting through the door. I sat down at my desk in the corner, wiped the water from my brow, and then I realized that all the teachers were at their desks. No one but me had taught a class that period. And no one was heading out the door to teach a class this next period. It seemed they didn't teach in the rain. But how could they spare a moment? How would they ever meet the Ministry of Education's curriculum goals if they wasted a second? They wanted me to be a miracle teacher while they hid in the staffroom so as not to get their hair wet?

I WOKE UP THE NEXT MORNING and ran hard through the fields as usual to bleed the stress. I didn't know how to teach. I felt so awkward up there saying things the students didn't understand, just staring at each other half the time. And teaching without books! This system's a mess. The Ministry of Education had these stratospheric expectations and then the first day was wasted with no teaching and more class hours were wasted while it rained. The students got their ears twisted if they answered a question incorrectly. The cool mountain air seared my lungs. My quadriceps were wobbly when I arrived back at my house. But the run didn't do a complete job. It hadn't flushed out my mind. After I bathed, I sat down at my table to eat breakfast and my chin began to quaver. It became hard to see clearly, like I was underwater. My bottom lip felt heavy. I was on the road to crying. I couldn't believe I was going to cry. When was the last time I had cried? Why was I going to cry? Where was the blood?

CHAPTER TWO

Hostelers

CRYING AT MY BREAKFAST TABLE, I thought that maybe I should just leave—go back home. Maybe teaching is not for me. But I didn't have time to consider any further. Shortly, a student would ring the hand bell and everyone would assemble to recite "Our Father." I had no time for a pity party or a deliberation, only a quick decision. Stay or go? I wiped the dust off my shoes and walked up the hill. I robotted through the day, not thinking, just going to classes and going through the motions. I hadn't really made the decision to stay as much as I knew that I couldn't quit.

After school, I had the time to try and figure out why I was broken down. Teaching was perplexing. I didn't know when classes would start, apparently I wasn't supposed to go to classes at all when it rained, students didn't understand me, some of them had no books, the Ministry of Education set ludicrous goals in its curriculum, and the list went on. Yet I wasn't even a trained teacher. And on top of that, I was expected to be a miracle teacher.

It seeped in though that even if I had been a teacher with experience, I would still be confused. It wasn't just teaching that was new for me, but it was also teaching at Ngoana Jesu that was requiring so much coping. The culture of the school was altogether different from anything I'd known, and further, it was only a slice of the larger culture that I was now in and also had to adapt to. So how had the enthusiasm of my first day in the village at the initiation ceremony degenerated into this despair? Well, everything was different here: language, job, flora and fauna, people, food, how socks were cleaned.

It felt like starting life over.

It rained again. I was sitting in the staffroom when the drops turned from a gentle patter on the tin roof into a static riot. The path to the classrooms was turning to mud again. The bell rang. 'Me 'Malimpho and 'me Albertina rushed into the staffroom, closing the door behind them and keeping out the tempest. I saw on the new class schedule on the wall that 'me 'Masamuel had a class to attend in the next period just like me. But she wasn't moving. According to the timetable, ntate Lemphane was to teach too. He also remained seated at his desk, next to the door. Ntate Lemphane had shown up just this week, late because there had been some disagreement about his paycheck. When he first arrived the women made some jokes about how grateful he must be to see me: "You're not alone as a man in the staffroom!" And I was glad ntate Lemphane had arrived too. But he had been quiet so far. He didn't speak much more than me, and he never joined in the women's gossip, and I had yet to get to know more than his name. We just looked across the room at each other from time to time while the women were chatting. I didn't understand what they were talking about, and it looked like ntate Lemphane was deliberately not paying attention. Even though we didn't talk, there was something about ntate Lemphane just being a man that encouraged me to watch what he did and take his actions as cues. None of the women were getting up to go teach their scheduled classes. I had my stack of books ready to go, and all I needed was to grab a piece of chalk on the way out, but ntate Lemphane was slouched in his chair, flipping pages in an agriculture textbook. I looked behind him, out the window, as much as I could since it was beginning to fog, as something in my mind began to clear up.

I was at a watershed moment, and I knew it. If I walked out that door to teach a class in the rain I'd be the only one.

I saw some rat droppings on the floor in the corner of the room. There was a tear in the plastic floor covering near the door. I had noticed in the previous days that whenever the door was opened, it caught the flap and tore bigger. How big would it get? And what a strange way to cover a floor, with this plastic sheet.

It was so lazy to sit in this chair. It was such a waste of time to leave the students to sit in their chairs in the classroom until the rain stopped. It might not stop until tomorrow.

There was a lizard high on the blue wall, above the timetable, up near the rafters. It was totally still.

What did 'me Albertina's hair feel like? She put some chemicals in it and brushed it straight back off her forehead in a hairdo I heard the women call a "pushback." It shined. Was it soft? Brittle? Greasy? Stiff? With the noise of the rain on the roof, the women were also sitting in silence in the staffroom. It was too loud to hold a conversation. We were all a little uncomfortable at our desks.

But I wasn't going to fight it anymore. I wasn't going to swim upstream and try to be the miracle teacher, the industrious one that tried to make the most of every minute by being the only teacher who ran out into the rain to teach. Wait, where did the miracle teacher expectation come from anyway? It was hearsay. No one at Ngoana Jesu had actually mentioned it to me directly.

With teaching it was the same as acclimating to every other facet of Lesotho life: mimic. Act like the child you are here and just follow the adults.

After about twenty minutes, the rain let up enough such that some teachers headed off to their classes. Only then did I. Slowly, I walked to class. I taught a brief lesson, and while I did I felt careless, but in a good way. As I walked back to the staffroom, I felt like for the first time I was in step with my surroundings.

I DID A LOT OF HIDING in my house in the early days. I loved the privacy, having no eyes on me. One day I made a cup of Ricoffy, a South African brand of instant coffee granules mixed with chicory, and the closest thing I could find to real coffee, and as I sipped it I stood by a window and stared out. A girl walked by, only a few feet away, and she looked in at me. I quickly turned away so she wouldn't catch me staring. I was brought up to think it was rude. I looked back at her before she had completely passed and saw that she was still looking at my window, but I could tell by the expression on her face that she wasn't seeing anything. So I went outside to look into the window and sure enough, I got nothing.

The glass in the window was slightly warped and dimpled—not high quality material—but it was the lace that caused the real distortion. Over the windows were thin lace curtains, and somehow, from the inside I could see out through the lace just fine, though from the outside they were as opaque as my walls.

Instantly, standing at the window, safe and undetected from behind the lace curtains, became my default position in the house. If I wasn't busy actually doing something inside, I was staring out at the hostel, which was only spitting distance from my house, and at the hostelers as they buzzed around. Within a few short weeks I had stared so much that I knew their daily routines.

In the early morning the first male hostelers came out of the hostel. They wore only underwear: red, black or green little superhero briefs. They walked directly over to the pig sty to pee beside it.

The hostel was split in two, and the girls lived on the north side, the far side from my vantage point. If I woke up early enough I saw the first girl to exit the hostel too, carrying a bucket. She walked over to the bushes near the eucalyptus trees and dumped the night's worth of pee. If the girls had to relieve themselves in the middle of the night, they urinated in the bucket rather than dare leave the hostel to relieve themselves. Dogs and men roamed at night. Nights were dangerous for girls. No one had indoor toilets, not the hostelers, not me.

Later, other girls woke up and walked right by my house toward their pit latrines. Most of them wrapped themselves in their blankets, but sometimes they too only wore underwear, and nothing on top. My eyes followed them as they walked right past my window, but I didn't feel creepy. Even though some of the girls were as developed as women, I felt no attraction. Their look was unfamiliar: the chocolate skin, the short hair, thick lips, narrow hips and bulbous buttocks. I was an apathetic observer.

On school days, I stood by my window and watched the hostelers get ready for the day as I brushed my teeth. They brushed their teeth outside with a cup of water in hand to rinse with, but they bathed inside the hostel, and they constantly came out of the doors to dump their bath water in the bushes or on their vegetable gardens. On the hostel steps they dusted off their black school shoes, and the boys and girls both combed their hair—what little curly black buds of hair they were allowed by the school to have.

Sometimes during breaks in the school day I came down to my house and got a peach from the tree next to my window. I stood inside eating my snack and watched the hostelers come down to get their own snacks. While some of them took peaches, I always saw a couple girls digging in the dirt near the hostel, and then munching on the chalky rocks that they had mined up. I later tried the rocks. They tasted like chalk. The peaches were better.

After school the hostelers hung about outdoors, spending only moments inside the hostel. As I cooked dinner I looked over my shoulder through the lace curtains and saw the boys playing soccer on a dirt clearing near the classrooms, most of them barefoot. Or some boys played *morabaraba*—a chess-like game—down at their toilets, where they had etched a game board into the concrete foundation of the latrines. It stunk horribly down there. I couldn't understand why they chose that as a place to hang out, except that maybe it was because the stench kept teachers and girls away. Some of the boys also played at stick fighting in the afternoons: each boy would carry two thick sticks—one for blocking, one for striking—and they would try to beat each other back.

The girls played their own games. They played chase, in circles around the hostel, or they hopscotched on a grid drawn in the dirt. They braided jump ropes from the summer's tall grass, and they took turns swinging and jumping until dark.

When night fell all I could see out my window was the window of the boys' side of the hostel, glowing orange from a candle on the sill. The flame flickered, and I imagined it was because of the hostelers singing inside. But I couldn't see anything. I could only hear. Both the boys and the girls sang every night. They had no television or radio, so they made music. One night the girls brought their songs outside and a few of them also brought their wash basins out, which they turned upside down to beat on for rhythm while the others sang and danced in a circle. I heard that one girl was the leader, and after she sang a line loudly the group repeated her words in a lower pitch. The girls laughed feverishly between songs and some of them screamed the names of other girls and other words I couldn't understand. Eventually, a leading voice emerged again and the girls fell back into song by repeating after her. Occasionally, girls clapped and ululated over the chorus, and they didn't stop until midnight. I was enthralled by the voices coming from the black outside. It was like nothing I had ever heard. It wasn't my idea of delicate female sounds, but a riotous party of sounds. Hidden in the darkness, I opened my door and set my camera down on the step to record video. There was no picture, of course, but the camera picked up the sound well. Inside, I played the video over and over to try to decipher the lyrics. The chorus went, *"Pula ea na"*—It's raining. I was sure of it. But the words made no sense because the sky was all stars. Maybe it was more a song of request rather than description, or more likely the teenage girls didn't care what they were saying, only that the melody was fun.

I KNEW IT WOULD HAPPEN at some point. Some hostelers knocked on my door. *"Koko,"* they said. I opened the door and found two girls, one stocky, the other tall. "We are your visitors," the stocky one said. I stepped over the threshold and closed the door behind me.

I wanted to keep my house to myself. There was so much pressure when I was outside being stared at, so I thought of inside my house as a kind of asylum where I could not only turn the tables and stare out, but also decompress and not feel self-conscious for a while.

We stood together awkwardly on my three square feet of porch. "We are asking for a book to read in English."

"Oh. OK."

I opened my door and went inside and grabbed a *Newsweek* magazine and returned to the porch. All around the world *Newsweek* sent its magazines to Peace Corps volunteers for free. I gave the girls the magazine, and they left.

I KEPT THE NEXT FEW VISITORS on my porch with the door closed behind me too. Then I remembered that even though it was private and comfortable being alone inside my house, I hadn't come to Lesotho to be alone. The last thing I wanted was to be alone. I really did want to get to know the hostelers, and I really wanted them to get to know me. It felt risky, but I began speaking with them at my threshold and leaving the door open. They would sneak glances around me and inside my house.

Moipone and Lipolelo, the stocky girl and the tall girl, came over again one day. I had heard the crunch of their feet over the gravel in front of my house before they knocked, and I decided to take a further chance. I closed the door to my bedroom. My house had two rooms: a front room and a bedroom.

"Koko."

I opened the front door.

"We are your visitors."

I stepped back from the front door.

They took the hint and inched inside. Moipone scanned my front room. We all were unsure what to do next, and then she said, "Where is your cell phone, sir?"

That's what I was afraid of. Were they looking for things to steal?

"I don't have a cell phone."

"You don't have? When you will you get one?"

Most everyone in Lesotho who could afford a cell phone had one. They were cheap to buy, cheaper than landlines. No homes in Tšoeneng had a landline telephone. People still mostly communicated by word of mouth, where a child would be sent as a messenger, or by note, often sent with the taxi and bus drivers. But I really didn't have a cell phone.

"I don't want a cell phone," I said.

"Why? They are nice."

"I know, but . . . see, if I had a cell phone I would always be talking to *makhooa*," I said. White people. People who looked like me. Foreigners. I would be tempted to call home often, or to call other Peace Corps volunteers. "And I don't want to do that. That's not why I came to Lesotho. I came here to talk to you guys."

Moipone's face told me that my explanation rang hollow. Those were my intentions anyway, and the girls left it at that.

ONCE THE DOOR of my hallowed house had been penetrated the trickle of hostelers knocking on it turned into a flood. A group of hostel boys came over one day and it was largest group yet that I'd let inside. Once in, they had little to say. We just stood together in the front room. They looked around, excited for the chance to see what their American teacher lived like, and I watched their eyes. I didn't know if they were innocently curious or looking for something to pocket. I still didn't know any of the hostelers well enough to trust them. And though I didn't have a cell phone, I did have some other electronics: a CD Walkman, a shortwave radio, a digital camera. I kept those valuables hidden in my bedroom closet.

A Form A named Khosi finally spoke up. He looked at my stove, a two burner that ran on a propane tank, and he asked, "Do you have *papa* in America?" *Papa* was the staple food in Lesotho. As Basotho usually described it, *papa* was "hard porridge."

I told Khosi that we didn't eat *papa* in America, and his eyes tensed. "Sir, what do you eat?" He was really concerned.

"We eat bread and rice and pasta and many other things."

"Do you not have maize in America?"

"We have maize, but usually we eat it whole, not ground into a meal and cooked like *papa*."

"Do you have Coke in America?"

"Yes. Coke actually comes from America."

Khosi looked skeptical about that. But at least America had Coke.

He looked away, for another item in the room to ask about. Khosi was only a Form A, a 13-year-old, but he was obviously the leader of this little group of hostel boys, perhaps because he had relatively good English. Whenever a student had exceptionally good English I asked where they had learned it. Khosi had grown up in the capital city and he said he attended an English-medium elementary school there. The village students who were only really starting to have to speak English a lot at school now because of me would never be able to master the pronunciation like Khosi, who had been speaking it, albeit not so well, since he was a child.

I could tell Khosi was from another place the first time I saw him. His school uniform wasn't torn or ill-fitting. Even the skin on his face had a smooth, urban shine to it. And his teeth glowed white.

While the boys were standing around in the front room, I went into the bedroom and got my camera from the closet. I hadn't planned on ever letting the hostelers even see my camera. But as with every next step I took with them, the moment caught me up. They were curious about me, I was curious about them. They wanted to get to know me, I wanted to get to know them. And I couldn't help but take some chances. I held it up and they immediately started posing for pictures. They didn't smile, but they stood tall and stared intensely into the camera's lens. I came to know this as typical Basotho style when posing for photos.

The real reason I had fetched my camera though was to see their reaction to the image of themselves on the display screen. Mine was one of the early models of digital cameras sold in the U.S., so I was pretty sure they hadn't seen any here in Lesotho. I showed Khosi and the boys the display of the photo I had just taken. They recognized themselves. They shouted, *"Khelek! Khelek!"* They stepped back and shouted some more, and then came up again to look at the display closer. They could've looked at it forever. I switched the camera to video mode, and I began recording. They posed for a still shot when I held the camera up. They stood tall, gazing seriously into my lens. I told them to speak. "Say hello," I said. I put the camera close to a boy named Thato's face. "Hello, sir," he said. After I went around to some of the other boys I stopped recording and they gathered around to see the display. When they saw the movement and heard their own voices speaking back at them, they jumped back and nearly threw themselves to the ground. *"Joee! Utloa!"*

That was why I had fetched my camera. I guessed they might get a real kick out of seeing themselves like that, and I didn't regret at all revealing that I had an expensive item stashed away in my bedroom. I was curious to learn about their exposure to technology. "Have you heard of the Internet?" I asked.

"Sir?"

"Do you know the Internet?"

It seemed their first time to hear the word. So I asked the backup question, "Have you ever used a computer?"

"No, sir." No. No. No, all around. But they knew of computers—they knew that word.

Khosi and another boy Thato, I knew, were from Maseru, the capital city, and yet they had never used a computer. If they hadn't, there was no way any of the other students had. This was something to wrap my head around: I was living among a group of teenagers in the 21st century who had never touched a computer.

KHOSI HAD GOOD ENGLISH compared to some of the other boys. Among them the range in fluency was wide. (Another hostel boy had answered "16 years" when I asked for his name.) Nonetheless, Khosi's English was not my English. It was strange and I didn't understand everything he said, even when I knew he was speaking English. It was influenced by Sesotho, of course, but it was also seasoned with the English spoken across the border in South Africa. And the English of South Africa is more closely related to British English than American English, which was why Khosi called corn "maize."

I was frequently confronted with differences in vocabulary between the English spoken at Ngoana Jesu and my American English. The students and teachers used peculiarly South African English words for some things, such as calling a pickup truck a "bakkie," calling marijuana "dagga," calling a barbecue a "braai," or calling erosion gullies "dongas." And they otherwise used British English terms for most things. A chalkboard eraser was referred to as a "duster," a pencil eraser was called a "rubber," Math class was called "Maths," and a period at the end of a sentence was a "full stop." Cookies were called "biscuits" and backpacks were called "kitties."

I didn't have a book to consult, or a person to guide me in learning this new lexicon. I just got confused and then picked it up through context as I went along. One of the causes of our trouble making name cards on the first day, I found out, was that I had asked them to tear a sheet from their "notebooks." They didn't call them that. They called them "exercise books," or sometimes just "exercises."

For me, it was disorienting to have come to Lesotho thinking I was going to teach English, but then find myself having to learn English, or a new version of it anyway. Yet really, I only had to read the history section of my Lonely Planet guidebook to understand why students and teachers at Ngoana Jesu spoke the English that they did. From 1868, when Lesotho became the British Protectorate of Basutoland, the British ruled the Basotho for almost 100 years. During that time they implemented a system of formal education in which British English was the medium of instruction. Young Basotho were taught English at school to the end that they could possibly be employed as civil servants under the British administration. Lesotho gained its independence in 1966, but it remains a member of the British Commonwealth, and Lesotho today has two official languages, Sesotho and English. The education and employment situations in the country have stayed remarkably similar to that of a century ago, when the British began governing. That is, the students still learn English in school, and English can help them get jobs in government, which is by far the largest source of formal employment in the country. Students also still take British style examinations in school, after grades 7, 10 and 12. The final high school examination in Lesotho is actually one created in and still administered from England, called the Cambridge Overseas School Certificate.

Lucky for me I had spent a semester studying in England during college, so I was familiar with many of the differences between American and British English, but there were often things that students and teachers said in English that I didn't understand and that I knew weren't Britishisms, or from South Africa. When students were leaving my house they kept saying, "I'm coming." I wanted to correct them: "No, you're going." It took some time to figure out that it was a direct translation from Sesotho—*Kea tla*—and that it actually referred to what they planned on doing. They planned on coming back.

It was this English that came from Sesotho that I found most mysterious, especially in these early days when my Sesotho was poor. And though I wanted to correct the Sesotho-English at first (I thought they should be taught "real" English and not say they're coming when they're leaving), I heard the teachers at Ngoana Jesu using the same expressions and so I realized that this was another place where I should just imitate, or at least not fight.

THE HOSTELERS ALWAYS CAME to my house in groups of two or three. In the front room where we hung out there was only a small table, two plastic chairs, and a bookshelf. At first I kept a careful watch while they were inside, and that made the visits uncomfortable, but slowly I came to realize that they weren't looking to steal anything. They were just interested in seeing what their foreign teacher lived like. What did he keep in his house? What did he eat? How did he decorate?

On one wall I had put up a map of Lesotho. I had bought it at a government office in Maseru. On the other wall was a calendar, which a friend from home had sent. Each month showed a view of mountains or rivers in America's national parks. "There are also mountains in America?" Khosi once asked, and so did many of the other hostelers, but otherwise they were uninterested in those vistas of nature. That was all they woke up to see every day of their lives. They would have been more excited to see pictures of city skylines, or even photos of people.

They were delighted to find the small photo album I kept on top of my bookshelf, and once they did their visits became less awkward because the photos always provided discussion topics. They wondered why one photo showed my brother's dog inside the house. "That is not good," said a girl. "Dogs are dirty." I remembered hearing a story about a past Peace Corps volunteer in Lesotho who had been run out of his village because he adopted a dog and kept it in his house. Basotho only owned and fed dogs so the dogs would work for them. Dogs herded animals for shepherds and guarded homes; they barked at and threatened to bite anyone who wasn't their master. You never petted dogs in Lesotho. Yet this volunteer had not only let his dog inside his house, but also kept it inside to sleep at night. The villagers suspected bestiality, and they forced him to leave. There was another photo in my album that showed my friend Katie wearing shorts, and one boy commented, "We would beat her in Lesotho, the way she is wearing." In Lesotho, it was totally inappropriate for women to wear shorts. Even wearing pants was dressing promiscuously, and female students and teachers at Ngoana Jesu were not allowed.

I could not tell some of the hostelers apart. And there was a group of girls in my Form A class who sat together toward the back and looked almost identical and I avoided even looking at them because I could not get their names straight. However, I began to feel less guilty about that after a hostel girl named Tšepang looked up from the photo album one day with a sigh and said, "Sir, have you ever noticed that all white people look the same?"

Every visit now the hostelers came in the door and went straight for the photo album, always finding something new and interesting even in photos they'd seen a dozen times. On one evening a whole bunch of hostelers were marveling at a photo of my cousin Chelsea sitting Indian style and one of them asked me, "Can you sit like this?" I said I could and I demonstrated. Then they started trying, but somehow none of them could get their legs to fold that way. One girl tried to get into the position by standing and crossing her legs and then lowering to the ground, but she just fell over. As I sat cross-legged on the floor, cracking up at their attempts, a boy named Tlhokomelo looked at my legs and asked, "When did you learn?" They had different ways of sitting. Women often sat on the floor with their legs straight out. Men sat on their haunches or on rocks or on a chair—they never truly sat on the ground. I couldn't remember learning to sit Indian style, of course. It was just a skill I felt practically born with, although I had never before thought of it as a skill.

MY PHOTO ALBUM remained the focal point of the hostelers' visits until exactly the day I got a radio that played CDs. It was a Sony, and it was white with two orange and black speakers. It ran on batteries. Nthabiseng, the one who had made fun of me for not knowing how to wash my clothes, and some of her friends were over my house one evening soon after I got it and they noticed it on my table. They all admired its shine and sophistication. Nthabiseng ran her fingers over the radio's surface.

This girl was so bold. She was likable, but bold. One time a couple days earlier a group of us were looking at photos and she stole a touch on my forearm. She lightly drew her finger across it, like to see if it felt the same as hers. I wondered what her impression was, but she said nothing. I had forgiven her in my mind for making fun of me on that first weekend, but also, I had to admit, it had kind of hurt. I was very insecure about not knowing how to do things that everyone around me knew. I didn't try to wash up at the water pump again for three months. I washed only in secret. I walked up to the pump to fill my water buckets and furtively noted the hostelers' techniques out of the corners of my eyes. They scrub waistbands by taking an end in each hand and rubbing one against the other. They hang pants to dry inside out, pockets exposed. They wash blankets by standing on them in a tub like they're squishing grapes. Then I returned to my house, closed my door, spread out my tubs on my concrete floor, and tried to copy their moves in privacy. I was embarrassed about being a 27-year-old who couldn't wash his own socks. I didn't need it pointed out in front of everyone.

So I couldn't help but find an opportunity for a little revenge. As the girls checked out my new radio and Nthabiseng ran her fingers all over it she asked, "How do you open it?"

I played dumb. "Open it?" I said.

"Yes. How do you make it sing?"

"Oh, I'm sorry," I said. "You don't know how to push buttons?"

IT HAD FELT LIKE me against the hostelers in the first couple weeks. It felt like me against this whole new Tšoeneng world, really. But the hostelers and I were becoming acquainted, and one day in church I realized that we had more in common than I had seen in the beginning.

Principal Tsita required the hostelers to attend church every Sunday, as our school was sponsored by St. Peter Claver Catholic

Church. Almost all schools in Lesotho were church-sponsored, meaning the churches established the schools and had members on each school board and hired the teachers, even though teachers' salaries came through the government. For me, not being Catholic, I still attended because I thought that attending church would be a good way to get to know people from the village.

Hostelers made their way up to the church in disparate pairs and groups, dressed in their school uniforms, some of the boys adding a tie to fancify their attire, and I latched onto one of them for the fifteen minute stroll through the fields around the school to the edge of the village, where the church was. The service started at 11 a.m., after an old man came out and rang a hand bell. St. Peter Claver looked like a sandstone warehouse, save for the tinted-glass cross over the entrance, and inside there were pigeons roosting in the rafters under the tin roof. There were rows of bare wood benches, and I sat with the hostel boys toward the back. Village men sat around us and in front of us, and in the very front were young boys from the village. All of us males were seated in the middle rows. Women and girls sat on the rows of benches to the sides. Families did not sit together in church. As with everything in Lesotho, people were kept separate according to age and sex.

The service began with a hymn, the men and women singing distinct parts. After I'd followed the motions of the rest of the congregation—crossing myself, kneeling at the priest's command until my knees were numb—we were singing another hymn when I noticed that the young boys in the very front were turned around in their seats and staring at me in particularly large numbers. More than a dozen of them were almost facing straight at me, dumbly gazing. An older man made a loud scolding whisper at them and they swiveled back toward the priest. A minute later I looked down and noticed, as if for the first time, my hands resting on the back of the bench in front of me. They were pink, almost translucent. Next to my hands were a hosteler's named Tumelo. His fingers were dark brown. They looked solid and substantial. Then between my eyes I noticed the glow of my own pink nose. I'd never thought of my skin as looking pink. It wasn't just my hands and nose that beamed among the congregation, it was every piece of skin that was showing. I scanned the room: a hundred Africans with dark skin and ruggy black heads; and then me: pink with yellow, stringy hair. We looked as different from each other as humans could. So it was only natural for the young boys' eyes to be drawn to me, the item that was not the same as the others in this picture. Of course they looked at me. I would've looked too.

When the service was over I walked with the hostel boys back out of the warehouse. Out front, between the church building and the road, the villagers lingered to chat. Here was my chance to get to know villagers. I said hello to a student's father named ntate Adoro whom I had met before because he was a member of the Ngoana Jesu school board. After that I felt awkward because I didn't have anyone else to greet—the only other villagers I'd met were the chief and witchdoctor, but I didn't see them and I wasn't feeling brave enough to introduce myself to anyone new—and then I started feeling people's eyes on me. I saw that the hostelers were pairing and grouping up again and crossing the road to head back to school. I latched onto a group and made my way west with them, through the fields toward the school, and there it dawned on me that they also had no one to talk to outside the church. The hostelers weren't from Tšoeneng either. They came to Ngoana Jesu from different parts of Lesotho: the capital; Mokhotlong up in the high mountains; Korokoro; and villages closer but still too far away so that they couldn't walk daily to and from school. They came for different reasons: because Ngoana Jesu was cheap; because it was easy to be admitted; because a hosteler had a relative who lived in Tšoeneng; because their parents knew Principal Tsita. (She and the other teachers were not from Tšoeneng either.) The bottom line was that the hostelers were all foreigners in Tšoeneng just like me. At first, since they looked the same as the Tšoeneng people, spoke the same language and so on, I lumped them together. Yet they didn't belong in the village either. We were all outsiders to varying degrees. In fact, maybe, just possibly, some of those young boys in the church had been staring at Tumelo.

IN THE LATE MORNING of Friday, March 5, the tin roof over the staffroom ticked as usual as it expanded under the heat of the rising sun. Little white pebble clouds appeared in the sky to the west. Soon the clouds became gray boulders, they grew taller and darker, until whirlwinds of dust started to whip through the fields and around the school and at noon lightning began to flash and rain started dumping.

These thunderstorms came through almost daily. It was the perfect summer weather pattern: just as the sun reached its peak and the day got too hot, you were cooled. Classes were interrupted, so you got to rest. I was getting used to that. After I had accepted that no teaching happened while it was raining, I came to enjoy the break. I loved to watch a storm play out, and after it had chased me indoors I would always stand by a window, watching the rain pelt it. Every storm built in the same way, emerging from the western horizon with innocuous and scattered cotton balls, and then consuming your world with dark and tempest. The thunder cracks sounded so threatening, but I felt safe inside. Lightning always accompanied the rain in Lesotho, and people were always getting caught in the fields, tallest thing standing, bolts touching down all around. Two people from Tšoeneng would end up being struck that year, and I started to understand that there was a good reason to stay in the staffroom during a rain. But rarely did the thunderstorms last long. A couple hours and the sky broke up again.

On this Friday the storm had dumped enough rain that after it swept off to the east, into the higher mountains, I heard a great rushing noise. I looked down to the river valley and saw a wall of water marching down the Tsoaing river bed. Tšoeneng village is located at the base of a mountain peak, and the fields which surround Ngoana Jesu Secondary School roll down to a river basin. After a strong thunderstorm much of the rain is shed into that river and it swells rapidly, sometimes like a flash flood.

From school and my house I could see the river and I could hear its movement, but on this day I had to see it up close. After school let out that afternoon I told the hostelers so, and some of them said they would go with me. I was happy to go somewhere with the hostelers, sure we would get to know each other even better off the school grounds, doing something side by side, outside.

We took a trail through the glistening fields and the green pastures between them. There were almost no trees around. Throughout Lesotho there were few trees. Nevertheless, from the school only one other village was visible, the village that was wrapped like a necklace under the volcano-looking peak called Kolo which was on the opposite side of the wide valley carved out by the Tsoaing River.

After only a mile's walk we were at the grassy banks of the Tsoaing, which were collapsing as the muddy current below pulled them in. We moved up river and climbed down and up numerous erosion gullies that emptied into the river. The gullies were common features of the Lesotho landscape, especially in the lower mountain areas like Tšoeneng, where the powerful rains had eaten out ditches of topsoil. That topsoil, which was the fertility of the agricultural land in Lesotho, was being washed down the Tsoaing into the Mohokare River, which connected to the Senqu (known as the Orange River in South Africa), forming the border between South Africa and Namibia where it spilled into the Atlantic Ocean. It all started here.

The Tsoaing River itself was about 50 yards wide where I stood, and as branches rushed by in the flow I asked the hostelers if they ever swam in it. About a dozen had come down with me. They all said they never swam in the river.

We stood at the base of what they called the old bridge. In 2003 the road through Tšoeneng had been paved for the first time and a new bridge had been built across the Tsoaing. It was a first rate piece of engineering that was suspended high above the water and had been financed, like the paving of the road, by the European Union. But here we were at the old bridge. It was a track of concrete laid across the river over culvert pipes which the water was supposed to pass through. It functioned poorly, however: the pipes were small and partly clogged. It was flooded and impassable now, as it was after every thunderstorm, and the hostelers said that a couple years before a minibus taxi had tried to drive over it after a rain and was swept off and over the waterfall that lay just a few seconds down the river, between the old bridge and the new bridge. Many passengers in the taxi had drowned.

We walked closer to the waterfall. I imagined the taxi tumbling over the edge, 15 feet down to the roiling, angry white water at the bottom. A girl named Maleshoane Ramokone said, "There is a snake that lives in there." She pointed to the roiling beneath the waterfall. "It eats people."

"Well," I said, "I want to swim."

"No! The snake will eat you," said Maleshoane.

I hadn't really wanted to swim. Still I said again, "I'm going to swim."

"You will die."

Being told that made me want to take the game further, so I started untying my shoes.

"No, sir!" the hostelers all began saying. "Don't go in."

I took off my shirt.

I was beginning to actually want to swim now. I was tired of being warned about the dangers all around me. Peace Corps: Don't eat food that flies have touched. But I ate that goat meat, and I lived. Peace Corps: Don't go running through the fields. Shepherds will attack you. But I ran almost every morning and the shepherds did nothing but stare and occasionally wave. And I was tired of being shown where I was unskilled. Nthabiseng: You can't wash your clothes. Principal Tsita: Sir Greg can't speak Sesotho. Now the hostelers: You can't swim in the river. If there was one thing I could do it was swim.

The female hostelers were still yapping about how I shouldn't enter the water. I really wanted to swim now. So I asked someone to hold my camera. Two boys grabbed for it. This made me think they really did believe in the snake, and that I was about to die. Still, I started to climb down the bank next to a willow tree. A girl went over and picked up my shoes. "They will be mine," she said.

What kind of snake could there be in the river that could eat me though? Did they mean crocodile? It made me think, but it didn't stop me. I put my leg in. The bottom, which I could not see through the murk, felt sandy to my toes and the wetness climbed up my pant leg. I worked to keep my balance as I walked into the stronger, deeper current. The hostelers had gone into a frenzy now, shouting warnings, which still only had the effect of spurring me on. They could tell me how to wash my clothes, but I knew how to swim. I lay back and let the current take me.

With my feet out front, and my hands under me, I took off downstream. Atop the bank to my right I saw the hostelers screaming and running to keep up. The river curved left, around a frothy rock ledge and through some rapids, so I stroked away from the rocks and then held my breath as my body shot through the turbulence like a stick. I navigated it without my head ever being sucked under. If that was the scary section, then the rest was straightforward. I dashed through a smaller set of speed bumps where the banks slightly bottlenecked, and then the river opened wide. I saw that there was a sharp left bend ahead, which would take me under the big new bridge, but I had no idea what lay below that so I swam to shore and trudged out of the water. Alive. No snake. Just a thrilling, quick little swim. The hostelers arrived a moment later, out of breath and full of chatter. I basked in the moment. I was proven.

Then Khosi said, "I want to swim." Of course Khosi did. The smallest boy was the bravest.

Along this stretch there was a sandbar twenty yards wide, only waist deep, where the current was light. So I said I would take him. He took his shirt off as girls warned him not to swim. I held his arm and walked him a few feet into the water and then sat him down. Together we bumped slowly down river.

We walked back up and Khosi said he wanted to "swim" again. Then Thato and some other boys wanted to try. If they weren't wearing shorts they just stripped to their underwear. I took them each, one after the other, into the water and held their arms as we cruised down. The water level was receding fast because the rain had been hard and short. The river was going back to a normal flow. Soon enough it was only knee deep through a football field-sized section, and the girls came into the water too. They also stripped to their underwear if they weren't already wearing a skirt, and some had bras on. 'Mapaseka, a 17-year-old in my Form D class, came running to me wearing only her skirt—nothing on top. "Sir, help me to swim!" she said. I tried not to look at her breasts as she latched onto my arm. She excitedly splashed as we made our way downstream, all the while saying, "Sir! Sir help me!" No one else—including the teenage boys—paid naked 'Mapaseka any extra attention. Only I seemed aware of the bare parts of her body. This was new though: I was aware of the bare parts of her body. Up until now, when the hostel girls had passed by my window in the mornings half naked I barely registered it.

By the time the sun was low enough to touch the side of Kolo Mountain, the water over the sandbar was only up to our ankles. It was still flowing though, and the hostelers were still in the water running and laughing and "swimming." And 'Mapaseka was still half naked.

We never saw a crocodile or any kind of snake. The air became crisp and we left the water. We walked uphill through the fields toward school, exhausted from the day, with the muddy water drying into a common crust on our skin. For that moment, I felt like I was one of them. I wasn't totally useless. True, I couldn't handwash clothes well or speak Sesotho like them, but they saw that I could do other things—not just sit Indian style but more useful things like swim. We only learn skills that are advantageous in the context in which we live. Give me time and maybe I can become competent in abilities that matter here in Lesotho.

CHAPTER THREE

Crocodile Burning

AS THE SCHOOL YEAR WORE ON, after I got used to missing classes because of the rain and all of the peculiar English words used at Ngoana Jesu, the salient obstacle to a smooth teaching day was books. The poor Form A students. I began thinking of them as the Lost Class. It was now the second quarter and the government had yet to bring them a single book. No one knew when these magical government rental books would arrive, but in the meantime all of us teachers continued to think up lessons and write them on the chalkboard. That way of teaching, every single day, got so draining and boring that I noticed teachers start to skip some of their Form A classes. Being such an inexperienced teacher, I probably had the hardest time coming up with learning material from scratch for the Form A's each day. How many times could I write sentences on the board and ask them to join the sentences with conjunctions? So I didn't feel so bad imitating the teachers in this respect. I felt bad for the students, but I had run out of activity ideas. And the Form A's had the lowest level of English. Khosi was way beyond most of his classmates. We couldn't just hang out and chat.

The Form D's had a problem with their books too, not because they also lacked books, but because of the level of books they were assigned to read. Our first book was a play, and here were the opening lines:

"If music be the food of love, play on
Give me excess of it, that, surfeiting
The appetite may sicken, and so die."

I had to read that again, to let the metaphor sink in. Then I thought of how I would explain it to the class, and then how I would account for the strange punctuation of the language. Shakespeare for my Form D's? Get real. Teenagers from a remote village in Africa who didn't even have a handle on contemporary English studying an archaic poetic form of the language? That was the decree of Lesotho's Ministry of Education, and I had no choice. I tried to prepare them on our first Shakespeare day. "He lived about 500 years ago, so the English is very old and strange, even for me." I tried not to come across negatively, but I couldn't help recalling that I had last read Shakespeare in college, where I struggled to decipher the plot points of *Hamlet*.

This first scene of *Twelfth Night* was only 42 lines, but we read it aloud and stopped every few lines so I could paraphrase and explain. The students quietly suffered through. It took more than that first 40-minute class period to finish the first scene.

As ill-suited as Shakespeare was for the Form D's, the book that we had to read in Form B caused me more mental anguish. It was a novel called *Crocodile Burning*, and the story was about the growing up of a Zulu boy named Seraki, set in South Africa.

Normally, the Form B students arranged themselves in the classroom like members of a choir—baritone boys in back, soprano girls up front—but days when we read *Crocodile Burning* the students had to gather in small groups. There were only seven copies of the novel among the class of forty students. They were supposed to buy all of their textbooks, but only a handful of students could afford to. So the students shared. Some sat, some stood and looked over shoulders, some stood and stared out the windows as we shuffled through the novel together. I had a student from one group read a couple paragraphs out loud and then a student from another group read the next couple of paragraphs, and so on. It seemed ridiculous to read an entire novel like this at the high school level, but without more copies of the book there was no other way.

I always thought of the Form B's as my first class. They were the first class I ever taught, anywhere. Further, there were a lot of hostelers in that class: Nthabiseng, Tlhokomelo, Maoto, Thobei, Tšepang the boy, Tšepang the girl, Maleshoane Rapeane,

Maleshoane Ramokone. And since I got to know the hostelers better than any village students during those first months, I got to know the Form B's better than other classes.

Reading aloud, we made it to page 9 of *Crocodile Burning*, where Seraki jumped onto the back of a grocery truck to hitch a ride across town and an onlooker said about him, "Look at that terrorist."

"Sir, what is a terrorist?" a Form B asked. I thought for a second, and then wrote a simplified definition on the chalkboard: "Someone who does things to scare people." Then, since this was only 2004, it occurred to me that I should give them the conspicuous example of the events of September 11, 2001. "The 9/11 hijackers were terrorists," I said to the class.

"Sir?"

"You guys remember what happened on September 11th?" They made no such affirmation.

I gave them a brief reminder of the events: Planes crashed into buildings, some of which were tall ones in New York, which then collapsed. Their eyes widened as I told the story. These Muslim guys were trying to scare and kill Americans, I said.

"Why did they do this?" a student asked. "What happened to the people in the buildings?"

I finished the story, through the invasion of Afghanistan, but it was all a surprise to them. This was the first they were hearing of it. An event that had rocked America and shocked the rest of the world, and dominated much of the world's news for some time, was never news at all in Tšoeneng.

I happened to have a *TIME* magazine with photos of the September 11th attacks, and I passed it around the class the next day. The students gasped and pointed to people in each photo, "Did he die? Did she die?"

"I'm not sure."

I came away realizing that Ngoana Jesu was not just a school in a village in a country on the other side of the globe where the culture was different from America's and technology was less advanced. I could have been living on a different planet altogether. These students had no idea of the place from which I came.

I READ AHEAD OF THE CLASS each day in *Crocodile Burning*, so I knew on which day I would have to talk to the Form B's about apartheid. The novel is set in Soweto, the famous black township near Johannesburg, during the twilight years of white rule in South Africa, and the story involves Seraki's older brother becoming politically active against the government and getting into trouble for it. So I thought I had better be able to speak knowledgeably about apartheid and South African history to the class. I was apprehensive about the discussion. It was going to be uncomfortable to stand up there as a white teacher in front of my black students and talk about how people who looked like me had treated people who looked like them very terribly. I was especially uneasy going into it because I'd seen that their grip on world events was loose to nonexistent. Despite that, I figured they would know a lot about apartheid since South Africa totally surrounds Lesotho—the border was only a half-day's walk to the east—and also, the rule of whites in the government of South Africa had only ended ten years prior. A few of the Form B's were more than 20 years old so they should have some recollection of apartheid, I thought. Even the students who were 15 or 16 had been alive during that period.

To prepare for the coming talk, I consulted my Lonely Planet guidebook, the only relevant book I had in Tšoeneng. The school didn't have a library, and in fact there were no public libraries in the whole country, and of course I had no access to the Internet. I perused the Lonely Planet's summary of the region's background, and I went to class with it nearly memorized: Apartheid means being apart, and it refers specifically to the separation of races. Different races couldn't marry, live together, work together, use the same toilets. Apartheid was a Dutch word, and the government which created it was composed mostly of descendents of the Dutch who had long ago settled near the Cape of Good Hope, at the very bottom of Africa, starting in 1652. Yet when these people imposed apartheid, they no longer called themselves Dutch. After a few hundred years they had begun to feel disconnected to Europe, and very connected to Africa, so much so that they began calling themselves Afrikaners, and their language Afrikaans. These Afrikaners imposed the apartheid style of government beginning in 1948, and it lasted for almost 50 years, all the way up to the time of Seraki and his brother in our novel, *Crocodile Burning*.

In class we hit page 44. The students read aloud, and we learned that Seraki's brother, Phakane, had come home from school one day jumping in excitement because he had become the new chairman of the Youth Action Committee. Although this filled Phakane with joy, it made his mother nervous. The Youth Action Committee was involved in anti-apartheid activities. "Since the government declared the State of Emergency after the troubles in 1986, anyone can be arrested [for anti-apartheid activities] and detained and the police don't have to give out any information," read a Form B student. Late that very night the police came and dragged Phakane from the house and threw him into their van. Eight months went by and no one heard from Phakane.

I didn't really want to get into it, but I had to. I checked the Form B's for an understanding of Phakane's abduction, and then I asked, "The mother was nervous about Phakane's anti-apartheid activities. What is apartheid?"

"It is the government for the Boers," a boy answered.

That was another name for Afrikaners, particularly for the subgroup of Afrikaners who left the Cape region to explore the interior of Africa. After Holland lost in the Napoleonic Wars in the early 19th century, the British usurped control of the Cape and imposed new laws on the settlers there, including the abolition of slavery. Some Afrikaners, still called the Dutch, emigrated to find new lands on which they could continue to live the way they wanted. And they took on a new appellation: Trekboers— "traveling farmers" in Dutch—or for short, just Boers.

"What kind of government was the Boer government?" I asked.

"The cruel one."

I would come to hear students use this adjective often when talking about Boers. *Maburu a khopo*. The Boers are cruel.

As the Boers trekked north from the Cape they ran into the Basotho. At first, the Basotho were hospitable and allowed them to stay on the land, thinking they were only passing through, but soon the number of Boers increased and they clearly weren't moving on. In fact, they began demanding to occupy more land. Decades of skirmishes and wars began, ending in the Basotho being pushed up into the mountains and losing much of their arable fields to the Boers. Finally, in 1868, King Moshoeshoe asked the British to annex his Basotho nation, thereby putting a stop to the overrun by the Boers. The British had been allowing the Boers to buy guns but disallowing the landlocked Basotho, which gave the Boers an insurmountable advantage. In that way, the Basotho remained undefeated and yet protected—they retained partial control over their country but had the aegis of the powerful British ensuring that the Boers encroached no farther.

Today, the land to the west of Lesotho, where Boers continue to own huge swaths of land, spreading farms, is still referred to by the Basotho as the Conquered Territories. And the Basotho think of the long ago wars when the Boers won those territories, along with the apartheid years, when they say, *Maburu a khopo*.

Our discussion in class continued. I asked the Form B's about Nelson Mandela, and specifically which year he had become president, but no one could answer. 1994, I wrote on the board. I asked what else they knew about Mandela. "He is a Xhosa," a student said. His tribe was important to them. I had been thinking of apartheid as blacks against whites, but really there were different blacks and different whites.

A boy raised his hand. "Sir, do you know Afrikaans?"

"No, not at all," I said. I was surprised by the question. Of course I didn't know how to speak Afrikaans. I felt the need to elaborate, and to hammer the point home, that there was no kinship between me and the Boers. "White people have different tribes just like black people. I'm from America, and it's very far from where the Boers are from. Americans speak only English. Do you know how to speak Zulu?" No one in the class answered. "You don't know how to speak Zulu for the same reason that I don't know Afrikaans."

I came out of the class feeling like the students were clear about me being different from the Boers, and for that I felt great relief and joy. I had never actually met a Boer myself, and it was clearly self-serving to throw them under a bus as a whole group of people, but the immediacy of my being alone as a white foreigner at the school and in the village made me abdicate the finer points of logical and sympathetic thinking. I also liked that the Form B's and I had gotten to know each other better because we had attempted a real discussion, which didn't happen often. Usually, we were just talking grammar or the plot points of the novel.

By the second quarter, the Form B students had made themselves at home in their classroom, and I began to feel more at home in there too. There were decorations on the walls. Near the door, students had stuck a paper on which was a handwritten prayer: "MAY THE GRACE OF OUR LORD JESUS, THE LOVE OF GOD AND THE FELLOWSHIP OF THE HOLY SPIRIT BE WITH YOU NOW AND FOREVER MORE, AMEN." Another paper next to the prayer showed a schedule for sweeping the classroom, as there was a different pair of students obligated to sweep each day. And also stuck to the wall was a similar schedule, but for cleaning the pig sties. There was no janitor at Ngoana Jesu. The students did all of the cleaning, even in the staffroom. On the back wall there was a poster of the South African soccer team Orlando Pirates, and also a boy named Thobei had put up his pencil drawing of a bus with gleaming rims and the driver hanging out the window wearing sunglasses and a cocky grin. The name of the bus was written on the windshield, *Khosi ea Bashanyana*—King of the Boys. This was the real name of a local bus, and students thought bus and taxi drivers were cool. The ceiling above was rotten and caving in from leaks in the tin roof, windows were cracked and the walls were dirty, but the students' decorations sometimes made me not notice that. Over the chalkboard a small, white plastic Jesus hung on a wooden cross.

In *Crocodile Burning*, Seraki joined a song-and-dance group in his Soweto neighborhood which began performing locally. Soon it became such a hit that it was invited to perform on Broadway, in New York! The Form B's were unimpressed. New York meant nothing to them, let alone Broadway.

On page 99, Seraki and his group arrived in the Big Apple and went sightseeing. Seraki and his friend Sipho took off alone to check out the Bronx and they ran into a crack dealer. A Form B student read aloud to the class the words of the crack dealer shouting at Seraki and Sipho: "Looks like we've got ourselves some real live monkeys here!"

I had read ahead for the lesson on this day, like usual, but somehow I had forgotten this line was coming. I quickly scanned the class, but no one was looking up at me for an explanation, so I let the student read on.

The crack dealer was a white guy, and his friend, another white guy, said directly to Seraki: "Come on, monkey! Let's hear some more of that jungle speak. You come needing a banana?"

But the Form B's still didn't react. So I let them finish the scene. Seraki attacked the friend of the crack dealer, and a brawl ensued. The New York police arrived to arrest Seraki and Sipho, and then a white woman yelled down from her apartment window, "You blacks are always causing trouble."

I hated *Crocodile Burning*. Who was this author? What was he trying to prove? Then again maybe I deserved it, since earlier I had essentially told the class that Boers and Americans had no relation and implied that Boers were bad but Americans were good. Still, the book was a lie. That would never happen. And now I had to explain it away.

"This book is fiction," I said to the class. "Fiction means the story is not true. I have been to New York. And there are many black people there more than in Soweto, actually. And I promise, if you ever went to New York, no one would call you a monkey."

I wondered about Lesotho's Ministry of Education. They asked the Form D's to read Shakespeare, the A's had no books at all, and they had chosen *Crocodile Burning* as a required reading text for the Form B's. Did they think the students would relate to this story because they were teenagers and they were black like Seraki, and because they also lived near South Africa? Well, my Form B's didn't relate at all. They didn't care for the book nearly as much as for the novel we read later in the year. Called *I Am David*, it was about a Jewish boy escaping from a concentration camp in Eastern Europe and making his way to Denmark. The book was honest and well-written, the narrative having believable adventure. The students talked of the story often outside of class. Some of the male students even started calling themselves David. I learned that the Form B's were like teenagers everywhere else in the world. They didn't care about race and politics, like the adults in the Ministry of Education did, or like I feared they would.

CHAPTER FOUR

Why Peace Corps

CROCODILE BURNING **WAS WRITTEN** by a white South African named Michael Williams, *I Am David* was written by a Danish woman named Anne Holm, and the Form B's also had to read a collection of short plays which were set in England. That book was called *Reaching Out*. The fourth of their literature books was a selection of poems called *Growing Up With Poetry*, and at last this book was edited by an African, but not a Mosotho. None of the books was produced in any way by a person from Lesotho, and none took place in the country. Lesotho produced very little literature, and most of what it did was in Sesotho, not English. A goal listed in the Ministry of Education's curriculum was to develop a "reading culture" among the students because Basotho culture was not a reading culture, and it never had been. Basotho had no written language until French missionaries arrived in the 1830's and learned Sesotho and transcribed it.

There is a funny story told by one of the missionaries, Eugene Casalis, about his struggle to get the father of the king of Lesotho to believe that words could be written. Mokhachane, the father of King Moshoeshoe, was a "scoffing and sceptical old man," according to Casalis. And he ridiculed the young missionary about his claim of being able to "make paper speak." It was a lie, the old man said repeatedly. "I will never believe that words can become visible."

King Moshoeshoe, on the other hand, believed. "We will prove it to you," he said to his father one day. "Now, think of something, and tell it to this white man; he will draw some marks on the sand, and you will see." The marks were made and then a man from the village who had learned to read was called over to speak the words written in the sand, which he did.

Mokhachane was, as Casalis described it, "more than stupefied." He covered his mouth with his hand and looked around at everyone as if to assure himself that he was not dreaming. "At length, after having exhausted all the interjections of his language, he burst forth into a torrent of invectives against his subjects and his family, for not having informed him of the miracles which were being performed in his country." As if they hadn't tried.

Maybe Lesotho was the perfect culture for me because I wanted to escape the written word. College had been full of books. I finished in 1999 with a degree in philosophy, and I began applying to graduate programs with the aim of becoming a professor, but then I backed out. I felt imbalanced, saturated from five straight years of heavy reading. I wanted to put books down for a while and touch the world. I needed physical contact, real interaction, to get to know some things for myself rather than through the words of others.

And I came to Lesotho to escape America also. I wanted to find out how people lived in a place that was as different from home as possible. I didn't dislike America in any way. I was just curious to see how people lived elsewhere.

From the time I graduated, I made my living building surfboards, and so I considered moving to the Atlantic coast of France where I could support myself by building surfboards and simultaneously settle into the culture there and learn the language. After some consideration though, I concluded that France was too much like California, and French was too much like English. I wanted to go to a strange place.

Madagascar. I would save my money and then spend a month or two there. I could surf and see weird animals with big eyes and the culture would be totally new. But a month or two was only traveling. I didn't want skim along the surface of a culture, I wanted to sink in, I wanted to live there, to spend enough time to get to know the place deeply, to learn the language.

Peace Corps. Two years in a place far away. That was what I

needed. And maybe I could be of some service to people along the way.

ON A MAY MORNING I opened my door to see some hostel boys crouched over a fire they had built near their vegetable plots. I walked over to find Tumelo, Tšepang, Taelo and Masopha warming themselves and roasting maize kernels in a pan. The kernels didn't pop, but softened and browned into a nice snack—*chechisa*, they said it was called, and they offered me some.

A silver film of ice coated the grasses that morning. I asked the boys how to talk about the frost. *"Serame se oetse,"* said Masopha. "Frost has fallen." Masopha was the hosteler who was the most enthusiastic about teaching me Sesotho. Whenever he came over my house he had a new word for me or a cultural cue. *Serame* was the first whiff of winter. I had long been told that it snowed in Lesotho, and finally now I was able to imagine it.

The afternoon became warmed up enough, but in the morning and at night my clothing no longer sufficed to keep me comfortable, even in my house. The concrete walls and concrete floor were icy cold and seemed to provide no insulation at all. In my house I was technically indoors, but I felt like I was as exposed to the temperature and wind as though I were camping in a tent.

That evening, after school, I stoked my propane heater for the first time. Nine hostelers crowded into my house to huddle around it. They didn't have a heater of any kind in the hostel. We were a herd of blankets worshiping a flame inside a metal box. I was wearing a Basotho blanket just like them because a few days earlier Masopha had noticed my blanket on my bed and asked if I knew how to wear it.

"I just use it for sleeping," I said.

"It's not for sleeping, sir!"

Basotho blankets are special. They're tough, made mostly of wool. They're square, and only six feet long or so, not long enough for anyone's bed, but they weren't supposed to be. My whole training group had been given Basotho blankets by the Peace Corps staff upon finishing our two months of training, but they never taught us how to use them. Unlike most blankets, a

Basotho blanket was a piece of clothing, and further, it was to be worn in specific ways. Masopha folded over the top of my blanket and then draped it over my shoulders. He put the opening at the middle of my chest and said, "Do not wear it like this. It is for the women." Then he shifted the opening to my left shoulder and said that was how men wear it. "I will teach you to tie the blanket without a pin, like the shepherds." He tucked one end behind my shoulder and tucked the other end under the first to make a bulky knot. Then he stepped back and began laughing.

He gave me his stick. "Hold my *molamu*, sir." I held the *molamu* high, playing along, doing as I'd seen initiates and shepherds do. "Where is your camera, sir? I will take a photo so that you can show the Americans how we Basotho dress."

My blanket was blue. I was told that it was the color worn by people from a northern district called Leribe, which was where I had done my Peace Corps training. Masopha wore a yellow blanket, which indicated that he was from the south, in a district called Mafeteng. Around the heater that evening, hostelers had all sorts of colors of blankets on, which to other Basotho gave hints as to where they were from. Except for red. No one wore a red blanket, as those were only worn by initiates, new men.

Masopha looked around the room at all of us crouched and facing the little propane heater and asked, "What kind of family is this?" Then he answered his own question, "An extended family. Sir, you have so many children."

A FEW DAYS LATER Principal Tsita walked into the staffroom and announced that it was time to go home for the winter. There was no set date for the end of a semester, not by the school, not by the Ministry of Education. Schools were just supposed to be open for 180 days per year. Each principal decided when to open and close the semesters, and Principal Tsita also decided when to tell everyone else when she would end it. Principal Tsita had given us a day and a half advance notice. Tomorrow we would go home until late July. The semester ended as it had begun: unexpectedly.

On my very first day—when I thought I would teach but all that happened was the students cleaned their classrooms and the teachers mostly got reacquainted with one another—I had been introduced to this desultory mode of operation. Things ran the same way throughout the term. I never knew for sure when I was going to teach a class, despite the timetable that was taped to the staffroom wall. Classes had been canceled or missed all the time. Weather caused a lot of problems. When it rained hard, a stream called Sebolu flooded just like the Tsoaing and students who lived on the other side of it couldn't cross to make it home, so the whole school was let out early during heavy thunderstorms and students rushed away to cross the riverbeds before they filled. Beyond the obstacles of the rain and the lack of books, if, for example, the two women who cooked school lunches ran out of firewood, the first two periods of the day were canceled so the students could go into the countryside and collect more. There were impromptu staff meetings called about a variety of urgent issues—which teacher would call taxi drivers to take the students to the sports competition, say. And the students would be left alone and clueless in their classrooms while the teachers were otherwise occupied. A parent of one of our students died, so we teachers walked into the village to offer consolation to the family. The students sat in their classrooms alone.

The hostelers hurriedly packed up and trekked off to their home villages that Wednesday afternoon and the school grounds abruptly became empty and soundless, save the odd donkey bray that wafted down from Tšoeneng village or the faint song of a shepherd that floated up from the pastures. I had a hard time sleeping that night. I'd grown accustomed to the hostelers' visits each evening and overhearing their songs across the way as I went to bed. The night was dark and the silence was loud. The hostelers and the teachers all had homes and families to return to for the winter, but I didn't. This house at Ngoana Jesu, out in the fields on the edge of Tšoeneng village was my home now, and truthfully, the hostelers had become the closest thing to family for me here. I was alone again. Still, I didn't exactly feel lonely. I was disoriented by the sudden disappearance of all the action around me, but I still wouldn't say I was lonely. I had feared that I would be lonely in Lesotho, and before I left America I had written a list of things to do to keep my mind occupied in case that happened: "Read a book. Exercise. Listen to music. Work. Write a letter." But I had yet to refer to the list. When I broke down in the second week of school I hadn't been lonely in the way I anticipated I might be. I had been overwhelmed and feeling alienated. Throughout the rest of the first semester the hostelers pursued me, never leaving me alone in my house for long. And now that they were gone I noticed their absence immensely, but I still didn't feel the need for distraction in the way I had feared I would.

The first semester of school, about three months long, had hit me like a tornado and not let up until today. It left me extremely tired. I'm in a state of exhaustion that is not as shallow as that incurred after a long run. It's running though the marrow of my bones. Mere sleep will not cure it, I wrote in my journal that evening. Then I studied some notes in my Sesotho memo book by the light of my paraffin lamp. I had started using it instead of candles because it gave off more heat. And the paraffin, or kerosene, was not too expensive. I then read a little from a *Newsweek* magazine and eventually, with a feeling of nostalgia for the presence of the hostelers, I fell asleep.

The next morning was eerily calm too. There was no clinking of the water pump lever. It was conducive to more reflection, about why I wasn't lonely, why I was exhausted, and why I was enthused by my new life in Tšoeneng despite the chaos that permeated it. I recorded more thoughts in my journal: This is the best job I've ever had, this whole Peace-Corps-volunteer-English-teacher-in-a-Lesotho-high-school thing, I wrote. It was the best not because it was straightforward, or easy. It challenged the heck out of me. I spent long hours at school. From 8 a.m. to 5 p.m. I was up there, and then bookending school, I helped hostelers with homework and studied Sesotho. It didn't pay well. At $250 a month my Peace Corps stipend was less than I'd ever lived on. Nevertheless, I called it the best because it was incessantly interesting. Every moment of every day I was learning something new, encountering something strange, dealing with something tricky. I was never for a second bored. I felt weary after a few months of such a life, and the school break was a welcome chance to recover, not an empty space where loneliness might creep in. I finally had a chance to take a full breath.

Within a couple days I was feeling relaxed and I started planning goals and activities for the break. I wanted to learn to teach better, because I really liked my students and I wanted to serve them well. So I planned to ask Peace Corps for books about teaching that I could borrow and study. And then I wanted to spend all of the rest of my time learning Sesotho and getting to know Tšoeneng village. I wanted to make the language my own, and make the village my home. I was excited about the next two months, June and July.

CHAPTER FIVE

Mugged

I ARRIVED IN LESOTHO in November of 2003 in a group with 23 other Peace Corps volunteer trainees. After a couple months of language and job and culture and health training we were disbursed to live in different corners of the mountainous country. There were about 80 Peace Corps volunteers in Lesotho in total at the time, but only our group was called to a conference in the capital city in early June, 2004. Some volunteers spent a full day of travel to get to Maseru, but for me the capital took only an hour and a half by minibus taxi. The hulk of Qeme plateau and some lower peaks separated Tšoeneng from Maseru. From my house at night, if I looked north I could see a slight glow in the sky from the electric lights of the city.

The conference was organized so we could reunite and discuss how our teaching jobs were going. It was comforting to commiserate with the other volunteers. We had gotten to know one another pretty well over our two months of training, and to hear that they had encountered many of the same odd practices at their schools and had felt many of the same frustrations was comforting, in the way that misery loves company. Sometimes at school I had felt like I was pushing English on my students. There were kids like Khosi who could speak some English and enjoyed learning more, but then there were many others who couldn't even ask to use the toilet in English and they didn't show any interest in getting better at the language. Yet students were beaten by the other teachers if they made English mistakes or if they were caught speaking Sesotho at school, and English was the only "failing" subject, that is, if you failed English, then no matter how well you passed other subjects you were not allowed to move on to the next grade. I felt uncomfortable forcing my mother tongue on the students who clearly didn't care to learn it. One of my closest friends in my group of Peace Corps volunteers, Ajith, said he also struggled with feeling imperialistic at times. But he realized that the students would be sitting in class learning the language with or without him, and that made him feel better about trying to motivate the students to improve their English. That made sense to me.

Also attending the conference were our Peace Corps supervisors and a couple of Ministry of Education officials. Ajith was teaching Shakespeare at his school too, and he took the opportunity at the conference to ask one of the officials why they had chosen Shakespeare for students such as ours. The official pushed the question aside, saying he had a very good answer to it, but that he would address it after the lunch break. We broke for lunch and the Ministry of Education official slipped out, never to return to the conference.

All was not so serious though. We volunteers joked about how so many of our male students liked to wear only one glove. It was something we had noticed at all of our schools. Were they imitating Michael Jackson? And all of our students seemed to share a nervous habit, something they did when they had to speak in front of their class, for example. They picked their noses. They all did it. Weren't they embarrassed? Didn't they know what they looked like when they did that?

And we talked about plans for the winter break. Ajith was considering traveling to Swaziland. Some others had even more distant destinations: Namibia, Malawi, Ethiopia. They were surprised that I intended on hanging around Tšoeneng, that I didn't want to travel to new places but rather I wanted to stay put, get better at Sesotho and get to know Lesotho more deeply. I wanted to make this place feel like home. I knew why I had come, and I knew that in order to continue feeling more comfortable here I needed to get better at the language and make more friends in the village. I had a mission, and it felt good to know exactly what I wanted.

AFTER SESSIONS WRAPPED UP on the conference's last day, two other volunteers and I chose to walk back to the Transit House, where Peace Corps volunteers slept while they were visiting Maseru. (No volunteers lived in the capital, and our travel there was restricted, since the city was by far the most dangerous place in the country.) We could have taken a ride in a Peace Corps vehicle, but it had been a long day of sitting. Nate, Amanda and I made our way down the main street, Kingsway, past Queen Elizabeth II hospital, and then past the tallest building in the country, the 11-story Lesotho Bank Tower. Taxis honked to offer rides but we said no thanks. We continued by the sandstone, tin-roofed colonial-style building of the police headquarters, and the park below it where you were not allowed to walk on the grass— just like in England—and overlooking the park was a bronze statue of a crocodile, which is the totem animal of the royal family's Bakoena clan. (Maybe there were crocodiles in the rivers.) Maseru is a city of about 200,000 people, far and away the biggest city in Lesotho. But in many ways it's still much like an overgrown village. Basotho on the sidewalk hawked apples, single cigarettes, cobs of roasted maize and lollipops. A couple people begged us for money. We didn't buy anything, nor did we give away anything. We only picked up some food, including a carton of ice cream, at Shoprite, a chain based in South Africa and the capital's one modern grocery store. None of us had tasted ice cream for months. Even though it was cold outside, we were excited for the treat.

Kingsway Street turned residential as we made our way west toward the Transit House. The sun slipped behind a stand of eucalyptus trees in front of us and the air temperature also dropped. Then Nate nudged Amanda and me to the side. "Let's wait up and let these guys pass," he said. Two guys came up behind us on the sidewalk. One of them looked over his shoulder at me as he passed. They were both small young men. After they walked ahead Nate said, "There's no need for them to come up on us like that."

Come up on us like what? I looked back at Nate's face. It was suspicious. Maybe he'd been listening too well to the warnings of Peace Corps administration about how dangerous it was in

Maseru.

On the first day we all arrived in Lesotho, on November 14, 2003, we had crossed the border in the dark. The only things that were lit up in the night were the road signs warning of AIDS. One read, "Doing it naked? Wear a condom." And I remembered that on the wall in the immigration office was a calendar for MKM Burial Society. Funeral services must be big business here, I remember thinking. And then we arrived at the Transit House. A guard let us in through a gate topped with barbed wire. Then the Peace Corps security adviser, an American man with a froggy voice named Mark, gathered us around. "If you feel like going for a stroll tonight, don't. For a run in the morning, don't. Stay in the compound. Maseru is dangerous."

But over the eight months since then I had learned some Sesotho and I had come to Maseru many times, yet I had never had a bad experience. I came to think of the place as benign, and its dangers as being exaggerated or only affecting people who showed obvious wealth or made themselves especially vulnerable by going out drinking at night or being in the wrong part of town after sunset. Not me. I didn't even wear my inexpensive watch when I visited the city.

We picked our walking pace up again and I stared at the guys that were now walking in front of us. I especially stared at the guy on the right. He was short, wearing a blue windbreaker, at the most 30 years old, but he could've passed for one of my Form D students. I looked at his right hand and thought, these guys aren't a threat. In fact, I'd like to get into a fight right now. I could easily handle this one.

We walked on for a few blocks, and the two guys got so far ahead of us that I stopped thinking about them and went back to thinking about ice cream. Then we crossed a side street, and I looked up to see the guys spin around simultaneously and brandish knives. Amanda shrieked. One went after her and the one in the blue windbreaker came at me. He said in English, "Give me your money!"

I looked down at his knife. It was stubby, perhaps a three-inch blade with a rounded tip and a black handle. He held it close to his body and said in clear English again, "Give me your money." As a reflex I said, "I don't have any money." He continued approaching me and I began backstepping. At the same time I was thinking about how weak the knife looked. It was so small and unshiny. Still, I found myself with my hands in the air, backing up, repeating, "I don't have any money!"

He repeated, "Give me your money!"

"I don't have any money! I don't have any money!"

I backed up and backed up until I was against a fence. Blue Windbreaker put his knife to my stomach. I froze, with my hands raised, knowing he could stick it in and spill my guts before I even felt pain. With his free hand, he deftly slipped into my left pocket and removed all of the contents: around 200 maloti in cash, my Peace Corps ID card, and a grocery/to-do list. After examining it, he stepped back and folded up his knife. Stupid, I thought, he's just disabled his only weapon. I could kick it out of his hand. I could kick him in the nuts. I could . . . Right then he turned and I watched the back of his jacket balloon as he ran back up Kingsway with his friend.

Nate came over and said to me, "Should we run after them?" Both of us started toward them. "Don't!" Amanda yelled. We had only made a few strides, and then stopped. What would we do if we caught up to them anyway? We would only be back at square one, again outmatched two knives to none. I rocked back and forth frustrated, debating, feeling powerless.

We came back together on the corner of Kingsway and Cenez streets. Are you OK? Are you OK? Did they take anything from you? What did they get from you? The whole mugging had probably taken less than a minute, but it was hard to say. Time warps when your mind is reduced to the single goal of not getting shanked.

While Blue Windbreaker had his knife to my stomach, in the back of my mind I had heard shouts and screams from Nate and Amanda. Now they told me that the other guy had gone behind Amanda to put her between him and Nate. He rifled through her back pockets, finding nothing. So he took her grocery bag. He got the ice cream!

This happened only two blocks from the Transit House. As we walked the rest of the way I joked at being especially pissed because they had taken our ice cream. But really I felt emasculated. Nate felt even more so. Amanda was his girlfriend, and while she was being manhandled he merely stood by and shouted. He felt emasculated and humiliated. Of course he shouldn't have because there was nothing more he could have done. The three of us convened inside the barbed wire security gate, not yet inside the T-House, to decide what we would tell others. There were twenty of our friends inside the door.

"Let's just keep it to ourselves," said Nate.

"You don't want to tell anyone?"

Amanda was quiet, but she was clearly shaken up and then she said she wanted to tell Peace Corps administration.

Peace Corps took us to the police station to file a report, and the police gave us a case number, but the new Peace Corps security adviser, a former Marine name Mike, told us that honestly, nothing was likely to come of it. Getting away with a mugging like that was too easy. All the police had to go on were physical descriptions of the guys (young black males) and their clothes (blue windbreaker and black jacket), and since no blood was spilled it was low priority. The police in Lesotho weren't as corrupt as in, say, Mozambique, Mike said. In other words, a bribe wasn't necessary to get them to even lift a finger on the case, but still we would most likely never hear from them again.

The next day Peace Corps reimbursed me for the money that had been stolen. Before I even got on the plane to Africa I told myself to expect to get mugged or robbed. It seemed to go with the territory. So each time I walked out of my house, and especially when I went to Maseru, I split my bills between pockets. That way, after a mugging I might still have some money to get a bus ride home. On that day I had small bills in my right pocket and big bills in my left. Blue Windbreaker had been lucky to choose my left pocket. He got away with the equivalent of $30.

While debriefing with Peace Corps staff and filing the police report I continued to spend the couple nights after the mugging at the T-House. But I wasn't sleeping well. My head on the pillow ran through the events of that evening on Kingsway over and over again. Should I have tried to kick the knife out of Blue Windbreaker's hand? Should Nate and I have run after them and tried to at least bean them with rocks? I just hated the fact that this guy had come up to me with that stubby little knife and took whatever he wanted, as I did nothing but raise my hands. I felt wronged and I felt like a pansy. And my humiliation was starting to morph into real anger.

I knew I would meet Blue Windbreaker again someday. Maseru was a small world. Even though I only came into the city to buy groceries every week or two, I already recognized many of the faces on the streets. There was the beggar who rubbed his tummy and said, "Money?" There was the guy selling apples and candy and phone cards who I learned had grown up in Tšoeneng. And some of the cashiers at Shoprite knew my name. So, while at the Peace Corps office, between meetings with staff, I researched knife fighting. I would not let Blue Windbreaker have his way with me again. We would see how he handled some of his own medicine. Each time I thought about confronting him my emotions flared. I imagined whipping out my own blade and watching him cower. But then through my Internet research I read guys say repeatedly that even the winner of a knife fight always ends up bloody. Blue Windbreaker wasn't worth a drop of my blood. So I considered a gun. I didn't want to actually shoot him, not because I didn't want him to die, but because I would end up with a small amount of temporary satisfaction and then a large police and diplomatic problem. I would just like to pull the gun out and stick it to his head and listen to him cry. What if he fought back and I had to pull the trigger? It could all go terribly wrong. I felt cornered, back to being powerless again. There was nothing I could do but try to avoid the guy.

A STORM WAS DRIVING cold rain at angles. I was back on the abandoned school campus, in my house, wrapped in my Basotho blanket. I sipped coffee and tried to stay warm, but there seemed no escape from the cold, even inside the house. When the first frost had hit in May I turned on my propane heater, but the hostelers and I had to practically sit on top of it to feel its warmth. Cold air was constantly whirling all around and whisking the heated air right back out through the space under my door and the gaps where my windows didn't totally shut.

The rain slamming onto my tin roof created a white noise that helped me concentrate on the book I was reading, Nelson Mandela's autobiography, *Long Walk to Freedom*. I felt like being captured inside someone else's story, and Mandela's book was an obvious choice. Living in Lesotho was, in a way, living inside of South Africa. In 1910, when colonies in the region formed the Union of South Africa, Lesotho remained a British Protectorate. The Basotho didn't want to be incorporated into the Union, as they suspected that the whites who ruled it, which included the Boers, would not treat them fairly. In 1961, the Union of South Africa became independent of the British Empire and took the name Republic of South Africa, but Lesotho remained separate, even as it gained its own independence five years later, and so it continues to be a tiny sovereign state surrounded by the richest and most powerful nation on the continent, a mountainous island floating in the South African sea. Relations between the countries were good, especially after apartheid. A South African once told me that they call Lesotho their 10th province to show their affection. I had still never been to South Africa, besides landing in the plane and bussing through to Lesotho when I arrived. Yet sometimes while in Lesotho I felt like I was in a part of South Africa, as when people talked prices in the market. Lesotho has its own currency, called the loti, or maloti in the plural. But not only is its value pegged one-to-one to the South African rand, when people in Lesotho talk prices they almost always give quotes in rand, not maloti. You ask, "How much is this head of cabbage?" They answer, "8 rand."

As I read Mandela's autobiography I felt a strange sense of kinship to him as I learned that he had grown up in a rural Xhosa village just south of Lesotho, right over the mountains down there. And then I came to admire him as he talked about being treated so poorly by whites under the apartheid system, eventually imprisoned for over two decades, only to regain his freedom and then power, and yet not seek revenge. He became the country's president but refrained from sticking it to those who had abused him. The extent of Mandela's discipline and the depth of his foresight astonished me. I found myself shaking my head at the book thinking, How could he hold back? I had revenge on my own mind, and for something so trivial compared to what Mandela had dealt with. I continued to imagine confronting Blue Windbreaker and doing something violent. I knew that I should have been taking inspiration from Mandela and emulating his forbearance, but I just wasn't there yet.

I read further in the book. I was whipping through it. No one was at school, so there were no hostelers interrupting, and the storm kept the villagers inside, so no students from up there came down to visit. I had nothing to do but read. The rain lasted for two days straight, and I spent those entire days reading. When the storm outside finally broke up, the book was over. But I didn't feel good. Instead of reflecting on how wise Mandela had been to try to form a fair and just country instead of merely enriching himself and his family in the short term, as so many leaders do, I came away somehow focused on perhaps the only fault I could find in his character. I wrote a cynical commentary in my journal. "Mandela was an absent husband to his wife and a neglectful father to his children. I don't care what kind of rainbow nation he had helped create for South Africa. Why did he abandon his family?"

I was in a mood that I couldn't shake. No storm could do it, no story could do it. I needed to move, to change the scenery.

CHAPTER SIX

Escape to Durban

WHILE IN MASERU for the Peace Corps conference, I had learned through email that a friend from home was going to be coming to South Africa. I decided to go and meet up with him. I decided to make that my change of scenery from Lesotho. My friend's name was also Greg, and he was coming in order to compete in a surfing contest in the coastal city of Durban. Going surfing with him would refresh my head. He had told me the name of the hostel where he would stay in Durban: Ansteys Beach Backpackers. That was my destination.

In order to get from my house in Tšoeneng to Durban I could go one of two ways. Tšoeneng is in the west of Lesotho. Durban is on the Indian Ocean, on South Africa's east coast. So all of Lesotho's mountains lie between Tšoeneng and Durban. One, I could exit the mountains and Lesotho at the western border and then travel north around the top of the range and then head east to the coast. Or two, I could take the more direct route east but have to bull my way straight through the mountains. That sounded like a slog, but still I chose that route because on that eastern edge of the Drakensberg escarpment was where Nate lived, so I could visit him on my way out, and I wanted to see the interior of the mountains anyway.

Transportation to anywhere in Lesotho spoked out from the hub of Maseru. So I took a minibus taxi to the capital, and then found a full-sized bus destined for Nate's place, called Qacha's Nek.

Lesotho is only the size of Rhode Island, and an airplane can fly across it in a half hour, but since the land is so crumpled with toothy ridges and breathtaking gorges, traveling by road takes forever. On the way up and deeper into the mountains, towns were very few but villages were scattered about, with motley quilts of fields between them. The fields had mostly been plowed by oxen, obvious because the furrow lines were so shaky. The road often followed rivers which had carved deeply into the heights. At times I could have walked as fast as the bus when it putted up steep sections. The road was paved for much of the way, but it went to dirt a couple hours before Qacha's Nek. All told, I had bobbed south and east through the mountains of Lesotho for ten hours that day.

I spent the next day with Nate and a couple of other Peace Corps volunteers hiking around, to a waterfall, to a cave where Bushmen had long ago painted red images of antelope and men hunting them, and then the next morning I crossed the border under another storm of cold rain. Snow had already built white caps on the surrounding peaks, which I could see through occasional breaks in the clouds. Nate would later tell me that the rain at the border pass also became snow soon after I left.

The border simply followed the eastern edge of the mountains. It was easy to know what was Lesotho and what was South Africa. Mountains was Lesotho, below the mountains was South Africa. Once on the South African side of the border gate—there was literally a single metal bar across a single lane road, which I walked around after a man in a booth stamped my passport—I saw how precipitously the mountains dropped off. I took the only transportation down the mountain that was available. Pickup trucks with camper shells acted as taxis there. I hopped in the bed of one and when it was full it started down the rough dirt road. Squished in the bed with me were two mothers and their children, two single women, and five men. Our destination was the nearest South African town, at the foot of the mountains, called Matatiele, a place where Basotho from Qacha's Nek sometimes traveled for shopping.

The passengers talked amongst themselves and the walls and windows of the camper shell soon dripped with condensation, and the air stunk of bad breath. I could only understand snippets of conversation. No one addressed me, though I got some looks. I looked forward to the day where my Sesotho was good enough to listen to a conversation like this and then just insert myself by saying something funny or insightful. Everyone's eyes would bulge with surprise. They would never have expected me to know Sesotho. That would be so cool. But today wasn't that day.

Riding in the back of the truck wasn't the safest way to travel. If the truck had overturned we all would have surely been crushed. But it was the only way, and we made it to Matatiele. The town had a Kentucky Fried Chicken. I understood why Basotho made the journey.

I got a minibus taxi from Matatiele. As we motored through town I saw proper tree-lined streets with houses and front yards for the first time since I had left America, and then the town abruptly ended. A few kilometers down the road a township popped up, where small box houses were stacked up in a large grid. This was an artifact of apartheid. I thought apartheid was dead, and it was, but the evidence was still so alive. Whites lived in the town and blacks lived in the township, where they were close enough to commute to work in the town.

The landscape varied as we drove on though. Here and there were farm houses surrounded by some trees, often eucalyptus, and then many acres of fields. Amid the fields was a cluster of huts where I saw black women outside hanging laundry to dry. The white families lived in the farm house and owned the land. The black families lived in the huts and worked on the land.

The cultivation was nothing like in Lesotho. The fields here were plowed in perfectly straight lines using modern tractors, not cattle. And the maize was tall and dense, not inconsistent. I also saw irrigation lines and sprinklers, whereas the fields in Tšoeneng were all watered naturally, by only rain.

The land greened and warmed until plantations of sugar cane appeared and the air became heavy with sea water smell. Then we pulled into the Durban taxi rank, but I'd yet to see more than a handful of white people during the whole ride, and most of them had been driving in cars beside us on the road. Everyone walking along the road had been black. Every other passenger sitting with me in the taxi was black. And now every person I saw in the

Durban taxi rank was black. Where were these white South Africans I had read about? It seemed their influence on the country far outweighed their physical presence. And later I did read a statistic that made some sense of why I hadn't seen many whites: South Africa was 80% black.

Finally though, in another minibus taxi I rode in to the Bluff, the neighborhood where the hostel was, I saw a white South African close up. I sat next to him in the front. He looked to be in his forties and had his left arm in a sling made from a plastic trash bag. He was unshaven, and throughout the ride he obsessively got things out of his backpack and put them back in. I had been eager to see my first white South African up close, but then I didn't try to speak with him because I concluded that he was crazy. Then he looked at me and asked, "Where are you going?"

"Ansteys Beach Backpackers."

"Oh, you'll get off soon. You'll walk up that hill."

He might not have been totally crazy, just poor and nervous. He kindly told the taxi driver where to let me off and I said thanks.

I hated to even think about race, white and black. In Lesotho, I wished people didn't pay so much attention to the color of my skin. But in South Africa, race was the overwhelming story. There was the separation of the races, the power one race had over others, the hope the people impregnated into the nickname they gave their country: Rainbow Nation. Thus far at least, I couldn't help but think of much else while I was in South Africa.

I walked up a road which turned into a giant staircase and when I crested the hill I saw a big ocean with a bowed horizon. It was such a welcome sight. I missed the ocean so much. I hadn't seen it in eight months. In my whole adult life I hadn't lived more than a mile from the beach, and eight months was easily the longest I'd gone without surfing.

Greg wasn't at the hostel yet. He was scheduled to show up in a couple more days. Luckily, when I checked in the clerk showed me surfboards I could use for free. "These ones are junky but those ones are OK," he said. And then he added, "You can surf, but the sardine run is on so they've taken the shark nets down. There are a lot of sardines in the water and a lot of sharks eating them." His words went in one ear and out the other. Did he say sharks? All I really heard was that I could use these surfboards for free, and I had noticed an older Town and Country twin-fin board that looked right for me. I quickly put shorts on and grabbed the board from the rack and ran the hundred yards to the water. Running with a board under my arm felt so natural, like I had just done it yesterday. I entered the water and paddled and duck-dove through the shorebreak and it certainly didn't feel like it had been eight months. I felt surprisingly balanced lying on the board. Then I rode two small waves, which was wobbly and awkward, but still I appreciated the glide along the surface of the water. My shoulders were already feeling mushy from the paddling though. I took one last wave in. No question, a session that consisted of three short rides had never felt so good. I walked up the sand in my shorts, dripping salty water, feeling cleansed.

I was also very hungry now. I loved how surfing could make you so hungry. I walked down the street to get dinner at a fast food joint. Marine Drive had a sidewalk, and I passed large and modern and spreading houses. Many were multi-storied, and all had gates at the end of driveways. The trees in the yards were palms and magnolias and oaks. Birds of paradise blinked orange and blue, white and black, from behind the gates, and bougainvillea meandered over walls. I recognized so much of the flora because it grew in Southern California too. The Bluff could have been any neighborhood back home, I thought as I walked. Until on a wall just above me to my left I saw a cat, then did a double take because it wasn't a cat. It was a monkey.

The hostel was just another of these big, modern homes. It was owned by a friendly white South African family who spoke English. Staying at the hostel with me were other travelers from Germany, Holland, France, Australia, England and America. I liked this because they looked like me and I looked like them, which meant they didn't stare. I was totally ignored in fact, a welcome change after the intense attention I got in Lesotho. I lounged on a couch with the other travelers—how I had missed having a soft couch to sit on. We watched television, or I read my book, *Les Miserables*. I surfed a lot, and in between sessions I ate hamburgers and pizza from nearby restaurants. This all seemed very un-African to me. Even the fact that I was walking around in my shorts seemed un-African. In Lesotho, shorts were clothing for boys. Men did not wear shorts. So I had only been wearing pants for months. I had even swum in the Tsoaing River in pants.

I got so comfortable on the couch and taking hot showers, eating fast food and hearing English or German that I soon forgot I was still on the African continent. The only time I remembered was when I looked at the decoration. The hostel was filled with African items: a big drum, a leather shield with a spear and a knobkerrie, a zebra sculpture, masks, big wooden spoons on the wall. But nothing else about the hostel, or the Bluff for that matter, told me I was in Africa. It was the change of scenery I needed.

Greg showed up and I accompanied him to his surf contest. It was great to see a friend from home, and when he asked about my life in Lesotho I had no idea where to start. I just said it had been really interesting, that I had been learning a lot. And I continued to sink into the very comfortable routine of surfing and eating familiar food and hanging out with an old friend. It was actually starting to get a little bit too routine.

ONE MORNING, sipping coffee and reading the local newspaper, I came upon a review of a new book titled *Soweto, Inside Out: Stories about Africa's Famous Township*. Soweto is the township near Johannesburg where much of that novel the Form B's were reading, *Crocodile Burning*, took place. A quoted excerpt caught my attention. A man was reminiscing about his youth:

"This Soweto is my world, home for 61 years, and a microcosm of this country and continent ... We used candles and paraffin lights right up to the time I matriculated. We carried water from a tap about 100 yards down the street. I remember the torture of watering the garden—so many trips to the tap, with the heavy watering can slashing my leg."

Sounded rough—I gritted my teeth as I read the passage. Then I snapped to: I remembered my life in Tšoeneng, where I used candles and a paraffin lamp to light my house, and where I also got my water from a pump up the hill. I knew that life, and it was hardly torture.

And right then I realized that I had been getting from Lesotho what I wanted. I wanted to experience things firsthand instead of just reading about them. I wanted to know about the world for myself. And because of Lesotho I knew from my own experience (an undeniable authority) that life without electricity and running water wasn't torture. I no longer had to read things like this and wonder if the writer was being honest or histrionic. This newspaper article had made me recall why I had joined Peace Corps and come to Africa in the first place. And it made me ready to go back to Lesotho for more, the good and the bad.

When I left Durban a few days after Greg arrived, I wasn't looking forward to the specifics of life in Tšoeneng: the cold up there in the mountains, getting stared at, having to cook all of my meals from scratch, only a plastic chair to sit on. But I knew that being scared or uncomfortable at times was the price you paid for experience. On the bus back to Lesotho I had the feeling that I was returning to something not entirely fun, but compulsively important.

PART II

Happiness is neither virtue nor pleasure nor this thing nor that but simply growth,

We are happy when we are growing.

- WILLIAM BUTLER YEATS

CHAPTER SEVEN

Motsie's Shop

FROM DURBAN I took a bus and made a half-circle around the bottom of the mountains of Lesotho and reentered the country from the west, which meant that I crossed the border at the Maseru gate. I hated Maseru. I wanted nothing to do with it and its criminals. I quickly passed through and got on a minibus taxi headed toward Tšoeneng and only noticed that there was some snow on the ground. Another storm, an even colder one, had apparently passed through while I was gone.

I was glad when I arrived safely back in Tšoeneng. People here had always been nice to me. Off the taxi, I walked down the dirt path through the fields to school and it was quiet. School was still on break and there were no teachers or hostelers on campus and my time was free for a couple more weeks. It was a long break, almost two months. As soon as I woke up each morning, I boiled water in my kettle to make a cup of coffee and then with the steaming cup in hand I sat in my blue plastic chair at my table, which used to be a teacher's table from a classroom, and I worked through one of the 30 lessons in a small hardcover forest green book that was my one and only written resource on the local language, *Everyday Sesotho Grammar*.

If anything was going to deepen my experience of Lesotho, and give me access to more friends besides the hostelers, it was the local language. I saw this from the very beginning, when I met the chief and the witchdoctor but I couldn't communicate with them, and when the teachers in the staffroom joked among themselves in Sesotho and I felt left out. And now I was on an empty school campus during break, and if I wanted to talk to anyone I had to go up into the village, and there, almost everyone spoke only Sesotho.

I had been working at Sesotho from my first day, but upon my return to Tšoeneng from Durban I resumed my study routine with increased vigor. It had always been centered around the little green book. After Peace Corps initially put me through two months of formal Sesotho lessons they sent me to Tšoeneng with only the little green book. It would be my teacher from that point.

The book was "intended for Europeans," it stated in its preface, and was written by someone named M.R.L. Sharpe in June, 1951 at Morija. The place was just a half-day's walk from Tšoeneng to the east. It was where the first European missionaries settled in Lesotho, and also where the country's first printing press was established. Each lesson in the little green book I spread out over a couple days. By this time in July I had navigated through all the fundamental lessons, although I couldn't yet fluently produce the language structures in conversation, and I was soaking up some of the extra reference material in the back. The past tenses were puzzling to me, and I was working on one that the book called "The Imperfect." It could be used like the Past Continuous tense of English. *Ke ne ke nahana* means "I was thinking." But it could also mean "I used to think," so said the little green book. I needed to listen for how people used this verb tense in order to be able to use it correctly myself.

For many years, I had wanted to learn another language. I tried Spanish in high school, and then German in college, and right after college I took a French class at a community college. Yet I never felt like I got more than a weak handle on those languages through learning them using a book in a classroom setting. I needed to be in the country where people were speaking the language all day, all around me. I didn't even particularly care what language I learned, whether it was a common European or Asian language, or a little known African tongue. I was most interested in the process of living in the place where the new language was spoken and having to learn it in order to survive.

I also felt like Sesotho was the first truly foreign language I had tried to learn. I hadn't noticed before, but with the European languages English shares so many obvious roots. Our word "pants" is similar to the Spanish *pantalones*. Our word "father" is similar to the German *vater*. Our word "judge" is similar to the French *juge*. In contrast, I was hard-pressed to find cognates in Sesotho. "Pants" is *borikhoe*; "father" is *ntate*; and "judge" is *moahloli*. I also discovered how similar the syntax is between English and the other European languages. Often when translating from English into a European language, you can keep the same word order. You just have to replace your English words with their equivalents. So, to say, "That man is tall," in Spanish you say, *"Eso hombre es alto."* But in Sesotho I had to learn to speak in a different order, and sometimes I also had to omit words, or even add parts of speech that didn't exist in English. To say, "That man is tall," I had to say, *"Monna eo o molelele,"* which translates literally as, "Man that he tall."

When Peace Corps gave me the little green Sesotho grammar book I wondered why it was so old. It had been published during colonial times. Had they over-ordered back in the 1960's when the first volunteers came to Lesotho? So I searched through every bookstore in Lesotho (there were only a handful) for a newer volume, but found none. Apparently, learning Sesotho just wasn't a popular thing for foreigners to do.

Still I wished I had a more up-to-date resource because the little green book was teaching me how to ask ridiculously outmoded questions such as, "Do you know the price of wool to-day?" and "Have you paid your dog tax?" And phrases like, "We were disputing over a concubine," and "He is abnormal, a cripple." The book contained short stories that conjured up images of an era long past: "The visitors came from England. What a long journey it was! They sat on the ship for two weeks. Afterwards they went by train for three days." Another story went, "The police have caught the murderers. They will be hanged on Wednesday." And then in one it was written, "The pump will not work and we are short of water." At first I resented that the language was obsolete. Then it occurred to me that much of the language was in fact not obsolete at all in Lesotho. Someone, somewhere in the country had probably been saying at the very moment I was reading: "This pump won't work! We're short of water!" Lesotho wasn't exactly a place that had ridden a wave of technological advances over the last half-century. People in Tšoeneng still plowed their fields with oxen, they rode to nearby villages on horseback, they cooked in cauldrons over wood fires, they lit their homes with candles and paraffin lamps, and they sheared their sheep and sold the wool.

I EVEN FOUND LESOTHO in 2004 to be remarkably similar to the descriptions of it by Eugene Casalis in the 1830's. He was the missionary who had recounted King Moshoeshoe's father reluctantly being amazed by written language. He wrote a memoir about his 23 years living in Lesotho, called *The Basutos*, and in it he also mentioned that King Moshoeshoe's obstinate father admitted that the missionaries were good for one thing: they introduced sugar. So that is where the obsession started, I thought. Whenever a hosteler baked bread, they added so much sugar that it tasted more like cake. And when a teacher made a cup of tea, they stirred in a minimum of four spoonfuls. It tasted like hummingbird feeder syrup.

I found Casalis's memoir in one of the bookstores where I did *not* find a new language book. I loved reading it. I identified with so many of his observations, and I felt like I was seeing the origins of customs that I had been noticing. 'Me 'Masamuel once brought her daughter to school and I offered the girl a pen to draw with. I put it into the girl's left hand and 'me 'Masamuel barked at her, "With two hands!" The girl quickly wrapped her other hand around the pen to receive it. Then I read in Casalis's book where he learned the same lesson: "Politeness also requires that, when a gift is accepted, however small the object may be, both hands should be extended to receive it."

He had been living in Lesotho 170 years before I was, yet it was the same culture, and it also looked like the same place. He described a fertile country "where the grass attains such a height that it is necessary to destroy it every winter by means of fire," but which possesses scarcely any large trees. The only trees near my house were pine, eucalyptus, peach and acacia that had been planted upon the building of Ngoana Jesu Secondary School.

Trees that grew on their own were all down by the river: willows and olives. It is these tree species that Casalis mentioned seeing.

He saw things I did not see, however. "The wild beasts caused me much uneasiness during this journey," he wrote. "I found the borders of the Caledon infested with lions, and one of my best draught oxen was carried off by them." The Caledon was the river that the Tsoaing flowed into just a two hour walk east of Tšoeneng. But no lions infested its borders upon my arrival in 2003. Casalis talked of encountering other wild fauna—elephant, leopard, hyena, ostrich, rhinoceros—but these had by now been hunted out of the area. In common with Casalis, I did hear the cry of jackals at night, I saw rock rabbits near the summits of mountain peaks, and I came across antelope from time to time. I was told that there were baboons that still lived deeper in the mountains in caves, but I never saw them. And I never saw a monkey near my home, which wasn't right because the name Tšoeneng means "place of the monkey."

In the end, reading Casalis's book made me feel like I was following in a big brother's footsteps. He had also arrived when he was a young bachelor, and he tried very hard to learn Sesotho. He wrote about this with a spirit of discovery. "There are in the idioms of this language words magical, on account of their poetry, metaphors, sometimes naive, sometimes brilliant or full of fire."

EACH MORNING I studied my little green book, and then I tried to apply its lessons as I walked up to the shop in the village in the afternoon. It was a perfectly balanced routine—input, then output—and I improved a lot every day. I would buy only one or two small pieces of food at the shop so I had a need to walk up there again the next day, so I had a legitimate reason to get out of my house and into the village to practice my Sesotho each afternoon. On each trip I encountered a new person, I was confronted with new vocabulary during our brief conversations, and I stumbled through the new grammar structures I had gleaned from the little green book. The shop wasn't far away (perhaps a quarter mile), but each trip still took at least an hour because there were so many people who wanted to chat along the way and because I was open to the tangents. Being sidetracked was actually the purpose. Each trip was a tiny adventure, a little mission of language discovery.

From my house I took the dirt path that led to the paved road. The path was at times lined with poplar trees and giant aloes (actually they were agaves, but the Basotho always called them aloes), and it bisected fields of pasture grasses and cultivations of sorghum, beans and maize. I walked north and uphill on the paved road past St. Peter Claver primary school, past St. Peter Claver health clinic, past St. Peter Claver church. These were all on the same grounds, and sometimes I spoke with people from the St. Peter Claver compound. There were teachers, nurses, children. And sometimes there were young couples on this stretch of road walking down toward the river to get away from the village and flirt in private. The first person I could count on seeing was 'me 'Matšepe, as hers was the first house along the road. I always seemed to catch her with a bucket of water on her head as she was returning from the spring, but she still smiled and strained her neck to carefully turn her head to have a quick chat.

"*Sir Greg. U phela joang, ntate?*"

"*Kea phela, 'me. U phela joang?*"

She was on the school board at Ngoana Jesu, so she always called me "Sir Greg." But just feet from 'me 'Matšepe's house was the village bar. Here men and women sat on wood benches out front drinking home-made sorghum beer out of plastic jugs and oil cans, and as soon as they saw me they called out, "Thabang!" Most people in the village called me in this way, by my Sesotho name. Greg was difficult for them to pronounce, and when they tried, it came out "Greka," or "Gkreeck," or even "Crack." Those who knew some English thought my name was Crack because that was the English word they knew which sounded most like Greg to them. Sometimes people also called me "Kereke" because that was the Sesotho word that sounded closest in pronunciation to Greg. *Kereke* means church. It was logical that they would look for words that sounded like my name because their names were usually plain descriptive words. 'Matšepe is a woman's name that means "mother of Tšepe," in other words her son's name was Tšepe. *Tšepe* just means iron in Sesotho. So her son was Iron and she was called Mother of Iron.

My Sesotho name, Thabang, means happy and the drinkers at the bar always shouted out an invitation as I walked by, "Thabang, come drink!"

"Sorry," I said.

My students who lived in the village were all around and they would see me. Or for sure they would hear the news that I had been drinking in the bar because some of the drinkers were parents of my students. I didn't want to set a bad example.

"Then buy me a beer," they would say.

"Sorry."

"Then give me one rand."

A jug of beer cost one rand (about fifteen cents). "Sorry."

Some of the parents I often saw in the bar were the same ones I heard Principal Tsita and the other teachers talk about being late in paying for their children's school fees. They just sat on those benches all day and drank. The men also rolled cigarettes between gulps, and the women snuffed their tobacco. Still, they were friendly people. "Then just come here, let's talk," they would say.

That was what I was open to. I quickly discovered that drunks speaking Sesotho were just like drunks speaking English— their words blended together, which made them hard to understand, except that they also repeated themselves often, and they didn't listen very carefully, which meant that my Sesotho mistakes went almost unnoticed. The alcohol had made them less self-conscious, and so when I talked to them I felt less self-conscious. My favorite drunk was a man with the darkest face in Tšoeneng. It was truly black. He also had a deep scar on his cheek. As a hat, he wore a jackal pelt, so when you spoke with him you had so much to observe: the deep pigment of his skin, the crude marks of the stitches across his cheek, the bloodshot eyes of a drunk, and then the muzzle of a jackal with two holes where the animal's eyes once were. Over the years I never did learn this man's name. He didn't need a name as far as I was concerned because there was no one else who looked anything like him.

On the road right next to the bar, taxis stopped to pick up passengers on their way to Maseru. The taxi drivers asked me,

"Are you riding?"

"No."

"Where are you going?"

"To the shop."

There was no need to specify. There was only one shop in Tšoeneng, and in front of it there were some big rocks where groups of boys and men from the village liked to loiter. Some of them were my students. Others were boys who didn't attend school, or young men who were home on break from attending school elsewhere, or adult men who had no jobs, or shepherds who had no animals to look after at the moment. The rocks were a good spot to watch the occasional vehicle pass on the road. The guys' heads would follow each car like meerkats. Since the taxis stopped here to pick people up, the guys could banter with the taxi drivers. "Hey Sek'hoama, I'm going to beat you!" They always gave out joking threats of violence. I greeted the guys on the rocks even though they intimidated me, and then sometimes they responded with, "What are you going to buy me?"

Being begged was such a common occurrence. It happened almost every time I walked to the shop, and most times I walked anywhere else. I never got totally comfortable dealing with it. Even the youngest children had learned to say in English, "Give me some sweets." At first I politely said to everyone, "Sorry." But that didn't discourage anyone, and during this time, my first break between semesters, it finally started to irritate me. When adults begged me I began to retort acidly, "Why don't you ask me for a job instead of money?" But I stopped that because it didn't make me feel any better. And it didn't stop the begging. I tried out more creative ways to deflect the requests. Recently, I had learned the word for poor person, *mofutsana*.

"What are you going to buy me?" a guy on the rocks asked me.

"Sorry, I can't buy anything. *Ke mofutsana.*"

He laughed. It worked. Calling myself poor was like a mouse calling itself a cat. It was a crazy idea and an obvious contradiction. People had told me that they believed that all white people were rich. End of story. So what I said was surprising and absurd, and while the guy thought about it I could keep walking without feeling rude.

This was the best solution I had come up with. I didn't want to give out money to everyone who asked, I didn't want to try to discuss why I didn't want to give them money because my Sesotho wasn't good enough yet, and I didn't want to refuse impolitely. I was very much aware that my safety and comfort here was in their hands. I was alone and vulnerable, and I felt even more so after the mugging in Maseru, and I didn't want to piss anyone off.

On my walk back from each trip to the shop I tried to recall whatever new Sesotho words I had heard during my exchanges and I repeated them aloud so I could search for them in my Sesotho-English dictionary once I got home. It wasn't hard to figure out the spellings because Sesotho is spelled phonetically. It also uses the Roman alphabet, just like English, because Casalis and his colleagues had been the first to write the language down. Usually, I found the words in the dictionary. Just that simple act of walking to the shop was always a thrill, and whenever I set out I felt some butterflies. What were people going to ask me this time? Even if I didn't like the questions I had to try and be tactful, and do so with a very limited range of vocabulary. I got better each time, partly because I raced back home to look up new words and expand that range of vocabulary, and I recorded my discoveries in a small memo book. It grew to read like a traveler's log. And I felt like I was exploring Lesotho through its language.

INEVITABLY, being that I was mostly on my own with learning Sesotho, I would make some mistakes in the process. I would embarrass myself. In the village shop the counter was a barricade between the customer and the food items. Customers weren't allowed to pass behind the counter and browse the shelves. You had to know what the shop generally carried, or crane your neck to see, or ask if they had something.

On one trip, I asked the girl behind the counter, Selloane, if I could buy three pears. *"Ke kopa pere tse tharo."*

She trumpeted out a breath, and then said in English, "Do you know what a *pere* is?"

"I think so."

Selloane was the shop owner's oldest daughter, and she attended school near the capital, so she had an urbanized air to her. She often looked bored working at her father's shop in the village. "A *pere* is an animal, abuti Thabang!" she said to me. "You ride it … you sit on it … it's like a donkey … ntate Santu has a *pere*." It was obvious by Selloane's tone that I had screwed this word up before and she couldn't let it slide any longer. Normally, she was pretty forgiving of my Sesotho.

On one hand, I knew immediately the mistake I had made: The words for both "pear" and "horse" were spelled *pere*, but they weren't pronounced the same. One was pronounced with a long middle *e* and the other was pronounced with a short middle *e*. Only I never could remember which was which.

But ease up, Selloane! "Horse" and "pear" were certainly different things, but they weren't as different as a "sheet" and a "shit." Basotho trying to speak English, like her, conflated the pronunciations of these two: I once heard someone say, "I'm washing my shits." So my gaff with "horse" and "pear" had to be put into perspective.

As usual, when I got home I looked up new words I had heard on the trip to the shop, or words I had had trouble with. I opened my Sesotho-English dictionary and found *pere*. The first meaning given was "pear." The second was, as expected, "horse." But the dictionary (the only Sesotho-English dictionary I knew of, published around the same time as my green grammar book) gave no indication as to any difference in pronunciation. Nor did it mention how a third meaning for *pere* was to be pronounced. A third *pere*? The dictionary only gave its English translation: "anus."

SELLOANE'S SCOLDING OF ME for my mispronunciation didn't discourage me from walking up to the shop every day for the rest of the winter break. I even continued buying pears, just hoping I wasn't buying anuses. I had nothing else to do, nowhere else to go but the shop. I found myself being a little less intimidated by the young men who loitered on the rocks in front of the shop, and I started to sit down with them for a bit. One day while I was sitting on the rocks, serendipity struck and Selloane's father, ntate

Motsie, the shop owner, pulled up in his rusted baby blue Toyota pickup and said, "Thabang! Let's go!" He motioned for me to hop into the bed of the truck. A man and a woman had just gotten off a taxi with a heavy stove they had purchased in Maseru and ntate Motsie was transporting them through the countryside to the distant hamlet where they lived, Thabana Tšoana. I climbed into the back, along with another guy, Teboho, for the ride.

Ntate Motsie loved his beer, and by the time we reached our destination he had about finished his quart of Castle (a bottled lager, not the homemade sorghum brew), surely not his first of the afternoon. Ntate Motsie also loved his voice. He talked the couple's ear off the whole way and threw comments out to everyone we passed on the dirt road.

After we dropped the couple and their goods off we got back into the truck to return to Tšoeneng, when ntate Motsie noticed me carefully observing him hotwire his truck and said, *"U tseba ho khanna?"*—You know how to drive?

"Yeah, in fact, I had a car just like this back home," I told him.

"You don't know how to drive!" he shouted back at me. Then he and Teboho had a good laugh.

It's rare for folks in Lesotho to know how to drive. There are so few cars—ntate Motsie's was one of two I'd seen in all of Tšoeneng. That was why students thought taxi and bus drivers were cool. And since I was young, and spoke Sesotho like a babbling toddler, I could see where his disbelief arose. But in America it's strange for someone to wait past their 16th birthday to test for a driver's license. Everyone knows how to drive back home. It's not a prestigious skill. I felt no desire to try to make Motsie believe me.

Ntate Motsie drove on for a few seconds and then he braked. He looked at me and said in a suspicious tone, "You know how to drive?" Then he got out of the car and told me to do it—if I knew how.

I hadn't driven for almost a year, and everything was on the opposite side of the dashboard like England, but I eased up the clutch, gave it some gas and we were on our way. *"Ho!"* yelled ntate Motsie. "He knows how to drive!"

As I drove us toward Tšoeneng ntate Motsie kept repeating, "He knows how to drive! He's a man!" I waved at a couple of my students we encountered on the road who were as equally astonished at my amazing abilities behind the wheel of a car. They waved and smiled and shouted. Then I hit a rock and he took it back. "He doesn't know how to drive! Thabang, you're not a man!"

We were almost to the village. It was dusk, so I turned on the lights, and that got him back on my side. "*Ow!* He knows! He knows!" If I knew how to turn on the lights too, then man, I knew.

I walked back to my house in the twilight feeling energized, thinking that this was what I had come to Lesotho for, to meet people like Motsie, to learn a new language by practicing it in real life situations, and to make a strange place like Tšoeneng feel less strange.

CHAPTER EIGHT

Eating without Maseru

WHEN SCHOOL REOPENED IN LATE JULY, Tšoeneng looked like an entirely different land compared to when I arrived in January. It was dry and dead now. The paths were sandy brown, the fields were yellow, and many of them had been cleared of crops. It was the nadir of winter. That was why there had been such a long break in the middle of the school year: winter—June and July—was harvest time. I went to teach the Form D's first, and I asked them how they'd spent their break and many said they'd been in the fields with their families gathering ears of maize and heads of sorghum.

For the Form D class, the second semester opened with a treat. I had connected them with pen pals in an American high school where my friend Steve taught. I chose their class because they were the oldest, and their English was the best at the school. The Form D's had written letters to the American students first, back in March, and the replies had just arrived.

I opened the envelope and began passing the letters out. There was a palpable energy in the class. The students rapidly unfolded papers and began reading. I wondered if the Americans' replies would satisfy, and I recalled the day in March when the Form D's had written their original letters: I had felt the need to warn the students not to beg. Don't ask your pen pal for money or gifts, I said. I just suspected that might be a temptation. "Just tell them a little bit about yourself and then ask some questions. What kinds of questions can you ask?"

"I can ask if they are learning Sesotho in school like we are learning their English?" said a student.

"What is their staple food? As *papa* is our staple food, do they also eat *papa*?" said another student.

"I will ask if they look after animals," said Tumelo Sello. I knew that he meant did they herd cattle and sheep and goats and donkeys in the pastures, just like he did.

I refrained from answering any of the questions because I wanted the Form D's to get their answers from their pen pals. Now was the time. The sound of crinkling paper filled the air, but it soon became accompanied by sighs of confusion, and I saw grimaces on the students' faces. "Sir, I don't understand," said 'Mamonaheng as she raised her hand. I figured it was a problem of vocabulary, maybe slang. She pointed to a line and asked me to decipher it. She couldn't read the handwriting in the first place. It was horrible, sloppy scribble that would've gotten one of these Form D's beaten by their teacher. Even I could barely read some of it, and I became embarrassed for my fellow Americans. I imagined the Form D's wondering: How were Americans so rich if they couldn't even write clearly?

Basotho students were taught to take the format and appearance of their writing more seriously even than the content of their messages. The Form D's had written their original letters with uniform and lightly stylized script, where all the words aligned perfectly along the left hand margin, and exactly one line had been skipped between the address, the date, and the salutation. The ideas in the Form D letters may have been hard for the Americans to understand, but they had been presented in impeccable penmanship.

Why was the American handwriting so bad? Maybe because so much communication was being done through a keyboard on a computer these days. Handwriting just wasn't important for them anymore. Moreover, in general, Americans are taught to prize creativity and individuality more than format. Handwriting was probably never as important in America as it was in Lesotho.

Many of the American students had stapled photos of themselves to their letters, and some had included their cell phone numbers. The Form D's were impressed by that because only one student at Ngoana Jesu now had a cell phone. One letter also included a dollar bill.

Tumelo Sello called me over to interpret his pen pal's response to his question about looking after animals. The American boy's reply: "In my country people don't look after animals, they look after cars. I have a Chevy Camaro."

TUMELO SELLO WAS OLDER than the 11th grade students in America, and so were most of the Form D's. Hlalefang was the youngest at 16, and 'Mapaseka was only 17, but the ages of the rest of the class ran all the way into the early twenties. They were older for various reasons. Masopha and Ntheka had missed a year of school while they went up the mountain for initiation. Lerato Thaki lost a couple years because his parents couldn't afford to pay school fees. He worked as a security guard down in Mohale's Hoek to earn the money and then he returned. Lerato's cousin, Maleshoane Thaki, had been out of school getting married and having her first daughter. This class was not a group of children; in terms of age and life experience, they were all young adults. And together, we were more like peers. I was only a few years older than them. But that was evened out since we were on their home turf, which made my relevant life skills fewer than theirs.

Such a relationship allowed us to have discussions that I couldn't have with my younger classes. Maleshoane Thaki asked in class one day, "Why is America so rich?"

"That's a difficult question," I said. "It's like why is Lesotho so poor?"

To my surprise, the Form D's immediately began raising their hands to answer that, a question they didn't find difficult at all. "We don't have any mines," one of them said. "There are many people in Lesotho, but the land is not enough," said another. "We are uneducated," was yet another response. The answers sounded straight out of their Development Studies textbook, not that there wasn't truth to them.

Then Maleshoane contributed an idea that seemed her own. "We are poor because of jealousy." She told the story of a man from a village called Ha Mantšebo who had worked hard and farmed efficiently, growing successful groves of peach trees among other things. He became very wealthy, until other villagers who envied his riches robbed and killed him.

This was why I began to focus more on the Form D's in the second semester. If my first semester was mostly about the Form B's—because they were the first class I ever went to, because there were a lot of hostelers in that class, and because they had books—then my second semester revolved around the Form D's. Instead of me only teaching them, there was much more potential for exchange with the Form D's. I taught them English and they gave me insights into their culture and explained local things. I had seen the very groves that Maleshoane referred to. They always caught my eye as they were the only significant groves of fruit trees I'd seen in Lesotho, and I'd wondered why.

In their letters to the Americans, many of the Form D's had asked about food. I had an idea: I could make some American dishes for them and they could make some Sesotho food for me. I still hadn't tried many of the things they ate. When I mentioned it to the class, they jumped at the idea. We settled on a schedule for the lunch exchange. Each Tuesday a group of three different students would gather down at my house.

What was American food? Hamburgers? French fries? I started with bean soup and grilled cheese sandwiches. I was limited to what I could find in the Shoprite grocery store in the capital and what I could keep without refrigeration. They loved it. "I will write about this day!" said 'Mamonaheng after eating the meal. All three of the students asked me to take their pictures at my table with the food displayed.

For the second lunch exchange I chose spaghetti. I was still boiling the noodles when the students knocked on my door. They came in and I heard Masilo whisper to Potso in Sesotho, "It looks like Chinese food."

I spun around: "These are not Chinese noodles!"

Basotho generally didn't like Chinese people. Now I felt I had to explain the food. "They are Italian noodles, technically. But since many Italians came to live in America, spaghetti is kind of an American dish too. My mother cooked it for my family a lot when I was young. The noodles are not Chinese!"

I was really hoping for another success, and I expected it to come easily since the first group had been so impressed with mere bean soup and grilled cheese. I sat the students at my table and I served the spaghetti. But the toast was burning in the pan, so I rushed back to the stove.

Then I heard laughter. There was more whispering. I walked back to the table to find red sauce splattered across Potso's white school shirt and noodles on the floor. None of the three students looked up at me.

They didn't know how to use a fork. I never considered it. And spaghetti was difficult even if you did know how to use a fork. I demonstrated how to stab the noodles and spin them into a ball. "Only try a few noodles at a time," I suggested. But they were holding the utensils so awkwardly, like they were alive and wriggling, and they continued to splatter sauce. So I took it another step down. "When I was young my mom would chop the noodles for me," I said, and I chopped up Potso's noodles. Then I chopped up Masilo's noodles. But when I went to Khauhelo's plate she put her hand over it. "I am not a child," she said. And she went on struggling to spin spaghetti onto her fork and get it up to her mouth. The hungry boys cleaned their plates long before she was finished.

Now for the exchange. After the first lunch, 'Mamonaheng had brought me *mochahlama*. It was bread made from maize, she said. It tasted less chewy and more crumbly than bread made from wheat. After the second lunch, Khauhelo presented me with *likhobe tsa mabele*—sorghum grains that had been boiled soft. The taste was very mild, and the grains, which were a little smaller than peas, were sticky. Every food the other students brought me was also made with either maize or sorghum.

Lipabi was roasted maize that had been finely ground and mixed with sugar. It was so refined that I had trouble eating it without breathing some in and coughing. *Motoho* was a sour drink brewed with sorghum meal. Nthabiseng Mokhele, the chief's daughter, was the student who gave it to me, and she said it was to be drunk from a bowl. She also gave me a plastic bag of brown sugar (Basotho always used brown sugar) to go with the *motoho*. Sprinkle some on top and stir it in before drinking, she said. I saw Basotho pour mounds of sugar into their *motoho* when they drank it, but I found it tastiest with only one spoonful added.

There were innumerable other ways the Basotho ate maize and sorghum. The fields in Lesotho were mostly planted to these two crops, which also happened to look a lot alike. They were both tall grasses. I couldn't tell the difference between the two when I first started paying attention to the fields during my morning runs, but as the summer went along and the plants grew bigger I learned that the leaf blades on the sorghum plants were a little narrower than on the maize plants. Once mature, the two were easily distinguished because sorghum formed a heavy head of grains at its apex while maize only had a flimsy tassel with pollen on top. Once upon a time, Basotho ate more sorghum than maize. Sorghum is a species indigenous to Africa. These days, however, they use sorghum primarily to make drinks: the sour drink, *motoho*, and beer. For eating, the staple is maize, mostly in the form of the hard porridge they call *papa*.

I DIDN'T KNOW how to cook *papa*, and this was a problem. There was nothing else substantial to eat in Tšoeneng. If I didn't cook *papa*, then I had to travel to Maseru to buy other foods to cook, foods like those I made for the lunch exchanges. And this was what I had been doing throughout the entire first semester. I took a minibus taxi to the capital almost every weekend. I went to Shoprite and bought cereal and milk, bread and cheese, pasta and marinara sauce. I bought as much as I could haul back to the village in order to get me through the following week. Usually, on Monday, Tuesday and Wednesday, I made grilled cheese sandwiches for dinner. I had to use the cheese before it rotted. Without refrigeration it turned into a smelly greasy blob pretty quickly in the summer. Then I made spaghetti later in the week. By the weekend, I was completely out of food and yearning for Kentucky Fried Chicken. That was my weekend meal. On Saturday morning I rose early to get to the road to flag down a taxi. I arrived in Maseru in time for an early lunch at KFC before hitting the grocery store again. I had never eaten KFC in America, but it tasted like water in a desert on those days in Maseru. I got to know the menu well, and I tried a variety of items, though my favorites were the "Twister", which was a fried chicken breast wrapped in a tortilla, and a simple three-piece chicken meal with French fries. There was a "Mini Loaf" option instead of the fries. It was a miniature loaf of white bread, and Basotho often chose it, but I always went for the fries. My mouth reveled in the oil and salt of the fries and fried chicken.

Come the second semester, however, I was afraid of Maseru. I wanted to avoid the place, as good as KFC tasted. I also wanted to make Tšoeneng my home, and every time I went to Maseru to do my shopping I felt like I was betraying the village. No one else did their shopping in Maseru. No one else could afford to. The hostelers, when they saw me walking toward the road on a Saturday morning would shout, "You love Maseru!"

So I needed *papa*. I asked Nthabiseng to teach me to cook it, the Nthabiseng who had sort of taught me to wash my clothes. She didn't make fun of me once during the cooking process, which turned out to be very simple. She took scoops of water from my bucket and poured them in a pot. "How much water do you put in?" I asked.

"This much for one meal," she said. But I knew I wouldn't remember just by looking, so I measured by dipping my index finger in. The water covered just over my first knuckle.

Once the water was boiling she turned the flame down low and added maize meal. "How much maize meal do you put in?"

"This much."

She had no measurements to give, so I took the stick she was using to stir (really, it was a stick from a tree outside) and I tried to inculcate how stiff the porridge felt, how much resistance it was putting up against my rounds with the stick. I needed to remember this stuff if I was going to cook it myself.

Nthabiseng put the lid on the pot and stepped back to let it simmer. I had to ask how long she would cook it for, despite knowing she would have no precise answer. Lucky for me, Tlhokomelo piped in. He was in my house too, hanging out. "Ten minutes," he said. Khosi was there too. He added, "And you stir it once after about five minutes."

When the *papa* was done, Nthabiseng gave the porridge one last stir. It was thick and sticky now. She pulled the stick out and the bottom half of the stick looked like it was covered in snow. She turned the fire off and replaced the lid.

That was how to cook *papa*. And once I learned, my gastronomic life in Lesotho was transformed. I would cook and eat *papa* most days for the next few years.

Even before Nthabiseng showed me how to cook it, I had been eating it every day at school. Two women from the village cooked enough *papa* in a cauldron to feed the hundred-odd students and teachers lunch. *Papa* tasted like stale air. My first impression of it was not good. I thought it was mashed potatoes, but when I tasted it I discovered a sticky, bland, slightly bad flavor in my mouth. Luckily, the *papa* was always served with a side: beans, peas, cabbage or other boiled greens. That was the school lunch Monday through Thursday, and then sometimes on Friday we had samp, which was boiled whole kernels of maize. Like rice for a Korean, maize was eaten every day with every meal. Basotho had their *papa* with potatoes, pumpkin, eggs and meat. For a special breakfast, they ate *papa* with milk.

As anybody's taste gets exacting about foods they eat often, Basotho could be exceedingly discriminating about their *papa*, which I always found funny since it consisted of only two ingredients, and that's if you count water. One day Nthabiseng was over my house while I was cooking and I had added too much maize meal to the boiling water, so I poured a little more water into the pot. "No!" she scolded. "Sir, no!" You don't add water after you've added the maize meal. I suppose, if you screw up the ratio, then you're supposed to suffer through eating your mess. But I often heard people complain about the way others cooked *papa*. The teachers, especially 'me 'Masamuel, criticized the school cooks. "It's too dry," was the most common lament. And 'me 'Masamuel would bellow for a student to take the plate of unacceptable *papa* off her desk, away from her sight, and back to the cooks. You had to stir the *papa* well or else you would get little clumps of dry maize meal hidden in the porridge, and in order to stir well you needed a proper stick. There was a special name for a *papa*-stirring stick: *lesokoana*. In fact, after Nthabiseng showed me how to cook *papa* the first time, she and some other girls took me out to find a stick that I could whittle to the proper length and diameter (about the length of my forearm and as thick as my thumb) and have for myself. And to truly finish the stirring off right you were supposed to pat the top of the porridge flat with the back of a plastic serving spoon, replace the lid, and let the *papa* steam for a few minutes before scooping to eat. Around the walls of the pot, a crust formed, called *lek'hok'ho* in Sesotho. It was something the Basotho were superstitious about. Girls were not allowed to eat it. Women could, boys could, men could, but not girls. It would cause them to grow a big butt. That was the long term effect. Immediately, it would cause them to fart. Basotho and *papa* . . . the customs and the stories were endless.

SO I WAS SET now that I could cook *papa*. Motsie's shop always had maize meal in stock, which you could buy in paper sacks of 1 kilogram up to 5 kilograms. Curiously though, he rarely stocked the most common side dish for *papa*. Only in about one in ten trips to his shop did I find heads of cabbage sitting on the counter (marked in pen on the outer leaves with the price: 5 rand, 7 rand). And he never carried any other forms of *moroho*. If *papa* was the king of food in Lesotho, then *moroho* was the queen, always by its side, adding a green splash to its white mass, kicking in with some flavor. *Moroho* was essentially any boiled leafy greens. It could be cabbage, collards, rape, chard, spinach, choy, mustard; Basotho grew them all. And that was why Motsie didn't sell them. Everyone had a plot of *moroho* at their house. Even the hostelers had plots of *moroho* surrounding the hostel.

The weather was warming, so a couple of hostel boys helped me get a plot going just southwest of my house. They got spades from the school storage room and dug up a raised bed about 4 feet by 8 feet. They uprooted some young plants from their own plots and settled them into mine. I did not know my *moroho* at this point, and when I asked the boys what these plants were called, they said spinach.

By early November, I was eating *papa* and *moroho* for dinner most nights. And somehow, somehow, to my own shock, I was enjoying the meals. I was eating *papa* twice a day, with lunch at school and then again with dinner on my own, and yet it didn't feel monotonous. I guess I had grown to like *papa*. And also, surely my mind was tricking my taste buds a bit, convincing them that the *moroho* tasted good since I had a hand in growing it. I sat down at my table each evening with my plate of white and green, I took a pinch of *papa* and with my thumb I scooped some *moroho* up with it and shoveled it into my mouth. I not only ate Tšoeneng food, but I also ate it like Tšoeneng people. In terms of feeling grown up and proud and independent, and also adapted, there was no bigger step, no more significant indicator, than being able to feed myself. The taste was miles beside the point.

SCHOOL FED ME lunch. I fed myself dinner with mostly *papa* and *moroho*. But I bought food for breakfast at Motsie's shop. He usually had some loaves of bread, sometimes he had a dusty jar of Black Cat peanut butter (I think I was the only one who ever bought peanut butter), and sometimes he had boxes of Jungle Oats oatmeal. I bought those whenever they were available, and at times I bought sorghum meal in order to cook a real Sesotho breakfast of *lesheleshele*, which was similar to cream of wheat. When Motsie had fruit in stock I snatched that up. There were often pears, of course, but also sometimes apples, oranges, or bananas. Never were there peaches. Never. Peaches were like *moroho*: you didn't find them for sale because everyone grew their own at home. One day I had gone up to the shop hoping for bananas and struck out. On my way back I met Masopha, the Form D hosteler who liked to teach me Sesotho things, who had taught me to wear my blanket, and who had eaten grilled cheese sandwiches at my house for the first lunch exchange. "Sir, where are you from?" he asked.

"The shop."

"Why don't you send me to the shop?"

"I have feet. Why should I send you?"

"Don't you know that in Sesotho we say, 'Children are for sending'?"

He was 20. I wanted to say, "You're a child?" But I knew that he was a child, for all intents and purposes. That was the relationship between a teacher and student in Lesotho, even though in terms of years we were both in our twenties, and in terms of physical stature we were the same height.

A couple days later I still wanted bananas, so I gave Masopha a couple rand and sent him to the shop. He came back empty-handed. "They are not there, sir. But on Saturday I'm going to the Chinese. They always have bananas," he said. "The Chinese" was a shop in a nearby village which was owned by some Chinese immigrants. I asked Masopha if I could go with him to the Chinese because I wanted to see them myself. They were the closest foreigners to me in Tšoeneng.

We started on a trail through the maize fields over to the paved road. The journey would be about a four mile walk from Tšoeneng south to Kolo. I asked Masopha if the Chinese knew Sesotho. "No, sir," he said. "The Chinese only know money!"

Ntheka and Tšepang both laughed. There were four of us taking the walk. The three of them were hostelers, and all around 20 years old. For moments it felt like I was taking a trip with friends, though the fact that they were my students never was completely out of mind—every time they addressed me as "sir" I was reminded.

The tar on the road was still black and smooth. It was the first tar to ever be laid down, in the fall of 2003, just before I arrived. When we reached the new bridge I looked down at the river which zigzagged sedately through its sandy bed and was much clearer than the day I had swum in it.

"The Chinese know some few words in Sesotho, that's all," continued Masopha. "They speak some words in Sesotho, some in English, and some in Chinese."

"*Abutiya, abutiya. Uena, you stealing too much. Ting, ting, tao,*" said Ntheka. And the three boys chuckled some more.

"Do you guys like the Chinese?" I asked, in Sesotho.

"Ah," said Masopha. "They are greedy. And they sometimes sell you the food that has expired. Basotho have died from that food, you know."

It wasn't right, but each insulting word the boys said toward the Chinese brought me a small sense of relief. As the only other foreigners around, I felt a strange sense of competition with them, even before ever meeting them. If the Chinese were disliked, it seemed more probable that I would be liked.

On the ascent up the other side of the river valley we saw a wild cat in the fields. The boys ran after the small orange creature, throwing rocks. I followed. But it escaped us by diving into a hole under some boulders.

Back on the road I continued prying about the Chinese: "Where do they live? Do they live in Kolo?"

Ntheka answered, "They live in town at Mafeteng."

"So they drive to Kolo every day?"

He said they did. "You will see. They have a white bakkie."

I had heard that there were lots of Chinese in Lesotho, relatively speaking. Later I read that there were about 5,000 Chinese in the country in total. Lesotho's population was only 2 million, so a group numbering 5,000 was significant, especially considering that the other 99 percent were African. But not just African—they were all of the same tribe, the Basotho, and spoke the same language, Sesotho. They looked alike: their faces were dark brown and roundish, their hair was in tight black curls, and they were not very tall as a people. For the Basotho, in fact, it was easy to spot an African from another part of the continent, especially those from up closer to the equator, with their purple-black skin, square heads and long bodies. *Makoerekoere*, the Basotho called these other Africans, because when they spoke their languages it sounded to the Basotho like, *"Koere-koere."* (Basotho said English sounded like, *"Qwesh-qwesh."*)

After about two hours we reached Kolo and I saw the square cinder block structure that had one wall hand-painted in blue letters, "Top Star Shop." High, small windows were protected with iron bars. In front of the entrance a handful of young Basotho men were offloading stock—bags of maize meal, bags of wheat flour, heads of cabbage, tanks of propane—from a white Isuzu pickup truck, a "bakkie," as a Chinese man with gray hair stood watch, smoking a cigarette.

We went inside. Top Star was at least five times as big as Motsie's shop. It even had shoes and radios on the shelves. I found bunches of purple grapes in the fruit bin, which seemed so exotic at the time. The guard spotted me looking at the grapes and approached. He was a Mosotho man in a jumpsuit, combat boots and carrying a shotgun. He pointed to the grapes and said the Sesotho word for them, *"Morara."* I said, "Oh." Then he pointed again, *"Morara!"* I took the hint and parroted, *"Morara!"*

I decided to buy some, along with some bananas, and a bag of cookies. The Chinese cashier, who looked to be in her thirties and was fashionably dressed in blue jeans, punched in numbers and then said nothing to me except to point to the price on the register. I had said nothing to her either: I had wanted to greet her, but I couldn't decide whether to do so in English or Sesotho. She probably didn't know much English. And wouldn't it sound self-centered if I greeted her in English anyway? But since Masopha had said the Chinese didn't speak Sesotho well, I didn't want to put her on the spot, or look like I was showing off my own Sesotho. And of course, I knew no Chinese. I just gave her my seven rand. She bagged my items, I picked them up, and I walked outside. It felt so unusual not to have greeted her. That would never have happened with a Mosotho cashier. Basotho always, always greeted one another. And I wondered what the Chinese cashier had thought of me, as surely she hadn't seen another foreigner in her shop for quite some time, if ever.

I stood at the store entrance to wait for the boys, as they waited in line to purchase jugs of paraffin, which they used in their stoves at the hostel. In front of them in the line was a Mosotho woman, who began arguing with the Chinese cashier. The two women exchanged heated words, yet I couldn't discern what the argument was about. I took a few steps closer to listen, but as they went back and forth I realized that I couldn't even pinpoint which language they were speaking—it didn't sound like Sesotho; it didn't sound like Chinese; it certainly wasn't any English that I knew.

The Chinese cashier called over to a Chinese man hunched behind a counter slurping noodles. He looked about her age—I figured they might have been siblings, and the man who had supervised the unloading of the truck was their father. Looking up from his noodles lazily, the young Chinese man mumbled something to the cashier which seemed to mean he didn't want to get involved, because then the guard came over. The Mosotho woman held up a bag of cookies and her words for the cashier grew louder. The guard spoke calmly with the Mosotho woman and then he spoke with the Chinese cashier, as a sort of mediator. Motsie didn't have a guard in his shop, but every Chinese shop I ever saw in Lesotho had armed security. I was learning why. All three people continued shouting until the woman left the store with her bag of cookies in hand. I hadn't noticed if she paid.

I asked Masopha what the disagreement had been about. "Ah," he said. "The Chinese hate when you cheat them." I didn't understand. But I decided not to pursue it. I realized that I didn't really care why they had argued. Just the fact that they had not gotten along gave me a winning feeling, though I'm sure the Chinese cashier had no commensurate losing feeling. The reality was we were on different journeys in Lesotho: I had come to make friends and live vulnerably in a village; she had come to make money and live behind armed guards.

On the road back toward Tšoeneng we shared my grapes, which had seeds. This made them seem even more exotic. "Do you think Chinese women are beautiful?" I asked the boys.

Masopha: "They don't have buttocks."

CHAPTER NINE

Lemeko the Climber

IT'S SURPRISING HOW FAST you can get used to circumstances that are beyond your control. My first semester had been so stressful, particularly those first few weeks, but the second semester was now careening toward an end and I barely noticed the days tick by. Many things which shocked me early on, I no longer blinked at. They were my new normal. Students picked their noses while they talked to me, all the time, in mid-conversation, while staring straight at me. And though I was astounded at first, I gradually started taking advantage of the different manners, and I started picking my nose freely as well.

I had gotten used to the teachers speaking Sesotho in the staffroom. Whereas in the first semester it offended me because I didn't understand most of what they were saying, now I paid their conversations full attention. I kept my memo book at my desk and I jotted down unknown words. After school, I looked them up in the dictionary at my house. My brain was more focused on Sesotho than it was on teaching these days. Sesotho was my interest, teaching was my job.

Sometimes I couldn't find one of the teachers' words in the dictionary. The hostelers were my next resource. On their visits in the evening, I showed them my Sesotho memo book and asked for translations. All of them were game to help me, but I preferred to consult with those hostelers whose English was best, which usually meant the older students. Masopha, a Form D, had a hand in my language learning more than the rest. His English was only fair, but his enthusiasm for teaching was above and beyond.

Without my asking, he had brought me his little sister's primary school reading books. They were tiny, about twenty pages long, with big color pictures of balls and chickens and shoes, the word for each being underneath the drawing: *bolo, khoho, lieta*. The vocabulary was easy for me, but on the pronunciation I could improve. I read aloud and Masopha corrected my errors, which were often related to the *q* sound. *Q* is a click where you pop your tongue off the roof of your mouth and then make a *k* sound. I also struggled with the tones. In Sesotho, the word for "you" is the same sound as the word for "he" or "she," but "he" or "she" is distinguished by a higher tone. The difference was so subtle to my ear. Even the difference between *ts* and *tś* was taking me a long time to detect. Still, often I mistakenly said I lived in Tsoeneng instead of Tšoeneng, and when I did people did not understand me. *Tś* is an aspirated sound, like the sound you make to show you don't believe something: tshhhh!

Masopha did more than help with my pronunciation problems. Late at night, my candle would be burning low, my eyelids so heavy, and Masopha would be telling me another Sesotho folktale: Kholumolumo was a dinosaur-like monster that ate up all the world's people and animals except for one pregnant woman, who had hidden herself in an ash heap. When the pregnant woman gave birth she named her child Senkatana. The boy quickly grew to be a man. Meanwhile, Kholumolumo, so fat from eating every living thing, had got itself stuck in a mountain pass. When Senkatana saw this he thought it his duty to slay the beast. But when he stabbed it in the gut he heard a chicken squawk, and then he heard people shout. So he cut the monster open gently and found everyone still alive in its belly. Senkatana had saved the world.

Masopha was from a village across the river called Ha Motlokoa, but his older sister lived in Tšoeneng. She was married in Tšoeneng, he said. In other words, her husband had grown up in Tšoeneng, so when she was married by him she became part of his family, there. "She wants to meet the ntate Greg that I've been telling her about," Masopha told me one day. So we walked up to the village to her house.

A thatched hut and a small square house with a tin roof were surrounded by a well-swept dirt border. Basotho kept grass away from their houses because they feared snakes. They even grew a wild garlic plant, *konofolo*, next to their front doors because it was supposed to ward off the evil slithering creatures. *Konofolo* had been planted on either side of my door before I arrived. 'Me 'Malijeng was out front standing over a big black cauldron. "You see where I'm cooking?" she asked. "On the ground. I don't have any . . ." She mimed pushing buttons, as one might on a microwave oven. Everyone seemed to have the same perception of me, of Americans: we used machines to do our chores, even to cook our food. She pointed to the fire beneath the cauldron. "I gather dung, I gather wood. And I burn. In fact, I've just come from gathering wood now." She laughed at the explanation she had given me.

'Me 'Malijeng had high puffy cheeks which squished her eyes almond just like Masopha's. The resemblance was obvious. She wore a dress with a bath towel wrapped around it, a common way of dressing for married women in the village.

Then she greeted us. *"Bo-ntate, le kae?"* It had to be done at some point. Basotho and their greetings: they had a million forms, a million words to greet with, and it always got done at some point in a conversation. I loved how you could start talking to someone and feel the greeting just hanging over the top of your heads, waiting for it to drop, knowing that at some point there would be a pause in the flow of words and then, "So men, how are you?"

She put down her *lesokoana* and left the cauldron of *papa* and led us toward the square house. We walked past an empty stone corral. 'Me 'Malijeng's husband was out to pasture with the sheep, Masopha said. She sat us down inside and then returned to her cooking outside. I looked over the room. The metal cupboards contained dishes and tins of grains. The poster on the wall of the Kaiser Chiefs soccer team was probably her husband's. Behind me was a curtain that cut the small, single-room house in half, delineating the kitchen and the bedroom—I could see the corner of a bed behind the curtain.

She came back in with two plates of food. My plate was piled with scoops of yellow *papa* alongside an oily gravy of tomato and onion, and chunks of mutton. 'Me 'Malijeng didn't have a plate for herself. She was feeding us, and talking.

"We were given that," she said, pointing to a 50 kilogram sack of maize meal in the corner that she had noticed me looking at. The sack was printed with "USA," in red and blue, and below the initials was a message, "Not to be sold or exchanged." I knew it must have been a donation from the United Nations World Food Programme, which made sense of the yellow *papa*. Basotho grew white maize; however, they received donations from America in the form of yellow corn. They didn't like it as much as their white maize, but at least it was free.

"What does this 'USA' mean?" she asked.

"United States," started Masopha.

"Of America," I finished. "That's where I'm from."

"America? They grow maize there?" she asked.

"Yes, especially the yellow kind."

"How is it in America?"

"It's nice."

"Is it better than Lesotho?"

I had trouble with this question. I was asked it often. "Um, it's not better, it's just different."

"Oh, it's different," said 'me 'Malijeng. She pondered that for a second. "I want to go to America with you. I can do house cleaning work. I'll wash dishes. Wait, do they use machines?"

Domestic work was the only type that most village women knew, so sometimes they sought jobs as maids in the homes of wealthy families in Maseru or in South Africa. Otherwise, they stayed in the village and kept their own house as their husbands herded or farmed or sought their own work elsewhere, sometimes over the border in South Africa, usually at a mine. Masopha and 'me 'Malijeng's father worked at a mine in South Africa.

Masopha was listening, eating *papa* and gravy and leaving his meat until last. 'Me 'Malijeng continued to ask questions. She asked about the foods we ate in America. She asked about how to travel from Lesotho to America.

"You ride an airplane over the ocean," I said.

"Ha! I'm afraid to do that."

"Then maybe you could take a boat."

"I fear the water, that's the problem!"

Masopha had finished his *papa* and gravy and tossed chunks of mutton into his mouth. I got to the mutton and found it very oily and salty, but a good complement to the bland *papa*. Only after all the food was finished did 'me 'Malijeng bring drinks. Masopha downed his whole cup of water in just a few gulps. Meal over.

"But are there chickens in America?" she asked.

"Yes. We eat them, and we eat cows and pigs too."

"Do you eat horse?"

"No, we don't eat horse."

"Do you eat donkey?"

"No."

"You don't eat donkey? It's nice ... and soft. It smells like fish."

I couldn't believe donkey meat smelled like fish. Nonetheless, the visit with 'me 'Malijeng was enlightening, and it was the kind of thing I wanted to do every day. 'Me 'Malijeng was curious, I was curious. I was so glad Masopha had brought me up there. I was lucky he had taken to teaching me and getting me out of the house to explore.

I WANTED TO SEE more of the village. I wanted to get to know more people. In the absence of invites, like to 'me 'Malijeng's, I still went up to the shop almost every day after school. I walked slowly, I loitered out front and next to the bar, talking to whoever was around, hoping Motsie might take me for another ride. And I looked up into the village and thought, That's where I really want to be.

Then I saw a sign, a way to get myself into the village. T'soeneng wrapped around the base of a mountain, and just above the houses and huts, where the slope steepened, there were a handful of huge golden boulders. They looked like a god had kicked them off the sandstone cliffs above, and they had come to rest among the tall grasses. The boulders called to me like a beacon.

When I learned that Peace Corps was sending me to Lesotho, and I read up on the place and learned that it had the nickname

Mountain Kingdom, I decided to pack along my rock climbing shoes. It was early summer now, and warm enough to use them. I slung my red rock shoes over my shoulder and headed for the boulders one day after school. As a destination, the golden boulders would require me to cut directly through the village. I could see people's houses, I could have chance conversations, but I wouldn't be suspiciously wandering. I walked through the fields to the paved road and then, instead of following the road up toward Motsie's shop, I crossed it and walked through the Catholic Church grounds. I followed a path past the clinic where a couple of government-paid nurses worked and the church building, and then I walked under cypress trees, next to a barbed wire fence, and beside a sandstone brick building with busted out windows. The building looked long abandoned. I then connected to a wide path that passed by a small cemetery, where crudely shaped stones were posted at the heads of lumps of dirt. Full names were etched into the stones. Many of the last names were Mokhele or Adoro. Some had Christian middle names: Benedict, Augustina, Daniel, Clementina. Often there was a date of death but no date of birth. And a couple grave sites were much more ornate than the others, with painted wrought iron cages around them.

A switchback took the trail to the left and up a steep rocky incline beside a wall of the spiky arms of giant aloes. Though Lesotho had few trees, it had innumerable aloes. As the trail leveled out I noticed a group of men perched on an outcrop to my right. I greeted them and they asked where I was going. "To the rocks," I said.

"Why?"

"So I can go to the top of them." I didn't yet know the Sesotho word for climb.

"So you can get a good view of the village?"

I said yes, as I was in the habit of doing whenever my elementary Sesotho prevented me from giving a complete and nuanced answer. With that I continued toward the boulders. The path was now weaving among homesteads high up on the mountainside. There were no roads in Tšoeneng save the paved road that bisected the village. There were only dirt paths leading from house to house, or shooting between a corral and a row of aloes. Some paths were wide enough for a car, while others were so narrow that you had to walk single file. On either side of my path there were both round stone-walled huts and square concrete-block houses. A soil and dung mortar was used on most huts and houses, but sometimes cement was used. Usually, the stone houses had thatch roofs, made of the tall grasses called *mohlomo* that grew on the mountainside just above them. The concrete-block houses had corrugated tin roofs. Some homesteads consisted of multiple small buildings, like a few huts and one house, like Masopha's sister's place. There may have been one hut originally, but then as the children grew and the family gained wealth they built more. Often, one hut was used solely for cooking. The women built a fire right in the center, and in the winter the whole family spent mornings and evenings there to keep warm. Near the cooking hut there was always a gray ash heap.

When the path up the mountain climbed above the village homesteads it went by ruins of stone huts from long ago. After crossing a wide ditch, the trail rose entirely above the village and onto a more level meadow where there were only shepherds tending their animals, and my boulders. I followed a shepherd's path. I knew it was a shepherd's path because I was stepping over brown turdlets left by sheep, plops left by donkeys and patties left by cattle. When I was new to Lesotho I had to pay careful attention so as to not step on poop. Now, I could walk up the mountain—or through the village, or on the paved road, or at school even (there were animal droppings everywhere)—without consciously watching my step. It was like I had acquired a sixth sense to avoid stepping on the mines of crap. Of course, Basotho were born with this sense. I don't think I ever saw a Mosotho step in animal poop.

There were two boulders that were significantly bigger than the others and looked best for climbing. They were sandstone—orange with some yellow and black—and I started on the southern one, the biggest of all. The rock's surface was smooth in places, rough as coral in others, and the first few times I pulled on the holds they broke off in my hands—no one had climbed here before, no one had pulled on this rock. The few shepherds that were grazing their animals nearby, among the tall *mohlomo* thatching grasses, the prickly pear cactus and red-berried shrubs, migrated closer to me and my boulder, but they said nothing.

The boulder had three facets: an impossibly overhanging side, a gently sloping side that was slick, and the side I chose to climb—almost straight up but full of good holds. It would take a few minutes to figure out, but I was confident I could make it up before the end of the day. More holds popped off in my hands and I dropped to the ground. Then I got half-way up and couldn't figure out where to go and had to downclimb before my arms were totally exhausted and I couldn't hold on and I had to let go and fall to the ground. Underneath the route I was working on were shrubs to both sides and rocks directly below that would snap my ankle if I landed wrong. But I downclimbed safely. I stood beneath the route shaking out my aching forearms and considering strategy when a shepherd's face appeared over the ledge above. He was smiling gloatingly. He must have run up the sloping backside in his rubber boots. He motioned for me to try his way, around the back.

I gave a puff of breath, and then I ignored him. I pulled onto the rock face again and saw how crazy I must have looked, trying and failing to get to the top of the rock by its steep side when there was a gently sloping side you could walk up around the back. Soon there were two more shepherds sitting on nearby rocks watching me and muttering. I knew I looked crazy, but that made me more determined, and by sunset I made it: there were no more loose holds to pop off in my hands, and toward the top I found jugs, really big handles carved into the rock that I could leverage to pull myself up and over the ledge where the shepherd had showed his face. At the top I turned around and saw the village spread out below like a skirt around the waist of the mountain, the black tarmac road running through the village, the patchwork fields stretching out past the village to a low spine of mountains in the west which was about to give cover for the sun. What a beautiful place I was living in. And this view of it could have been reason enough to climb.

THE MORE I CLIMBED the more I realized that as a ruse for cutting through the village and getting to see homes and routines and talk to people, rock climbing was a godsend. I started to do it a couple days a week after school, and then every morning once school closed for the summer break. All of December I woke early so that I could climb before the rock faces got too hot to touch. The climbing routine was paying big social dividends. When I was on my way up the mountain in the morning, shepherds and farmers would still be driving their cattle to the pastures and fields. One morning some men were already in a field and they called me over to take their plow, which I did as they snapped their whips to drive the oxen. I guided the plow through a handful of wavy rows, and the men taught me the words to describe guiding the plow (*ho tšoara mohoma*), and then they took over again. I passed women carrying pails of water on their heads, pacing between their homes and the nearby spring. They knew where I was headed now and they often warned me, "There are bees in the rocks, you know. And watch for snakes. They hide in the holes and they will bite you!" White smoke from freshly stoked cook fires rose thick through brown thatch roofs and straight to heaven in the still morning air.

The men who sat on the rocks near the trail up the mountain always called out to greet me. I found out one day why they always sat on those rocks.

"Going to the rocks, Thabang?"

"Yes."

"Do you know *morabaraba*?"

"Yes."

"Come play!"

On a flat rock they had worn a game grid where they tracked around a set of glass shards and small stones. This was the same game that the hostel boys played down near their toilets.

"Eat! Eat!" one of the men yelled.

"Block!" shouted another.

The game pieces are all referred to as "cows," and the aim is to gobble up your opponent's herd. *Morabaraba* grids were etched into rocks all over Tšoeneng, all over Lesotho, and nearby you could always find the cows, a half dozen light-colored rocks and a half dozen dark-colored rocks, or a half dozen bottle caps and a half dozen glass shards.

Only two men played, but *morabaraba* was very much a spectator sport. The other men surrounding the players constantly shouted advice, or criticism: "You're being whipped!" The two players made a few moves and then one of them swiped all of the cows off the grid. I'd played *morabaraba* with the boys at school down at the toilets and up at another grid they made near a classroom, and I'd seen that no one ever waited for their full herd to be eaten. As soon as a player sensed he was going to lose he capitulated by swiping the cows off the grid. I guessed that saved face, and time. Often a player swiped his cows off the grid after only a couple opening moves.

"Do you want to play?" the losing man asked me.

I'd never won a *morabaraba* match, an unmanly statistic in Lesotho, like not being able to stick fight, or having a high voice, or being afraid of dogs. I'd heard that skills in *morabaraba* were so respected that some chiefs chose the best players in the village to be their advisers. So to avoid self-incrimination, I declined the offer. "I'll just watch," I said.

"How much is one dollar?" one of the guys asked out of nowhere.

"One dollar is seven rand."

"I'll be here tomorrow, and you bring me seven rand and I'll bring a dollar."

"You have a dollar? Where did you get a dollar?"

"Someone gave it to me."

I said I'd bring the rand, but I suspected that the next day he'd show me a piece of Monopoly money, or maybe he was related to the Form D student who had got a dollar in her pen pal letter. Sure enough, the guy actually showed up with a real dollar bill that next day, which I exchanged with him for seven rand, but I forgot to ask who had given it to him.

I saw the *morabaraba* men almost every time I took that path up the mountain, but I started trying different routes through the village. On the way down I was sometimes drawn to pass by a stone hut with no windows, but lots of sound coming from within. Mostly, I could hear drumming, and also women singing.

There was no door on the hut's entrance, but it was dark inside and I couldn't see anything so I approached the hut to peak in and a woman appeared at the threshold: *"Tsamaea, ntate Thabang!"* It was 'me 'Makopano, the school cook. "You can't see in here," she said. "It's only for women. No men." I respected that and I left, but it made me more curious. Every time I passed by the hut, and the singing was coming from within, I slowed and I wondered why no men were allowed.

Sometimes I came down the hill and passed by Motsie's shop. There, I could always count on the dark man with the jackal pelt on his head demanding to examine my red rock shoes. "What are they made of? Do they prevent slipping? How much did they cost?" And I could always count on him finally demanding that I give him the shoes. It was our routine.

"You rock climb?" I would ask. "I've never seen you."

"I do. Give them to me."

He looked mean with his dark face and deep scar and dead animal on his head, but he was also drunk and I knew that the demand was just part of the routine. Eventually he started offering to trade his hat for the shoes. I liked his hat, but I only had one pair of rock shoes and I couldn't give them up.

MOST PEOPLE THOUGHT my hobbies were irrational. Trying to climb up boulders from the steep side? Where bees swarmed, where snakes hid? Throwing yourself into the river when it was flooded? (I had swum in the Tsoaing a number of times after thunderstorms now. After each downpour I checked the river, and if it was full enough I ran down, with hostelers in tow, to shoot the rapids and help the hostelers swim in the shallower parts.) But I preferred being thought odd to being thought of just as the white teacher at the school down there in the fields. At least people in the village were getting to know something about me, something deeper than the color of my skin. Maybe it was even better that they thought I was irrational, that I enjoyed dangerous activities, so they would be a little scared of me. I felt fairly safe in Tšoeneng now, but especially after I got mugged in Maseru I didn't mind if people thought that messing with me was risky.

Not everyone thought my climbing habit was weird though, and by the end of the year I had acquired a partner. It wasn't Masopha, although he and some other hostelers had come climbing with me from time to time. It was a village kid from my Form A class named Lemeko. The boulders were near his house, and he'd see me walking on the path to them, run out and ask to come along. "Call for me whenever you pass my house so I can climb with you," he asked. But soon I would pass his house and call for him and his grandmother would say that he'd already headed up to the rocks. I would arrive at the boulders to find Lemeko already latched onto one.

He was short, really short. 'Me 'Malimpho called him "the dwarf." And after Lemeko started climbing with me often she referred to him as "Greg's dwarf." She would ask me in the staffroom: "Did you go to the rocks with your dwarf yesterday?" The other boys played soccer on the school grounds every day after school, but Lemeko rarely joined them. He was smaller even than most girls in his class. But size didn't matter much in rock climbing.

One summer morning I watched Lemeko hop on and place his left hand precisely on the rock and then cross over with his right to a hold farther along. This traverse was our favorite route. His progress was smooth and balanced. But the ledge grew narrower and smoother, and then Lemeko arrived at the crux, where the hand holds disappeared altogether for a few feet, and the places for his feet were no bigger than a dime. He climbed barefoot, but his toes were covered in skin as tough as leather and he was able to grip parts of the rock with them better than my shoes. The challenge for Lemeko was the hand holds. He had to stretch his left arm as far as possible to touch the next hold, and it would be troublesome to bear his weight on such an outstretched arm. He placed his hand and then grunted as he swung his weight onto it, but his fingers strummed the lip and he dropped to the ground.

He stood below the route and slapped his pumped forearms.

We had started searching for new boulders up near the cliffs on the mountain's summit together and around the backside, and over in Kolo and beyond, and Lemeko taught me the names of plants along the way. One was called *tšoekere*—literally, sugar—which dangled sweet white crystals that crunched like candy in your mouth. Nevertheless, the boulders near his house remained our favorite. And Lemeko finally gave our favorite route a name. I had lent him an issue of *Climbing* magazine, which he read closely. He was an excellent student, spoke decent English, and he noticed that all of the rocks in the magazine had names. "What are our rocks called?" he asked.

"I don't know. In my head I call them the traverse one and the vertical one. But I haven't actually named them. You should name them."

The next day we climbed he told me that he wanted to call his favorite rock the Pacific Traverse. I didn't ask why. I just accepted.

This route on the Pacific Traverse followed a ledge about six feet off the ground. As Lemeko stood below it looking at his forearms and shaking the ache out of them he asked, "Do you know the wrestlers, sir?"

"Who are the wrestlers?"

"Like Undertaker, Batista, Triple H, John Cena?"

"Oh, no. I know the old guys though, like Hulk Hogan, 'Macho Man' Randy Savage and Andre the Giant," I said. "I used to watch wrestling on TV when I was young, but I haven't seen it for a long time. How do you know about wrestling?"

Lemeko said he sometimes stayed with his uncle in Maseru, and his uncle had a television. "When I'm there I cross the whole night watching the wrestling and also the films. Do you know Walker, Texas Ranger? He is too strong!"

Lemeko looked at his chest and flexed it. I laughed inside, a gentle laugh. Lemeko was 13 years old, but he could have passed for a fifth grader.

We were climbing the Pacific Traverse on another afternoon when a couple of older shepherds came over. You could tell they had attitude from the start. They leaned on their *molamus*, in their rubber boots, from a little distance and made comments to each other, laughing, but not saying anything directly to us, until one said, "Hey you Lemeko, is this your sir?"

"Yes."

Finally, one of the shepherds stomped up to the rock, egged on by his friends. He grabbed onto the first holds in a mocking way and pulled his body up and down. He started to move left. The first part of the PT is pretty easy, full of big holds that your hands fit around like ladder rungs, but immediately those jugs run out, and the real PT begins and the holds are only the width of a fingernail. Then the shepherd's rubber boots began skipping off the rock—a shepherd never took his boots off—and quickly his fingers lost their grip too. *"Ai!"* the shepherd shouted as he hit the ground.

Lemeko hopped on and the shepherds watched with a new appreciation. He worked his way through the traverse with obvious technique and I overheard one of the shepherds whisper, "He's like a cat."

I was so happy for Lemeko that he had found climbing. There were now two of us who headed to the rocks every day with ulterior motives.

CHAPTER TEN

This Is My Village

I LOVED THE SUMMER BREAK, December and January. I climbed early in the morning and then, if no thunderstorm built in the afternoon, I sat under my peach tree and read Sesotho in the shade. It was tranquil at my house. I looked down across the fields to the Tsoaing River and Kolo Mountain. I could hear myself think.

And I had plenty of time to expand what crops I grew. My initial plot of *moroho* was now accompanied by chili peppers and tomatoes, which the hostelers and teachers had helped me plant in a new bed right up against my house, along the west-facing wall. They grew feverishly, soaking up the radiation from the yellow facade of the house.

Though the hostelers were gone now, students from the village made the walk down to school to visit me sometimes. One day a Form D named Lerato Thaki came down and noticed my clump of green onions at the edge of my *moroho* plot. He showed me how to separate them and replant them in a row. I loved learning about plants and being able to provide myself with more food. On that day the late afternoon was cool enough such that I decided to rock climb one more time before sunset, so I grabbed my shoes, locked my door, and Lerato and I walked up toward the village and the mountain. We crossed the paved road and entered the church grounds. We followed the path between the barbed wire fence and the cypress trees and Lerato pointed to the seemingly abandoned sandstone brick building, the one with the busted out windows, and said, "That is where the priest was murdered."

"The priest was murdered?"

"Yes, sir."

"When?"

"Maybe 1960-something."

"Really."

"Yes, sir. He was the white priest."

"Oh. Who murdered him?"

"Men from the village. They wanted to steal his money."

Lerato was one of the smartest students in his class, in the whole school, and he seemed trustworthy. And he didn't seem like the kind of guy who would pull my leg about this. But my immediate reaction was that if it was true it felt like something I should have been told about in the very beginning: I wasn't the first foreigner to come to live in Tšoeneng. In the 60's a white priest stayed here, until he was robbed and murdered in his home. Had Lerato told me something he was supposed to keep secret?

When I got to the rocks I asked Lemeko if he had heard about a white priest that had been murdered at the church. Yes, he knew of the story. Why hadn't anyone told me about this? I asked him for details, but he didn't know any more than Lerato. "I will ask my grandmother," he said.

Father Menard was the priest's name, and he had come from Canada. In 1966, the man was in his quarters on the church grounds when some men entered. Some of them were his friends and some worked at the church. They robbed him and killed him right there. Did Peace Corps know about this? Why did they send me to a village where the last foreigner had been murdered? Maybe they did know, but since a generation had passed they thought it was safe now and Tšoeneng deserved a second chance. Or maybe they knew the rest of the story. The perpetrators fled. All but one escaped and never showed their face in the village again. The one who was caught, however, was beaten to death by Tšoeneng people on the spot.

That part of the story was relieving. Maybe Tšoeneng people were embarrassed of the event, wanting to live it down, and that's why I had never heard of it until now.

Tšoeneng had seemed so safe, compared to Maseru anyway.

That's where the *tsotsis* were, the criminals, up in the city. Down here everyone was cordial and genuine, they were hardworking and honest. Maybe not. My image of the village was fractured. But maybe the priest had brought it upon himself, like the Chinese. Did he know Sesotho? Did he hang out in the village or did he hide in his home? Was he liked by the Tšoeneng people? "Tšoeneng people liked Father Menard," Lemeko's grandmother said.

Not the answer I was hoping for. If making friends and speaking Sesotho wouldn't keep me safe, then what would? How did I not end like Father Menard? I felt vulnerable once again. I felt like a fledgling nation in need of allies, in need of protection by stronger forces.

I WENT TO THE CHIEF'S HOUSE. I had meant to visit the chief at his home ever since I spent that first day with him at the initiation ceremony, where we had gotten off to a good start, I thought. But I had yet to get around to visiting him. The work at school consumed so much of my time and mental energy, and since the chief didn't speak English I was always waiting for my Sesotho to get better, so we could have a real conversation when I visited. I didn't want to have to bring Principal Tsita or a student with me to translate. And before I knew it months had gone by, with me living in the chief's village, but me not paying him any visits or outward signs of appreciation.

In the meantime, I had seen him from time to time elsewhere. Once there was a running competition between Ngoana Jesu and a school from a nearby village. The entire student body and all the teachers from the other school, Tholo Secondary, had walked to our school. The chief from Tholo had even come, and he sat with our Chief Thabo on a low hill above the running field, watching kids run barefoot through the grass as fast as they could.

But I needed to visit him personally, at his house, to show some effort, to make sure that he knew I respected him and to make sure he was on my side.

When I showed up at the chief's door, uninvited and unannounced, it was open and I found him at his table studiously writing in a notebook. He looked up. "I've just come to say hello," I said. He grinned, saying with his face, This is an interesting surprise.

"Kena, ntate," he said. And then he told me to take a seat at the table with him. His wife was also in the room, and the chief gave her a look, to which she responded, "I haven't cooked anything."

"Bring us drinks then," said the chief.

I asked him the question I had prepared in Sesotho. I had learned that he once worked in a South African mine, so I asked him about that, *"U ne u sebetsa maeneng?"* But as he answered I got distracted by how coarse his voice was, and I thought about how it was probably from breathing the dust over all those years down in the mine.

'Me 'Malebusa, the chief's wife, returned with cups of a very sweet red drink. I gulped mine and tried to think of something more to say. I looked around the room. On the wall there was one of the free calendars the Fahida store in Maseru gave away, and there was also a plastic clock. "The clock is pretty," I said.

"It is broken," said the chief.

I looked at the time and yes, it was wrong. "I'm always late for meetings because I don't have a good clock, or a watch." My arm was resting on the table and he looked toward my wrist. "This watch is pretty," he said.

"You like it?"

"Yes. It's nice."

It was nothing flashy, just a $30 plastic Timex Ironman. Principal Tsita had once said to me, "Ntate Thabo isn't a rich chief." And now I was seeing how true that was. Most chiefs had bigger houses and many animals. Chief Thabo's house was as small as mine, with only two rooms. It wasn't bad looking, with fresh white paint on the front wall, and especially with the trellis near the door holding up a grape vine. There was a plot of vegetables in the back and in the front, between the house and the road, there was a large stone corral. But the corral was empty, with just a dark floor of decomposing dung. Chief Thabo may not have had much, but he was still the chief, and surely I would be much safer in Tšoeneng if he had my back.

Unfortunately, there was a minor patch to mend in my relationship with Chief Thabo. At that running competition some months earlier, I had been standing next to 'me Albertina when she turned to me and introduced me to a man who had just walked up and said something to her in Sesotho. "He is from the chief," she said. "And he says the chief is asking for 20 rand because he wants to buy the visiting chief a gift."

"Why is he asking me and not other people?"

"He has also just asked me. I told him I don't have any money. You can say that too."

I thought for a second. I didn't know if this was normal or some kind of attempt at extortion, but I was very sensitive to people seeing me as a money bag, and I wanted all of my relationships to be genuine and never influenced by any exchange of funds. Chief Thabo had seemed like a nice guy, but I didn't really know.

"Me too. Tell him I don't have any money."

Later, after I had read Eugene Casalis's book and talked to some people I came to understand that I hadn't maintained a principled relationship with my chief that day, but instead I had bucked the rules of the chief system in Lesotho. In Lesotho, instead of paying a tax as Americans would to their city coffers in order to salary a mayor, Basotho voluntarily provided labor and small gifts of money from time to time to support their chief. Chiefs received very minimal salaries from the government because their traditional support came straight from the people of the village in this form. Asking a villager for a few rand to help show a visiting chief hospitality wasn't anything extraordinary or shady. And now that I knew, I wished I had given Chief Thabo the 20 rand.

I didn't know how I could make up for that blunder at this point, until he said that he needed a watch and that he liked mine. Perfect.

But I wanted to get to know the chief too. I looked around the chief's house some more and tried to carry on the conversation. On the end of the table I noticed something that looked beautifully crafted. Part of the object was a cow's tail. The hair was white, and the skin had been stitched around a stick. Copper wire was wound and shining at the top of the leather. At the butt of the stick's handle a bust had been carved, and the bust looked like the moai statues of Easter Island. The artifact was obviously handmade, but by someone with excellent coordination and imagination. "This is pretty," I said to the chief, and I pointed at the object. Unfortunately, my Sesotho didn't allow for more elegant commentary at this time.

"You like it?"

"Yes, I like it very much."

Then I didn't see anything else to comment on and I didn't have any other Sesotho questions memorized and I couldn't think of more to ask. I had finished my drink and figured I should let the chief get back to whatever work he had been doing in his notebook. As I stood up to leave, the chief handed me the cow's tail. "It's called a *lechoba*," he said. "We do this with it." And he waved it as though he were shooing flies. "It's for you."

"Oh, no," I said. I hadn't meant to imply I wanted him to give it to me. I just really meant that it was beautiful. But he repeated, "It's yours." And since I didn't have the Sesotho to explain my thoughts I said, "Thank you," and I went home that day carrying the most ornate fly swatter I would ever own.

I was doubly indebted now. But at least it appeared that Chief Thabo was my ally. When I got home I immediately wrote a letter to my mom asking her to use one of the signed checks I had left with her to buy and send a Timex Ironman. My chief needs a watch.

THERE WAS ONE OTHER PERSON I knew I had to visit: the other powerhouse in the village, Witchdoctor Santu. He was the leader of those who seemed most dangerous, the initiated men. He took the young men of Tšoeneng up the mountain to circumcise them and train them to fight. So a few days later I dropped in on him at his house. Immediately after I arrived, the witchdoctor asked his young daughter to serve me food, just as Chief Thabo had asked his wife. "I have only cooked *papa*," the daughter, whose name was Khauta, or Gold, said softly.

"Go and cook something to go with the *papa*," Witchdoctor Santu said. It was then obvious to me that in Lesotho you were always expected to feed a visitor to your home. I felt imposing.

As we waited for the food, Witchdoctor Santu and I talked as well as my Sesotho permitted. It was awkward and halting until he left the room and returned with a small photo album. Photo albums worked like alchemy on stymied social occasions. Most of the photos were of the witchdoctor himself. He was never smiling. Instead, he was always striking a proud pose, and in various uniforms: a loincloth in one; a miner's jumpsuit with gumboots in another. Santu had also worked in South African mines just like Chief Thabo. It made sense. Santu breathed heavily and spoke with a hoarse voice, just like the chief. I was surprised to learn that so many men in Tšoeneng had worked in South African mines, but soon I would discover that mine work across the river was nearly the only paying job available to local men.

Witchdoctor Santu left the room again and returned this time with his passport. The name Santu was nowhere on the page though. The witchdoctor's real name: Lefa Adoro. His last name, Adoro, and the chief's last name, Mokhele, were two of the most common in Tšoeneng.

"How long does the journey take from Lesotho to America?" he asked.

"It takes about two days."

"*Hele!* That's far. What do you ride?"

"An airplane."

"How long would it take on a horse?"

"You can't ride your horse. You have to cross the ocean."

People were always interested in how you traveled between our countries, and the concept of crossing the ocean was one they couldn't wrap their heads around. Almost no one in Tšoeneng had ever even seen the ocean.

Both Witchdoctor Santu and the chief knew no English, but the conversation with Santu was a little easier because he asked more questions. And he brought out artifacts to talk about. After Santu's daughter brought me *papa* and beans to eat, the last artifact he brought out to show me was a book of laws, *The Laws of Lerotholi*. Lerotholi was king of Lesotho, or Paramount Chief as he was known then, at the end of the 19th century. He was the grandson of Moshoeshoe. These laws were a codified list of customary rules, especially dealing with land tenure and the role of chiefs in Lesotho. I don't know why the witchdoctor chose to bring that book out, except that it was probably the only book he owned. "Can you read?" he asked me.

"Yes."

"In Sesotho?"

"Yes."

"Read to me then!"

I opened the book, which Santu had covered with newspaper, and I started in on a section about how the chiefs should allocate land, which I didn't understand well, but I was focused on pronunciation anyway. Santu corrected me here and there, but he was generally impressed. "*Ai*, you can read Sesotho." Little did he know—thanks to the phonetic spellings of Casalis and his fellow missionaries—Sesotho was fairly easy to read. When it came time to leave, Witchdoctor Santu sent me home with the book, telling me to continue learning the traditional laws. And he told me he would soon visit me at school so I could take his horse for a ride.

THE VISITS to the chief and the witchdoctor had gone better than I hoped. At night, I still locked the metal bars covering my front door, and I kept a big stick next to my bed, but I wondered who would be suicidal enough to come attack me when the chief and the witchdoctor were on my side. Yet I lived off the edge of the village, out in the fields. I was alone out there, the only one on the school grounds. They could attack, but they wouldn't get away with it.

Around my home was very quiet. And that tranquility was something I relished. When students from the village came down to visit they often asked if I was bored. I said I liked the quiet. I had lived all my life in cities, and I found the absence of noise at my house so welcome that I could feel it, like my ears were taking breaths of clean air.

I heard a curious buzzing sound one December morning.

School was still closed, so the air had been clean silent except for faint animal noises—the grunting of pigs in the sties next to the hostel, the squawking of ravens in the eucalyptus trees, the distant bray of a donkey in the village, the occasional sound of cow bells wafting up from the fields. The campus was empty. I had been quietly drinking coffee at my table and studying Sesotho. Yet this buzzing outside . . . it was a machine, some kind of engine that grew louder and fluctuated in pitch.

I walked out of my house to see two motorcycles ride by on the dirt path above the classrooms. That was unprecedented. I'd never seen a motorcycle in Tšoeneng. I looked to the sky. There were no clouds to the west, which meant no thunderstorm this afternoon. I went back inside my house. But minutes later I heard more motors buzzing. I walked back outside to see more dirt bikes passing and now there were a couple vehicles parked on a grassy patch next to the path. I put on a shirt and headed up to check out what in the world was invading my space. By the time I got up to the path it was a parking lot of SUV's, trucks, Mercedes vans, and big white people standing around. Gas cans and coolers and soft drinks lay on the ground. They were speaking a little English, but mostly Afrikaans, and I could see the plates on their vehicles: all South African, many from the neighboring Free State province. This was weird. I had yet to see another foreigner in Tšoeneng. And these Afrikaners were tramping all over a grassy area where sheep often grazed and on the dirt which our students used to grow vegetables for agriculture class. They acted like they owned the place.

It was strange to see any foreigners in Tšoeneng, but I felt extra attentive seeing Boers. I didn't know what to make of them. I had never really met one personally, only having read about them and seen them from afar, so I couldn't shake the prejudice of thinking they were the ones responsible for apartheid. And now they were in my front yard, driving all over it.

A dirt bike raced up and pulled off the track. He took off his helmet and a white woman handed him a bottled drink. His hair was wet with sweat. He grabbed a gas can and poured some in his tank and then sped off west, kicking up dust. More dirt bikes and some quads roared up, some making a pit stop, some just flying past.

I saw that they had spray painted orange blazes on the trunks of Ngoana Jesu's pine trees to mark a route. The racers were rutting up our dirt path and sending grit into my mouth. I couldn't believe these people had invaded Tšoeneng. Did Chief Thabo know about this? Was it some kind of sanctioned race? Did he approve? I felt territorial. I also felt offended, on behalf of Tšoeneng people because of the history between these two groups. The Boers had expelled the Basotho off much of their land, and now they were riding their dirt bikes over the rest.

The whites and their vehicles were all on the south side of the dirt track. Some Tšoeneng people had come down from the village, having heard the noise, and they stood on the north side of the dirt track, in a field of weeds and sorghum stubble. Whites over there, blacks over here.

I walked over and stood with the villagers on the north side without speaking to any of the whites. I had chosen my side, but the villagers still assumed I had insider's knowledge about people who looked like me. One asked me, "Why do some machines have two wheels and others four?"

I did know the answer. "The ones with four wheels are easier to ride."

Another villager then asked me, "Why are the Boers so thick?"

Boers are big people, at least as big as Americans, and giant compared to Basotho. "They eat a lot of meat," I said. It was as well as I could explain things in Sesotho. It was fun being able to serve as a sort of interpreter of the sights.

The Boer women wore jeans, some even shorts, and shirts revealing their shoulders. This was in contrast to the village women in tattered dresses and shirts with sleeves, towels or blankets wrapped around them. The white women were showing their skin; the black women were covering theirs. I was standing next to a village woman and her daughter now. The woman pointed to a white woman and asked me what was on her back. It was a tattoo of a rose. Basotho sometimes tattooed themselves, but only with small black circles on their cheeks, or little marks on their hands. But because of this I knew the Sesotho word for tattoo and told the woman it was such.

The curiosity of the Tšoeneng people started to rub off on me. I was beginning to feel less territorial and more curious myself. It was entertaining seeing such people and such machines. This was like a free spectacle brought right to our door step. When a motorcycle rider took off from his pit stop doing a wheelie, accelerating incredibly fast, his back tire blowing up dirt, I marveled at how skillfully he handled the bike.

I wondered why I had felt so territorial earlier when the real locals, the Basotho, didn't seem to. Was it because I had been reading so much history, which made wars that happened centuries ago seem like yesterday? Maybe for the Basotho the taking of their land by the Boers was largely forgotten, or at least the emotions had faded. Or maybe not: I heard on the radio that evening that this race was an official event called the Roof of Africa and one racer had to abandon after being injured because some shepherds had apparently moved route markers (rocks spray painted orange) to direct the rider straight up an impossibly steep slope. He flipped his bike, and a helicopter airlifted him to a South African hospital with a broken back.

As I stood on the north side with the villagers, I noticed a few whites take second glances at me. Why is he over there with the villagers? I thought they were thinking. But they never tried to talk to me, and in the end I never tried to talk to them.

As a few of them started leaving to meet their riders at the next pit stop, I was feeling less offended by their presence, but still something bothered me about how they showed up out of nowhere, drove all over our fallow vegetable plots, made a bunch of noise, ignored the locals, and left trash. (Not that the Basotho never littered, but the Boers were visitors.) The village woman next to me spotted a plastic bottle that had been left behind. She whispered to her daughter, "Go fetch that." The girl ran across the track to the south side, grabbed the bottle, and ran back to her mother's side. The woman took it from the daughter and examined the bottle and smirked like she'd won a prize.

PART III

Too many regulations have been made for [the Basotho], without having any just idea of their history, their customs, or of what they stand in need.

\- EUGENE CASALIS

CHAPTER ELEVEN

Government Books

WHEN I WALKED into my first class in January 2005, my second school year, all of the Form E's sucked their teeth. This was Masopha's class, last year's Form D's. The girls of the class said to me, "OOWOO!"

"What is it?" I asked.

"You are fat," a girl said.

"I'm fat?"

But they were smiling, so I asked, "Is that good?"

"YESSSS."

Of course it was. Rarity brings value. Being fat in a place where everyone is skinny is worth something. Though fat was an overstatement for me. In December, at the end of the last school year, I had punched a new hole in my belt to keep my pants on my withering waistline. I was skinnier than I'd ever been. I'd almost exclusively been eating *papa* with *moroho* or another side. However, over the school break, around Christmas time, my mom and aunt visited. They rented a car and we traveled around South Africa and through Swaziland together for a couple weeks, all the while eating good food at hotels. Wealthy South Africans eat meat for breakfast. In Lesotho, I had eaten meat once a week at the most, like on a special Sunday when I went up to Maseru. But by the time I got back to Tšoeneng and my mom and aunt headed back to America, they had fed me so extravagantly that I no longer needed a belt at all to hold up my pants. I'd never experienced such a weight fluctuation, and I was now heavier than I'd ever been.

The day before, on the first day of the new school year, only about sixty students had shown up to sing the hymn at morning assembly. *"Lentsoe la ka ke lena: Jesu"*—My word is this: Jesus. I was getting to know some of the lyrics. The students sang in separate parts, like usual. The girls' voices were all high, and the boys' voices were all low; the girls led, while the boys echoed. I sang only when the boys did. I had practiced often inside my house and while walking out in the fields, so that now I could almost sing as deeply as them. I dropped the side of my mouth and put out the most guttural sound I could. It was close—not quite there, but close—to what the boys sang like at the initiation ceremony.

I knew there must have been about fifty additional students still out gathering their belongings in the village, asking relatives for tuition money, and in a few months the assembly hymn would be sung by a much fuller group, for that was how school had started my first year.

In the afternoon, while seated at my desk in the staffroom, the sun beat down on my neck through the window directly behind me. The varnish on the wood deck of my desk became so hot that it stung my forearms when I touched it. The tin roof overhead pinged as it expanded and the hot still air inside put me to sleep. But I knew that the sun's position in the sky would change, and by April I would be taking my chair outside to seek out the sun's rays. I knew I wouldn't teach that first day either.

I went home without teaching any classes, and I hadn't expected to. I knew the routine. I was now oriented this second time around. Students were busy cleaning their classrooms, and we teachers were occupied with divvying up the year's new classes. I simply followed my classes and would teach English to Forms B, C, and E. And then there was gossip.

"*Ho thoe* Maleshoane has become pregnant and has gotten an abortion in the village."

"*Joee!* This is the second time!"

"*Re tla* promote Thato. He has sponsorship."

I understood some. At least I knew the names now and the terms. To promote Thato was to send him to the next grade level even though he hadn't passed. Sponsorship is where the government pays a student's school fees because he is an orphan.

Not everything about the new school year was like my first though. Physical things had changed. Principal Tsita had hired men to erect a barbed wire fence around the school grounds, and they were finishing the job as school reopened. She said the fence would help stop shepherds from throwing rocks through the classroom windows, and also stop the shepherds from grazing their cattle on the students' vegetable plots. I had told Principal Tsita about the Roof of Africa racers driving over the students' plots, but it was only incidental that the fence would protect the school grounds from them in the future. She was more concerned with the shepherds and their animals. Principal Tsita thought the barbed wire fence would prevent the hostelers from sneaking up into the village at night too.

There was a new hostel on the school grounds. The small building next to my house couldn't hold all the boys and girls, and last year a handful of boys had spent the second semester sleeping in the kitchen storage room. Now the hostel by my house was filled with only girls and the boys had a new place. It was a thin concrete slab covered by a frame of wood beams and a skin of tin; it was a silver box that heated up like a brutal oven. The tin of the building shined, but it was cheap as a building could be. Everyone knew that when winter rolled around the new boys' hostel would offer no insulation from the cold. Good thing the boys were tough.

The hostelers had arrived on the opening day of school just like all the other students, but some hadn't returned from last year. I would learn that this was normal. There was a great flux of students in and out each year. Khosi, the small boy who'd been the first to swim, didn't come back. He enrolled in a better school in Morija. Tšepang Mosola, the guy who had gone to the Chinese shop in Kolo with Ntheka and Masopha and me, hadn't come back. I heard he had gotten married and was just working as a shepherd. Some new hostelers had arrived though. The sister of Lipolelo, one of the first hostelers to ever knock on my door, would now be attending Ngoana Jesu. And a girl named Mpatsi had arrived. She wore her hair in plaits, was small and cute, and the first time I spoke with her after school I discovered that her English was very colloquial. "How are you?" I asked.

"Fine and you?"

That right there threw me. Every single other student, and teacher for that matter, at Ngoana Jesu always gave the same greeting and response, which was the formal, scholastic, How are you? I'm fine. How are you? Mpatsi had shortened it, and with such a natural rhythm.

"How did you learn English so well?"

"*Eish*, my English isn't so good."

"Where did you go to school before coming here?"

"Khubetsoana. Do you know it?"

"It's near Maseru, right?"

"Right. So how do you find it here in Lesotho?" she asked.

"I like it."

"Really? Out here in the rural areas?"

"Yeah. You know, I grew up and lived all my life in cities so I appreciate how quiet it is out here. I like the views of the mountains all around and the river and the fields."

"It isn't boring? Without power and everything?"

"No. Not for me. Where I come from it's so loud all the time. I love how peaceful it is out here."

When Mpatsi returned to the hostel it struck me how different that conversation was from any I'd had with a hosteler before. We hadn't talked about anything new. I had answered the question of whether or not I was bored in Tšoeneng a million times. But Mpatsi had been able to understand my English almost perfectly, and I could understand hers. She asked questions like she could relate, maybe because she'd also grown up in a place with electricity and some other urban luxuries. It was nice to meet her.

Seeing new things of any sort on campus was exciting since Ngoana Jesu was such a small and poor school, even by Lesotho standards. Most high schools had well over 300 students, but we would never be close to that. We wouldn't even get to 150. About 10 kilometers down the paved road there was another village called Rothe and a fancier high school there called St. Barnabas. It had electricity, and any student from Tšoeneng with money preferred to attend there. Ngoana Jesu took students who couldn't gain admission to choice schools like St. Barnabas or whose parents were too poor to pay for them. We were always near the bottom academically, and we rarely beat other schools in running races, soccer or netball games. The name Ngoana Jesu translated from Sesotho as "Child Jesus," and we were kind of like that, just a meek baby of an institution.

It seemed, however, that by Principal Tsita installing the fence and building the tin boys' hostel, people were inspired to improve Ngoana Jesu in other ways. Students began calling for elections to choose class representatives. There had previously never been such a thing, and it seemed students got the idea from friends at bigger schools. We teachers obliged and made ballots and the students voted. They also chose members of an entertainment committee, which proposed to hold a "Miss Child Jesus" contest (never happened), a year-end feast for the graduating Form E's (never happened either), and a "Cultural Day" celebration in May (actually happened—students dressed like shepherds and initiates, and girls did dances while half-naked). A discipline committee was elected too, and its leader was Masopha who, from that point on, I nicknamed Officer Mokhele, which he liked. A uniform committee would make sure students dressed properly at school. This was an issue Basotho took seriously, and the committee would tackle urgent matters such as boys who dared to come to school without socks, boys who wore gray pants on a Tuesday (the day for khaki pants), students who hadn't combed their hair well, and later, girls whose hair was too long: Principal Tsita revoked the privilege of girls like Mpatsi to plait their hair and from then on girls had to shave their heads just like the boys. There was some complaint, but they soon complied. A debate committee was elected to run school-wide debates each Thursday. Sports committee representatives coordinated running races in the fields, soccer matches for boys, and games of netball (a British game a little bit like basketball) for the girls. A school magazine committee intended to write and print student stories and poems. With just over 100 students, nearly everyone was now an elected member of some committee. If bureaucracy was progress, then we were dashing into the future.

WHILE THE 2005 SCHOOL YEAR opened with tons of energy and new ideas, there remained one problem for which no committee had been formed to combat: the problem of the rental books. In 2004, the Form A class was the guinea pig, and the government finally got books to them halfway through the school year. I thought they would have the system in place and running punctually for this year, but after months, the guinea pig class had no books again. They handed their Form A books to the new Form A class and waited for their Form B books from the government, and waited and waited. One day in April I finally asked the Form B class, the class of Lemeko the climber, if anyone knew who the Minister of Education was. A student named Lefa raised his hand and snapped his fingers, "It is ntate Mohlabi Tsekoa."

"Today we are going to write letters to ntate Tsekoa, telling him that we are tired of trying to learn to read without any books."

Breaths caught. Respect for elders is a heavy rule in Lesotho. As you don't call a person who is older than you by their name—it has to be preceded by 'me or ntate—deference for someone in a high government office is exponentially greater, yet I had just asked my students to chide a government minister, one of the most senior figures in the whole country.

I was fed up. I had been teaching English to this class of students for almost a year and a half now, and a year of that had been without books. This was purely the government's fault, as it had chosen this class to trial the new book rental scheme on, and then bungled the whole thing. The scheme seemed promising when it was proposed. I thought so, and so did the other teachers. Few students could afford to buy their books (in my other classes, about one in five students were able to buy all their textbooks). It cost a student nearly 1,000 rand to buy all of his books for a school year. That was a heap of money in Lesotho considering a teacher's salary started at around 1,600 rand per month. The books were supposed to be rented to each student for the year for only 250 rand, or about $35. It all sounded like a good plan on paper. If only the plan had been executed.

Again this year we were working without books, and it had been such a pain trying to brainstorm my own new and interesting lessons each day, and to have to write them on the chalkboard. I was out of ideas, and my right arm was shot. The Ministry of Education was making my job impossibly hard. Principal Tsita wouldn't want me to stand for this, and I knew that from the beginning she had put hope in me to help improve Ngoana Jesu. I was ready to fight on the students' behalf, on Principal Tsita's behalf, on Ngoana Jesu's behalf. They were the little man, the powerless being trampled by the behemoth of government. Many students had long ago paid their 250 rand book rental fee. The government sat on their money.

In my early days in Tšoeneng I had been very eager to please. On my first school day I showed up early. I went to class in the rain. But I was more secure in my standing now, with Principal Tsita, with people in the village, with my understanding of the culture. I was beginning to think that I knew how things worked, or at least how they should work, and I was at last prepared to go after it.

"If a business took your money but did not give you the product you paid for, that would be stealing," I said. "Ntate Tsekoa has stolen from you."

Mouths opened at these brazen words. At least I knew they understood me. With some hesitation, with my guidance, the students began writing the letters of complaint to the minister. A couple students showed that they shared some of my anger, directly asking for a refund, but most politely requested that the honorable minister not delay any longer in kindly shipping out the books, please, sir. Maybe I was making them do something they didn't really want to. Maybe they had only written the letters I asked them to because I was older than them. I was also their teacher, and teachers commanded a lot of respect in Lesotho. Maybe the students felt pinned between respecting their teacher and respecting a government minister.

I left class with forty letters in hand, and I happened to run into Principal Tsita on my way back to the staffroom. I showed her the stack. "I just had the Form B's write letters to the Minister of Education about the rental books. I'd like to deliver them to his office personally tomorrow. Would that be OK?"

"*Ow*, ntate Greg," she said. She looked to the side, to the ground. She was caught off guard. "Ntate Tsekoa is a very powerful man. He can make things very difficult for our school."

The Form B's were probably the brightest group of students Ngoana Jesu Secondary School had ever seen. It just happened to have an exceptionally large number of driven and inquisitive individuals: Lemeko, 'Malefa, Tahleho, Khotso, Lefa, and on and on. And maybe Principal Tsita felt she owed me for doing my best to teach them to read and write the English language using only my head and a chalkboard for so many months, because she compromised. After thinking for a minute she said, "Instead of Minister Tsekoa, perhaps you can go to see ntate Mahloka. He is the Chief Education Officer for Secondary Schools and he is more directly responsible for our books anyway. But please, ntate, don't bring the letters. Just ask ntate Mahloka when the books will come. And ask him with a sweet tongue. Please, ntate."

THIS WAS MY FIRST TIME to see Principal Tsita afraid of anything or anyone. One day about a month prior, in March, she called for a Form D girl named 'Makoetje to come to the staffroom, and then a trial proceeded in Sesotho, which was always the language used when a serious matter was discussed or when clarity of communication was important. In my early days, the incomprehensible Sesotho allowed me to not pay attention to such discussions and concentrate on my lesson planning or homework correcting or whatever work I was doing at my desk, but as I got better at Sesotho I could follow when students were called in to the staffroom for a behavior problem like 'Makoetje's. I heard Principal Tsita tell 'Makoetje to lie down on the floor.

"*Ow*, madam," said 'Makoetje, a 16-year-old.

"You will take your punishment. Get on the floor." Principal Tsita pushed 'Makoetje's shoulder and then grabbed a stick off the windowsill. The girl slowly put her hands and knees on the dusty staffroom floor. "Look away," said Principal Tsita.

"*Ow*, madam."

Principal Tsita prodded her with the stick and the other teachers repeated, "Look away." But 'Makoetje couldn't get herself to give her backside to Principal Tsita for the impending blow.

Principal Tsita lost her patience and bent down and tried to strike 'Makoetje's butt from afar, but the hit glanced off the girl's hip. Principal Tsita then pushed down 'Makoetje's head and leaned over for another try, but again it was from a bad angle and weak. Principal Tsita's glasses had slid down her nose. She was now breathing heavily. She stood up and put her glasses on a teacher's desk.

"Look away!" the teachers were yelling now. "Take your punishment!"

'Makoetje seemed frozen in fear, unable to even hear the teachers' calls now. Principal Tsita got down on top of 'Makoetje and yelled, "Why did you lie? When will you tell the truth?!" And she lifted 'Makoetje's dress and started wailing on her bare buttocks. The other teachers were leaned over their desks shouting, "Why did you lie!" Principal Tsita grabbed the waistline of 'Makoetje's underwear and pulled it into a wedge, and she beat again and again on 'Makoetje's cheeks. She hit and hit and hit.

When she finally relented, she stood up over the crying girl. Principal Tsita's hair, which had been combed straight back, was tousled and there were beads of sweat on her forehead. Her eyes looked mad and scrambled. But she had kept order, she had finished the job.

THAT WAS THE PRINCIPAL TSITA I knew. She had her sweet side, but she was a fighter. I have a very distinct memory of the first moment I ever saw Principal Tsita. It was the day I arrived in Tšoeneng, before she took me to meet the chief at the initiation ceremony. Peace Corps had just dropped me off at my house and then there was a knock on my door. I opened it to find a small woman wearing a black dress and white blouse. On her head was a scarf. I thought she was a nun. It stood to reason because Ngoana Jesu was a Catholic school.

"Do you know who I am?" the nun said.

She then introduced herself as the school's principal and asked how I liked my house.

"I love it."

"Really? I'm sorry we are poor," she said.

We got in her white Volkswagen to drive up into the village to go to the initiation ceremony to meet the chief and Principal Tsita explained her clothes. In addition to her black scarf, she was wearing a black strip of fabric around her neck. "This is to mourn the death of my son."

Tšepo, at 27, had been in a technical school for electrical engineering and, in an apparent case of mistaken identity, he was seized by police officers and beaten to death just a few weeks before. Principal Tsita hugged the steering wheel to reach the foot pedals because she was so short. We bounced down the same dirt road that the dirt bikers would later race along. "I am Job. Every year another one dies. I hope this year is without more burdens." Her eldest daughter, who had been a medical doctor, was taken with throat cancer the year before. She lost her husband before that. She had three children left: a daughter in her twenties, Lineo, a son in high school, Leloko, and another younger daughter, Tlotliso.

Knowing where Principal Tsita came from, knowing what she had been going through, knowing what successful children she had raised, always tempered my understanding of how she could be tough on the students at Ngoana Jesu, and how they could respect her. And I felt a deeper understanding of Principal Tsita because my mother was also a widow—and I was also 27, the same age as Tšepo, the son she had just lost. Tšepo departed her world and then almost immediately I entered it. Principal Tsita began calling me her son. And she reminded me often to assure my real mother that she was taking good care of me in Tšoeneng.

I BEAT THE SUN out of bed the next morning. It was fall again and it was chilly enough that I could see my breath as I walked to the road and waited for a taxi. I arrived at Mahloka's office in the Examinations Council of Lesotho building around 9 a.m. I introduced myself to his secretary and twenty minutes later he opened the door to his office and invited me in. He didn't know what was coming. My students and my principal may have been afraid to talk straight to these bureaucrats, but I had no such trepidation. I would fight in their stead. I had nothing to lose.

Mahloka was a small man dressed in a suit, and he wore glasses. His office was roomy, carpeted, with a wide desk on one end and many books on shelves. *He* had many books.

"I was wondering if you know when the Form B books will be delivered," I said in English, once I'd greeted him in Sesotho.

"Your principal has been told when the books will be delivered," he said.

"Well, she said she didn't know and that's why I've come."

"The principals have been told," he said. I was surprised by his instant insolence.

"OK, well, last year we were told the books were coming for many months but they didn't arrive until the third quarter. We were then assured that they would be on time this year. But in January there were no books. Then in February we were told they would arrive in March. It's now the end of April and no books."

A pause, then the man pushed his glasses up his nose and said, "The orders have been placed."

"What does that mean? You don't really know when they'll arrive?" I had come prepared to keep my words sweet for Principal Tsita's sake. I didn't want to get her in trouble. But Mahloka was making it hard. Respecting authorities just because they were authorities was not my strong point. I had struggled with the issue a lot more when I was younger, enough so that in my eighth grade year the vice principal of my middle school decided to finally expel me.

"When the books are ready the publishers will deliver them through the booksellers," Mahloka said.

"So, you don't really know?"

"The booksellers will deliver them when they're ready."

"So, you don't really know then?"

"It can be any time from now." He had been standing behind his desk, but now he walked past me and toward the door. "I should learn more at the meeting today," he said. "I must go now."

I remained standing in the same place. "Can I stop by later to see what you learned at the meeting?"

"The meeting will take the rest of the day." He opened the door and stood aside for me to exit. My goal in Lesotho had always been to adapt and follow custom. I wanted to fit in as much as possible. But I had more questions for ntate Mahloka whether he was my elder, a government official, or whether or not he liked it.

"Perhaps you can answer this: The Form B students have been paying to rent the books for full school years . . ."

"As they should," Mahloka interjected.

". . . but they are only using the books for half of each year."

"Now you're making a political argument, sir. We should not enter into political arguments."

"How about the exams?" I continued. "Students are supposed to get two years to read their literature books before they write the JC exam after Form C, but this year's Form B's will only have the books for half of this year and who knows how long next year. Is anyone considering adjusting the exams because of the time the students have lost?"

"You are the teacher. Do what you must to see to it that they read," he said.

"Oh, so should I keep them in school over their winter break and through Christmas?"

"You do what you have to."

I took the open door.

I fumed as I walked four blocks over to the Peace Corps office. I considered what other angles of attack there were.

On a computer in the office I found the website for Lesotho's largest English language newspaper, *Public Eye*. Recently I had made the acquaintance of an editor at the weekly publication, so I sent him an email detailing the background of the book situation and recounting the conversation I just had with Mahloka. I asked the editor to print my words anonymously.

Peace Corps supervisors had reminded us volunteers often that we were here at the request and good will of the Lesotho government and we were not to involve ourselves politically or ruffle any government official's feathers. I knew I had taken a risk by even asking the Form B's to write letters of complaint to the Minister of Education. But as much as I was in Lesotho at its government's good will, I was also spending two years of my life teaching in one of its schools for free. On one hand, I wanted to do precisely this. I didn't care about making any money. On the other hand, I was feeling like a sucker if, while I was giving teaching and living down in Tšoeneng my best shot, the government officials up in Maseru were twiddling their thumbs in plush offices and ripping off my students. I wouldn't be a cog in that kind of machine.

AFTER SENDING MY EMAIL to the *Public Eye* editor, I poked around on the Internet for more information about the book rental scheme. I quickly discovered that the "Textbook Rental Scheme for Lesotho Secondary Schools" was financed by the International Development Association of the World Bank. On their Web site the motto "Working for a World Free of Poverty" was pasted under the World Bank logo. Below that was their stated mode of operation: "to provide low-interest loans, interest-free credits and grants to developing countries for a wide array of purposes that includes investments in education." I figured they would want to know how their money was being handled in the effort to eradicate poverty in Lesotho, so I immediately wrote an email to their New York headquarters telling them about the situation and offering to help them continue monitoring the project.

I wasn't surprised to find that the money for the books had come from overseas. The presence of foreign aid was everywhere in Lesotho. Education in the country seemed to be especially supported by outsiders. The Japanese government had recently finished building a huge wing of the Lesotho College of Education in Maseru, where teachers were trained. The Japanese also built primary school classrooms. I once helped ntate Thoahlane, the principal of Tšoeneng's primary school, prepare an application for the Japanese government's building program. For decades the Republic of Ireland had been the leading donor to the education sector though, as it had chosen Lesotho as the primary target of its overall foreign aid efforts. Among their many projects was a fresh white hall they had built at Masianokeng High School, where I periodically attended meetings with other local English teachers. There was a plaque out front that said it had been erected using

Irish money.

I suppose it made a certain amount of sense that the education of Basotho was funded by foreigners, since it was European missionaries who first introduced the system of formal classroom learning in Lesotho. The Europeans had brought education, and they took natural resources. Nearly half of the world's production of gold has come from white-owned mines located in South Africa. Mining company AngloGold has made enormous profits there over the years with the help of the migrant labor of thousands of Basotho men. In 2001, AngloGold built an entire secondary school in a Lesotho village south of Tšoeneng called Morifi, I suppose as a way of saying thanks for the labor of the students' fathers.

The U.S. Embassy in Maseru also contributed money to the education system of Lesotho with a Girls' Scholarship Fund, a program which paid tuition for a number of female students throughout the country. But why they chose to only support girls was a mystery to me. Girls were not being denied access to education in Lesotho by any means. At Ngoana Jesu, for instance, there were slightly more girls enrolled than boys. Moreover, in its annual Global Gender Gap Report for 2007, the World Economic Forum ranked Lesotho even higher than the U.S., saying, "Lesotho is once again the only country from the region to have no gap in education or health." If anyone, it seemed it was the boys who needed assistance. An article in the *Public Eye* newspaper by a local journalist named Mothepa Ndumo argued the same. "Little boys will soon become an endangered species as far as access to education is concerned, particularly in the rural areas where they are burdened with chores such as livestock herding. Little girls, on the other hand, perform household chores in tandem with their schoolwork." Maybe U.S. embassy workers weren't aware of this reality though, since they rarely traveled outside of urban Maseru. It is easy to just presume there is blanket inequality throughout poor countries of the world rather than getting your hands dirty and actually getting to know individual places. There was a gap between foreign donors and local benefactors that made me wary of this type of aid, more and more as my time in Lesotho went on.

THE WORLD BANK never responded to my email. I had to assume that either it hadn't reached them, or that they didn't really care what happened to the money they'd loaned little Lesotho. It was a drop in the bucket of billions they loaned out every year. Nevertheless, my letter to the editor of the *Public Eye* got printed in the following week's newspaper. In short, my letter said that the country's Form B students had no textbooks and it was the fault of the Ministry of Education. They had the money, they were supposed to have the books and be distributing them, but they weren't. And when I asked the Secretary of Secondary Schools about the books he couldn't give me answers. And just as I requested, it was signed anonymously as, "Concerned Teacher."

I brought the newspaper to class and showed it to the Form B's. They would otherwise never see it let alone know the anonymous letter was mine, since *Public Eye* newspapers weren't distributed out in the rural areas like Tšoeneng. I wanted them to know I'd fought for them. And I wanted them to see that there were things you could do if you were dissatisfied with a situation. They applauded. Literally, they gave me a round of applause, and I felt good. I felt like we were a team, trying to get government officials to do their jobs, trying to balance the power scales of rich and poor, urban and rural, senior and junior.

The week after that, a follow up article appeared in the *Public Eye*. They had sent a reporter to speak with the man the Form B's had originally written their letters to, the Minister of Education, Mohlabi Tsekoa. The reporter was denied a chance to talk with the minister. However, the reporter did show the minister's public relations officer my letter to the editor and asked for a response. The reporter quoted the PR officer actually admitting to harming the education of Form B's in Lesotho because of the books being so late.

Then on the front page of the Sesotho newspaper *Moeletsi oa Basotho* that same week was a cover story, "Education in Lesotho Falls." It detailed the government's bungling of the Form B rental books just as my letter to the editor had recounted it. Also that week, I turned on my radio to the state-run station, Radio Lesotho, as I usually did while I bathed before school, and the host of the morning news show *Seboping* was taking callers on the issue of the delayed delivery of the Form B books. Nothing had appeared in the media about the books before my letter to the editor, and now I couldn't help but feel like I had broken open the story.

I felt I had done something important and consequential, but when I told my mom about it she wrote back in an email, "Don't go pushing and making trouble. That should come from within. You are an outsider. They need to do their own work."

It *was* my work, I thought. I was the one in class every day teaching with no books. It was as much my business as anyone's.

And my brother Matt, when I told him of the situation, asked, "Why was it you who brought this issue up and confronted someone about it? Why didn't a Mosotho teacher ever go and complain?"

I gave him some ideas: respect for seniority, fear of being fired. Then I realized that the answer to Matt's question wasn't important. The important thing was the reality that prompted him to ask the question: I had tried to resolve a problem before any Mosotho had called it a problem. The Form B's hadn't asked me to help them write letters to the Minister of Education. Principal Tsita hadn't asked me to interrogate the Secretary of Secondary Schools. I had instigated it all.

THAT DIDN'T SIT WELL because it made me feel like a meddler. Over the years I ran across so many foreigners who were in Lesotho specifically to insert themselves into situations and tell the locals how to do things better. I met a nurse from Canada who was giving nutrition workshops in a town in the north called Hlotse. And I met another Canadian named Paul who had come as a volunteer economic adviser for Lesotho's Ministry of Finance. There was yet another Canadian, a young girl, who had decided that the people of a village called Ha Mpiti could improve their lives by building a fish hatchery, but when I met her she was in the midst of changing projects after she discovered there was no water available to fill the ponds. Oliver was a young German who had come to help a man named Reverend August Basson, a South African preacher and farmer. Together they encouraged the

Basotho to stop plowing their land. Rather, they told the villagers to dig individual holes in which to plant each seed—a technique they claimed was more productive and environmentally friendly. Another German, a short blond woman in her late 30's, was volunteering through GTZ, the agency the German government used to do its foreign aid work in Lesotho. She thought the Basotho needed to be saved from AIDS, so GTZ connected her with a local government worker in the District AIDS Task Force, except that the local DATF man rarely showed up for work. "I'm feeling frustrated and useless and bored," the woman told me. There wasn't much she could do without her local counterpart because she didn't know Sesotho. And this was a striking commonality among the meddlers: almost none knew Sesotho. And I wondered, if you really wanted to help people then, other than a warm heart, wouldn't step one be learning to talk to them?

Foreigners were everywhere in Lesotho telling people how to live better. Yet I met very few of them who were taking the time to learn how the Basotho already lived. They dropped in for a couple weeks or a couple months, and from their first day they set themselves up as teachers, never learners. I had been set up the same way, and I came to regret it. I was forced to step back and become a student. These foreign meddlers were presumptuous, and I didn't want to be like them.

I hadn't waited for my students or their parents to think of confronting someone about the books. I had asked them to confront someone. Then I confronted Mahloka. Then I threw Mahloka under the bus in the newspaper, but I didn't really know how much he was at fault for the book rental problems. Maybe the publishers were really slow. Maybe the World Bank had been slow in coming through with the money. I didn't know any of that for sure. I became afraid that I had acted like one of the very people that I internally derided, a meddling foreigner. That was the last thing Lesotho needed. There was already a cornucopia of those combing the country.

IN LATE MAY, days before the second quarter ended and schools closed for the winter break, the *Moeletsi oa Basotho* front page featured a photograph of Mohlabi Tsekoa, Lesotho's Minister of Education, in a suit and tie handing out the year's first Form B textbooks to uniformed students at Mazenod High School. The students had sung to celebrate the day, the article stated, and Minister Tsekoa was quoted congratulating his ministry for the benefits the rental books would bring to the country's students. He made no mention of the hundreds of hours those students had spent in January, February, March and April, sitting in class waiting for books, nor did he apologize for the previous year. The newspaper writer didn't bring it up either. Water under the bridge.

In late July, days after the third quarter had started, Principal Tsita and the other teachers at Ngoana Jesu gathered to cut open our boxes of books which had finally just arrived. We handed them to two mothers from the village who wrote numbers in the books before handing them to the Form B students. And then I went to class and we started reading as fast as we could.

CHAPTER TWELVE

Invisiblizing

HOW MUCH OF A FOREIGNER was I anymore? Every day I became more like the people around me. After school one afternoon I came back to my house and took my shirt off to change into more comfortable clothes and I looked down at my chest and I was disgusted. Why all this hair? Gross. It looked like a jungle, all of these tangles climbing up and down the front of my body. Directly, I grabbed a pair of scissors and began trimming. I cut the hair off until my chest was bare. There, now it looked correct.

I went on with my day. I went on with the next couple of my days, until one morning I put on my shirt and the stubble on my chest clawed at it, stuck to it, and then my chest started to itch. For the next few days it was like a poison oak rash that I couldn't stop scratching. It was then that I became conscious of the fact that I'd just cut all the hair off my chest. Why the heck would I do that?

All of the people around me were relatively hairless. Not just the young students. Basotho in general were not a hairy tribe. The women didn't need to shave their legs because barely any hair grew there naturally. And I'd seen the chests of the hostel boys while swimming down at the river, and I'd seen ntate Lemphane's chest while playing soccer. He had the most of anyone, but he only had a few little black swirls, nothing like the dodder I had.

I was trying to make myself fit in. And I had been doing so in less dramatic steps for a while. Look at the hair on my head. It was cropped almost as short as the local men, though it had been shaggy when I arrived. It had grown almost to my shoulders by the time I first cut it. I knew that I needed it cut, but how to get that done? There were barbers in roadside stalls in the taxi rank in Maseru, but they only had shears. I considered shaving my head like Basotho guys did, but I was afraid that my pink scalp would get burned. I preferred to just have it cut very short, to look close to normal. As I put the decision off and thought of how else I could get my hair cut it grew longer and longer. Finally, I wet my hair and grabbed my pair of little craft scissors and walked over to the hostel. I knew who I was looking for. I found Tumelo, a Form C boy who was fastidious about taking care of his plot of vegetables. He was always watering it, pulling weeds, transplanting seedlings here and there. I figured he would have the precision to give my hair a trim. "How do I do this?" he asked. I instructed him to just cut a line from above my eyebrows over to my ears and down to the nape of my neck, "like a circle around my head," I explained. But he held the scissors awkwardly. "Sir?" Tumelo said. I knew he'd never cut hair like mine before, nor had he ever cut hair with scissors. The boys cut each other's hair with razors or sheep shears. But then the way he was holding the scissors made me wonder if he'd ever used them for anything.

A handful of other hostelers had gathered around, and Nthabiseng picked up my wet locks and let them slide through her fingers and said, "Sir, don't cut. It is beautiful."

Tumelo even agreed. "It is too nice, sir. Don't cut."

"It's not beautiful for a man," I said. I knew that Basotho women tried all sorts of tricks to grow their hair long, plaiting it, combing in chemical straighteners, but men in Lesotho didn't have long hair. In fact, the school boys got punished by Principal Tsita if their hair was ever more than a quarter inch in length. I didn't want to be beautiful, and I definitely didn't want to be feminine, I just wanted to look normal. I demanded that Tumelo cut my hair. His hands were shaky. Still, he obeyed his teacher and he snipped and snipped until I had a jagged bowl cut. At least it was shorter. But it grew out fast, so a few weeks later I took the scissors into my own hands. I snipped and I snipped until it all felt about the same length, and then I cut it a little shorter around my ears and off my neck. I figured I couldn't do a worse job than

Tumelo, and it actually turned out decently. I cut my own hair every few months from that point on.

I was dressing like the guys around me too. I never wore shorts anymore, and my style of pants had changed. In America, I had preferred a loose fit, but the Basotho wore clothes tighter, so each pair of pants I bought in Lesotho to replace worn out ones were more form-fitting. Such style looked right to me now. And how clean were my shoes! I wiped down the leather with a wet cloth every morning, just as the hostelers were brushing and polishing their black school shoes. Also in the mornings I often ironed my shirts. After handwashing and drying on the line they were wrinkled, but no one wore wrinkled clothes. I had seen a couple students sent home for wearing school uniforms that hadn't been ironed properly. So I bought a slab of metal, a real iron, a heavy piece shaped like an arrowhead that I heated up right over the flame on my stove and then dragged across my shirts to press them out, so no one would see a problem in my appearance, so no one would have reason to notice me any more than they already did. Basotho took their clothes seriously, and so I had to.

Maybe it is my personality to try to blend in, or maybe after the episode of instigating the attention on the government rental books I was trying extra hard to not stick out. For me, fitting in might have been related to getting mugged in Maseru, or to finding out about the priest's murder. If you are invisible, you survive. I wasn't sure of the impetus, but the changes were real.

I HAD ALSO BEEN MORPHING in less outwardly obvious ways. One night, I tuned my small radio to the BBC. Out of the speakers: "Four American soldiers killed in Baghdad today . . ." I pushed a button to change the channel. I didn't want to hear about it. It was a bad saga from a faraway land, and it had no relevance to my life in Tšoeneng. Actually, I had a cousin in Iraq at the time, and of course I cared about his well being, but listening to radio news about the war wouldn't help. Anyway, I would be the only one in Tšoeneng paying any attention to the war thousands of miles away between America and Iraq.

I read a quote from John Steinbeck that captured my feeling

at the time. It came from *The Log from the Sea of Cortez*, his book about a journey through the Gulf of California in 1940, while World War II was raging elsewhere: "The world and the war had become remote to us . . . We had been drifting in some kind of dual world—a parallel realistic world."

I began to understand how my students had never heard of the terrorist attacks on the U.S. on September 11, 2001. Tšoeneng was in a world of its own, and news from outside of Lesotho or South Africa simply didn't penetrate the place. The longer I lived in this dual world, the more unconnected I felt to stories from the U.S. and the rest of the world, and the less I kept up on them.

As Peace Corps sent all of its volunteers free *Newsweek* magazines each month, I read most of the articles when the issues arrived with my mail in the early days. Later, however, I tired of hearing about the same three stories in each issue: there had been more killing in Iraq; Palestine still hates Israel; and China is on the economic rise. I just lost interest. I couldn't get myself to care. The stories were irrelevant. I began giving the magazines away immediately after I received them, usually to the hostelers because they liked to look at the photographs.

Rather than *Newsweek* and its news about the American world, I paid attention to the news of the parallel realistic world that I was currently living in through the local newspapers, mostly *Leselinyana* and *Moeletsi oa Basotho*. And rather than BBC, I woke up each morning with my silver radio set to 97.2 FM, Radio Lesotho. It began broadcasting at 5 a.m. with the national anthem. After the anthem they always played a special wake-up song that stuck in my head for hours: *"Ha ho na khomo ea boroko. Tloha mona le ee mosebetsing"*—There's no cow earned in sleep, get up now and go to work. Radio Lesotho was the state-run station where I'd heard people discussing the Form B book problem on their call-in news debate program *Seboping*. On that program in these days, in the second semester of my second year, the story that dominated the airwaves was how Monyane Moleleki had been chosen to succeed Pakalitha Mosisili as leader of the political party in power, the Lesotho Congress for Democracy. The very night that the committee selected Moleleki he was shot in front of his house in Maseru. Who had shot him? Who was jealous they hadn't been selected as the next leader? Most of the teachers at Ngoana Jesu conjectured that a man named Tom Thabane was somewhere behind the shooting. He had jumped parties for a couple decades in order to remain employed at the upper echelons of the Lesotho government. Late at night, Radio Lesotho played the songs boys sing at initiation school. I would blow out my candle, turn the radio loud in the total darkness and imagine the scene. Men together, blanketed, grinding their deep voices. I tested myself to see if I could sing that deeply yet. I was getting there. I loved to try.

The only news from abroad that got to me in Tšoeneng in those days was the death of Pope John Paul II. The King of Lesotho himself is Catholic. The pope's death was announced to the students of Ngoana Jesu by 'me 'Malimpho at the school's morning assembly, followed by a reverent group prayer. It was a rare collision of the dual worlds.

The collision of Hurricane Katrina with New Orleans, on the other hand, was a story that never reached my Tšoeneng world. I first heard about it when I returned to the U.S.

I kept in touch with my friends and family in America, but I did so mostly through letters. When I visited Maseru I wrote occasional emails at the Peace Corps office, as well as little stories that I posted to a blog. But the communication was mostly one way, from Lesotho out. I made very few phone calls. Since I didn't have a phone I had to borrow one, which I did every couple of months in order to call my mom. I didn't dislike my friends and family, or America or the rest of the world. Far from it. I was just really sinking into Tšoeneng. I had made friends there, so I didn't leave the village often. A girl named Stacey was the closest Peace Corps volunteer to me, and she lived about eight kilometers away as the crow flies. But between us were a lot of rolling fields, a stream, a small mountain, and no road. We got along well when we did hang out, but like me she enjoyed Sesotho and getting to know her village, and over the span of two years we visited each other only four times—two times each year.

Some other Peace Corps volunteers told me I was isolating myself there in Tšoeneng, and even the teachers at Ngoana Jesu encouraged me to buy a cell phone so I could stay in touch with

Americans. "They're cheap!" said 'me 'Masamuel. But I didn't want to try to stay connected to people who lived beyond Tšoeneng. I would have the rest of my life to stay connected to them. I would only be in Tšoeneng for a brief and definite time, and during that time I wanted to be there totally, immersed in my present experience.

THE IMMERSION IN TŠOENENG had one consequence that I never did totally understand. I started listening to rap music—50 Cent in particular.

This was especially inscrutable because it was at about the same time that I started liking Sesotho music. Masopha came to my door one Sunday afternoon wearing rubber boots and a blanket, and leaning on his *molamu*. This was his weekend attire. He had just come from home where he worked as a shepherd of his father's sheep and cattle. It was jarring at first to see him transform from a schoolboy during the week, wearing shiny black loafers, ironed pants, a dress shirt, and sometimes even a tie, into a herdboy on the weekends. But I got used to it, and Masopha somehow looked at home in both costumes. In his other hand he was carrying a black plastic cassette player. "I have brought the Sesotho music, sir."

The week before I'd heard him singing a song and had him teach me the lyrics. They translated, "People laugh at me even when I'm in trouble. But I trust in God. Problems are problems, and they'll get you too." The words are mellifluous in Sesotho, and I liked the feel of them rolling out of my mouth. Masopha came in and played the cassette for me, so I could hear the real song. The music was dominated by a melody played on an accordion. A simple drum set and a bass guitar accompanied the accordion, over which a man sang. He was called Famole, and one of the best known Sesotho singers, rattling off lyrics quickly until a group of men with very deep voices came in with a chorus. The music sounded repetitive to me and, all in all, unappealing. Masopha singing alone had sounded better.

On a taxi one day, I heard another Sesotho singer that sounded different. I asked the driver who it was and he told me the singer's name was Mantša, so at the taxi rank in Maseru I went to a music shop and bought his CD. I didn't want to listen to Mantša for pure entertainment. I knew that listening to the music and trying to decipher the lyrics, memorizing them and repeating them, would be good for my language skills. It was a form of homework.

50 Cent was no work at all. The strange thing was that I hated rap. "I'm so tough, so rich but grew up so poor, do so many women, blah blah blah." Rap must be the music genre with the worst lyrics of all time. But my friend Nate had sent me a CD with some such songs on it and, out of respect for him, I put it in my CD player. In spite of myself, I pushed the play button again, and again. I was eating that junk up. Within a few days I had a whole song memorized, and I was burning through D batteries playing it as loudly as my Sony could. "I wanna live good, so shit I sell dope for a four-finger ring and one of them gold ropes. Nana told me if I pass I'd get a sheep skin coat. If I could move a few packs I get the hat, now that'd be dope." I cussed with 50 Cent like I was protesting something. The words felt like freedom. In the moment, I had no idea why. I just felt it and went with it.

As I blasted the song, I thought about the hostelers hearing the bad words through my walls, but I realized that they wouldn't understand any of them. That wasn't the kind of English they learned. And there it hit me: the bad words and the slang were precisely what I liked about 50 Cent. In other words, the things I had hated about rap were now the very things I liked about it. I just missed the natural quality of it. Strangely, it reminded me of real American culture. Every day at school I had to teach in this simplified, stiff British English: "Hello, how are you? I am fine, madam. Will you please bring me your exercise books? I will use the duster to erase the chalkboard. Use your rubber to erase any stray marks. Write me a *lettuh*." I felt boxed up. I hated to speak English at all anymore because it wasn't my English. I had given in and allowed myself to speak in such a way as a means to an end, so that students would understand me, but that didn't mean I liked it. I'd rather have been speaking Sesotho because, though it may have been slower and more difficult, at least Sesotho didn't feel fake.

CHAPTER THIRTEEN

Playing with Mpatsi Fire

WHEN I DID THE 50 CENT THING inside my house, it was in private moments that punctuated the equilibrium of my life in Tšoeneng, which was primarily dedicated to ways I could be less heard and less visible. (That was why I did it inside my house, when no hostelers were there, with the door closed.) Outside, especially off the school grounds, I was always speaking Sesotho, and in the most authentic way I could, with a deep voice, using the conversational fillers that I heard others use, like saying *"E, ntate"* often while talking to a man, or *"E, 'me"* while talking to a woman, which was what people said in order to show that they were listening. And I tried to act as normal as possible in other ways, Lesotho normal.

But there were times when I wasn't sure what the normal way of doing things was. Back in February, I had taken six of the older Form E students to Maseru for a student workshop about the media held by a nonprofit organization called Transformation Resource Centre. It was at this event where I met the *Public Eye* newspaper editor who later published my letter on the government rental books. After the workshop, the Form E's and I were walking back through the city toward the taxi rank when Mpatsi, the new hosteler who spoke colloquial English, grabbed my hand. And she didn't let go. We kept walking, and she kept holding my hand in hers, and I looked around at the other students to see if any of them were watching. Was this OK? But they were all looking elsewhere. Mpatsi's hand wasn't soft, like an American girl's would be—she used hers to wash clothes and cook over fires. Still, the touch felt great, thrilling. It was a connection I hadn't made for so long. I kept walking, and Mpatsi kept walking beside me, holding onto my hand, swinging it in hers playfully.

Holding hands was something I had never seen a man and woman do in Lesotho, so I had no idea what Mpatsi meant by holding mine. But I often saw men hold hands. Men sometimes held my hand as they talked to me at Motsie's bar, and Lerato and Teboho and other male students sometimes held my hand as we walked from the school to the village or up the mountain to climb rocks in the afternoon. I came to understand that men held hands just to show they were friends. It felt awkward at first, but I got used to it.

Now when a girl held my hand I was confused. I was confused about relations between the opposite sexes in Lesotho in general. Men and women seemed to make no public displays of affection whatsoever. I never saw a man and woman hug, let alone kiss. I didn't know whether they never did, or only did behind closed doors. At school, I never noticed boys and girls flirting, yet it must have been happening. One day during the winter break between the first and second semesters of my first year, ntate Lemphane and I were standing near the vegetable plots of the hostelers and he said, "Did you know that the owner of this plot is married?" No. It was then that I learned that Tšepang Mosola had left school to marry another hosteler named Ntsatsi. I had never even seen these two hostelers speak to each other. Not once. But I'd seen them every day.

I told 'me Albertina, my neighbor, of the marriage news between Tšepang and Ntsatsi but she only responded, "You didn't know about those two?" There were almost certainly gestures and other subtleties that went on between students which could be read by other Basotho, like 'me Albertina, but not by me. But I had also been told that most sexual advances waited until after sunset and took place specifically in the dongas, the deep erosion gullies in the fields. Lesotho was an incredibly dark and therefore anonymous place at night, and it would have been easy for students to sneak off undetected into the fields and down into the dongas.

Though they were discreet when physical with one another, Basotho could be incredibly open when talking about relationships. A post office clerk once asked me if I was married. I told her I was because I knew where she was heading with the conversation. Still she said, "Well, you don't have a Mosotho wife. Do you want me as your Mosotho wife?" I told her no thanks. But she controlled my mail, and I feared she wouldn't take well to the rejection, so I opened up a package from America and gave her some of the candy from inside.

And then there was a girl from Tšoeneng who began showing up at my door on weekends. She was one of my student's older sisters. I walked her part of the way home after her visits because that was the custom in Lesotho, but I decided to stop being so hospitable after she said to me on one walk, "OK. I don't want you to buy me things. I don't care about money. But I will let you kiss me and do those things. Do you want to?" I had just wanted to practice my Sesotho.

It didn't matter who was listening. Basotho didn't touch the opposite sex in daylight but the adults at least were not shy to say anything in front of anyone. Some teachers from Kolo were visiting our school one day and as we all sat in the staffroom a fat female teacher who looked about forty years old asked me if I had a *motho*—a person—which meant, a girlfriend or wife. I told her I did, which was a lie, but when she asked where my *motho* was I blanked, and she seized the moment.

"I'll be your *motho*," she said. "Do you like fat or slim ones?" I didn't answer that, but she continued, "When should we meet?"

"I don't know," I said.

"Well, where do you live?"

"Here at school."

"Then tomorrow we can meet. What will we do?"

"I don't know." All of the other teachers were listening, breaking into grins.

"We will introduce ourselves. And then what?"

"I don't know." I was trying to look busy with school work.

"What do you like to do?"

"Read."

"It will be dark. We should conserve paraffin."

"OK, we can sing." I thought this was a funny suggestion, but no one laughed.

"Something more exciting," she demanded.

"I don't know. I have to go to class." I did. When I returned to the staffroom an hour later, the lady stopped her conversation with 'me 'Masamuel and picked up where she left off. The whole staff paused to listen.

"So what are we going to do? I'm coming tomorrow night, right?" I laughed. Was she serious? She was taking the joke a little too far. She was now standing over my desk. "You said you like big girls, right?"

"Wait, wait. I never said that."

Another Kolo teacher, a thinner one but also in her forties, then interjected from across the room: "Do you want this or that? Big or slim?"

Then the thin one came over to my desk and whispered loudly so all could still hear: "Are you shy? Do you fear women? We're offering two for free. Not a penny. Well, after two times it won't be free anymore. Do you want big or slim?!"

The big one: "Winter's coming!" She shook herself. "Go for the flesh!"

The thin one put her hands between the breasts of the fat one, "You can warm yourself right here."

IN SEPTEMBER, Mpatsi was washing a cabinet for Principal Tsita on the grass in front of the staffroom as I sat in a chair beside ntate Matlali. He was a new male teacher of about my age who Principal Tsita had just hired to teach some religion classes. Mpatsi had a rag and a basin of water, and she was scrubbing away. Principal Tsita walked up and said to Mpatsi, "Clean that cabinet well. Ntate Matlali is watching and he is not yet married, you know." Mpatsi looked away embarrassed and we three teachers laughed. I wondered why Principal Tsita didn't also mention that I wasn't married.

It was a mild afternoon, and soon the other teachers brought out their chairs to sit with us. Mpatsi had finished washing the cabinet and gone back to her classroom with the rest of the students for the 3:30 p.m. to 4:30 p.m. study hour, which ended each school day. Our conversation turned to who was the prettiest girl at Ngoana Jesu. "How about Makhokolotso?" asked 'me 'Masamuel.

"That little doll?" said 'me 'Malimpho.

"Yes," said 'me 'Masamuel. "I was once as skinny as she, and look at me now." 'Me 'Masamuel was the fattest of the teachers. And fat is good in Lesotho, you'll remember.

Ntate Matlali then suggested Nkaiseng, a friend of Mpatsi's in the Form E class. Whereas Mpatsi was smaller and cute, Nkaiseng was a woman, full of curves, so many that in America she would be called overweight. But that was how Basotho men liked their women. Nkaiseng had more than her girth going for her, for she was also light skinned. Ntate Matlali didn't say it, but I knew he liked that too. All Basotho, especially women, prized lighter skin. They wore hats in the sun. They carried umbrellas during the summer. Some bought whitening potions to rub on their faces. Principal Tsita once told us of a time her son brought the wrong girl home. "He wants to ruin our family's complexion with this black girl!" she complained. I thought it was so queer that Basotho talked about one another as being "black" or "white." The teachers often referred to a student named Lefa as "the black one," and they called a girl named Puseletso "the white one." To me, especially at first, all Basotho were the same color, black, and I was the only white one. I couldn't see the shades that they saw so distinctly and took so seriously. A slight difference in skin color was one way Basotho identified *makoerekoere*, Africans from elsewhere on the continent. *Makoerekoere* were "black."

The other teachers nodded their heads at ntate Matlali's choice of Nkaiseng. I voiced no nominations for who I thought was the prettiest girl at Ngoana Jesu. But I found that a name had popped up in my head: Mpatsi. Just the fact that I was thinking of a local girl as pretty was kind of surprising considering how in my early days I had trouble even telling the female students apart from the male students, especially after the girls were made to keep their heads shaved just like the boys. But Basotho girls were all I had seen every day for two years, and their look had become familiar, more than familiar—appealing. They were the only kind of girls I thought about anymore. When I closed my eyes and thought of a girl, I thought of a Mosotho girl.

The next day, ntate Matlali made a confession to me. Our desks in the staffroom were next to each other, and when the other teachers were out he leaned over and admitted that not only did he think Nkaiseng was attractive, he also wanted to propose to her. That's how it was done in Lesotho. If a guy thought a girl was attractive, his first step was to ask her to marry him. The girl was expected to say no, regardless of her true feelings, but from that point the courting could begin. "But I will wait until school is out before I propose," he said. That was a couple months away. Why was he confiding in me, the foreigner? Probably because I was the only other single male around. (Ntate Lemphane was already married.) His confidence invited me to open up.

"I've been wondering about that. Is it OK for a teacher to have a relationship with a student? I know of teachers at other schools in Lesotho who do this, but I didn't know if it was acceptable or if the teachers were just doing it no matter."

Stacey, the volunteer who lived closest to me, had told me of a teacher at a school near her who had impregnated a student. Everyone knew it, and he was still a teacher at the school. Another volunteer told me of a teacher at his school who made no secret of bedding as many female students as he could. The volunteer said girls were coming in and out of his house on campus all day, and every student and teacher at the school was well aware of it. A principal of another school told me she had begun her relationship with her husband while he was her high school science teacher. They were now both principals of schools, and married with children.

"For some it is OK," said ntate Matlali. "Because being a teacher is a good job. So the student's parents can be happy about that, if their daughter can marry a teacher."

Ntate Matlali had basically told me that teacher-student relationships were acceptable. In America, of course, the perspective was different. There, even if the teacher and the student were similar in age, like me and Mpatsi, both in our twenties, such a relationship was taboo. But what was acceptable for me now, living in this dual world, this parallel realistic world?

Which set of values do I follow? Do I use American values because I'm from America? Or do I use Sesotho values because I'm in Lesotho now, and because my aim in coming here has been to get to know the place deeply, to adapt and fit in, and to not impose an outsider's perspective?

MPATSI CAME OVER from the hostel to visit often in the evenings, sometimes in the company of other students, sometimes by herself. When she knocked on my door one afternoon in September she was alone. I let her in and closed the door. She asked me to play a song on my radio. It was a dance song, by a South African house group called Revolution. I put the CD in and pressed play. She was wearing a white shirt and a bath towel around her waist, and she started dancing lightly to the music.

"It hits nice," she said, and she turned up the volume.

Once the song was over she asked me to play it again. I did. Then she asked for another repeat. "You're boring me. I'm tired of this song," I said. And I walked over to turn it off. But she backed into me to block me. I stepped away and went to go around her, but again she slid and put her back against me. She could reach the volume and she turned it up a little more. Now she bent down and up in the rhythm of the music. I tried to reach around her to get to the radio's buttons, and as I reached around her my arm grazed her chest. I couldn't touch the buttons. I was too far. She pressed back against me again and danced. I slid to the left to pretend to try to reach around her and ... again and again. The song went on. We moved to the beat. Mpatsi was still pushing back into me when we heard a knock on the door.

"Koko."

My breath caught. We jumped apart. I turned down the music. Then, after a hurried scan of the room, I said, *"Kena."* The knocker, another hostel girl named Maleshoane Ramokone, opened the door. Without a word, Mpatsi rushed out the open door.

I WONDERED what would happen the next time Mpatsi visited and there were no other hostelers around, but a few weeks later exams started and she and the rest of the Form E's began spending their days at St. Barnabas, the bigger school 10 kilometers away that had electricity. Since Ngoana Jesu was registered with the Ministry of Education only as a secondary school, its Form D and E classes were technically illegitimate and the school was not capable of administering the Form E exam, for the Cambridge Overseas School Certificate. Fortunately, the principal of St. Barnabas had agreed to allow our Form E students to write their exams alongside his students. Our Form E's still used the Ngoana Jesu classrooms to study in between exams, and those who were hostelers still stayed at the hostel. I saw Masopha and Ntheka sometimes in the evening, but I stopped seeing Mpatsi at all. And I noticed that Nkaiseng wasn't around either, as well as another Form E girl named Setšoantso. All three of them slept in the half of the girls' hostel which faced my house, and always in the past there had been candlelight flickering in their window in the evenings, but these days there was no candlelight. After the sun set, their window was black and lifeless.

The hostelers were very independent. They cooked and cleaned for themselves and they watched over each other. The teachers who lived at school loosely kept an eye on them, but mostly the hostelers were living on their own. Especially the Form E's came and went as they pleased.

A Form E from the village named Lerato—the one who had helped me plant green onions, and who had informed me of the murder of the white priest—visited my house one day after school, in between his exams, and asked me, "Have you heard what has happened to your daughter, Mpatsi?" People from the village often referred to the hostelers as my sons and daughters.

Why was he specifically bringing me news of Mpatsi though? Could he tell I was attracted to her? I responded with a flat: "What happened?"

"She was beaten last night in the village, and it is said that her arm is broken."

I still tried to seem unconcerned. "Who beat her?"

"A taxi conductor."

I felt a tinge of anger.

He continued, "He had been giving her rides to St. Barnabas for free and she had been visiting him at night in the village, but then when he asked for sex she refused and so he beat her with his *molamu*."

The window! The lack of candlelight! Lerato was telling the truth. This all added up.

When I went to school the next morning, the news of Mpatsi's beating was the talk of the staffroom. I stayed out of it, which was easy because I often stayed out of those types of conversations, partly because my Sesotho was too slow to really keep up and partly because it was a women's game. Ntate Lemphane and ntate Matlali also didn't chime in. But the main reason I stayed out of this gossip session was that I didn't want anyone to see that I cared in a different way from them. I also felt like I wanted to distance myself from Mpatsi now. This story of her visiting the conductor at night and cavorting with him while she was cavorting with me was apparently true, and I felt betrayed, and I also felt foolish. All kinds of slurs were being thrown around the staffroom to describe her and Nkaiseng and Setšoantšo for how they had been sneaking out at night. *Likoena* was one slur. Literally, it meant crocodiles. But here it was used to mean prostitutes. And I didn't stand up for Mpatsi. Neither did ntate Matlali stand up for Nkaiseng. And I never got Mpatsi's side of the story because she never showed up at school again. It was like she disappeared from the school, and the hostel and my life, just after that day in my house with the music. I didn't know where her family lived, and I didn't try to find out. On one hand, I had done the research and I was convinced that getting involved with Mpatsi would be doing as the Romans do. (There was nothing wrong with it. In fact, it was a positive step.) On the other hand, I feared I was rationalizing. You can create a logic, however twisted, for any actions to stand on if you passionately desire to do them. Something in the back of my head kept telling me that it wasn't the best idea, that I had played with fire and by Mpatsi vanishing I had been spared getting burned.

Part IV

The whole object of travel is not to set foot on foreign land; it is at last to set foot on one's own country as a foreign land.

- G.K. CHESTERTON

CHAPTER FOURTEEN

America the Comfortable

WHEN I LEFT AMERICA, two years seemed like a long time to spend in Lesotho. During my first year living in Tšoeneng, the end was nowhere in sight. Now it was December, and my second year was over and I wanted more. I had suspected this would be the case, so earlier in the year, in May, I sat down and drew up a simple decision chart: I listed the positives of staying for a third year, and I listed the negatives of staying. Which added up to more?

If I stayed I would get to speak Sesotho for another year. I loved the progress I was making with the language, and I wanted to get to the point where I felt fluent. Also, I would get to follow my youngest class of students—Lemeko the climber's class—through their critical national exams at the end of next year. Finishing their Junior Certificate exams with them would feel like the proper completion of a story, one that had many bumps due to the government rental books disaster. And there were a couple of other projects that I had started on the side of my teaching job that I needed more time to see through. When I arrived the only extra books at Ngoana Jesu were some outdated math and English textbooks hidden on a dusty shelf in Principal Tsita's office. I couldn't imagine a school without a library, so I began collecting books and magazines and lending them out from my house. Currently, I had two shelves of books and a few stacks of magazines and newspapers. Some of the teachers borrowed too. Ntate Lemphane loved reading *Newsweek*. And friends and family were sending more materials. Two boxes of books from my Aunt

Lisa and the elementary school where she taught in the U.S., and one from my friend Amy, had arrived in the past couple weeks. More were on the way. I wanted to find a room at the school that we could fill with these books and periodicals, a room that would be like a real library, where students could browse and bury their noses in books on all sorts of subjects. A group of boys had already read all of the Hardy Boys mysteries on the shelves and taken to calling themselves the Hardy Boys. Principal Tsita said she supported the library idea. Off the school grounds, I had started working on another project with my Peace Corps supervisors, Clement and Rosalia. We were compiling a directory of hard information that would guide students after high school. Where could they train to become an electrician? What grades did they need to go to college? There was nothing like this directory in existence. Our working title was *Careers and Training Courses in Lesotho*, and we wanted to eventually get a copy of the directory into every secondary school in the country. But the research was taking longer than we thought, even as small as Lesotho was, and with as few vocational schools and higher education institutions as it had, and we would not finish it before my Peace Corps contract was up.

On the contrary, discouraging me from staying was that every once in a while I felt like I wanted to move on, so to speak. I looked forward to settling into a career path back in America and marrying, starting again that life in the other of the dual worlds. But I also knew that America wasn't going anywhere. That life would always be there waiting for me to pick it back up. What was another year away, especially if it allowed me to deepen my experience of Lesotho so much? Fact was, the staying side of the scale was much heavier, so I asked Peace Corps if I could stay longer.

Adding a third extension year was rare but not unprecedented among Peace Corps volunteers. Yet it wasn't only a matter of asking. I was only a third of the decision-making party. Besides me there was the school, and Principal Tsita had been saying since my first week that two years wasn't enough, that I should "renew the contract," so her support for a third year was a given. And then there was Peace Corps. I had to take a physical exam, which came back clean, and then the desk in Washington, D.C. would take a look at my situation and make a final decision.

In September, I was approved. I would stay in my house and continue teaching at Ngoana Jesu through 2006. Nothing would change. Except that Peace Corps offered to send me back to America for a visit for up to a month in between my second and third years. At first, I was reluctant to accept the trip. I didn't want to break up my momentum in Tšoeneng. But how would I explain to my friends and family that I had turned down a free chance to visit them? And I did want to visit them.

December came fast. The last quarter of each school year always raced by because of the exams, when students were left on their own in the classrooms to review the year's worth of notes, or "revise," as they called it. We teachers prepared the tests, then gave the tests, then marked the tests, in between shooting the old crap around and watering our plots of vegetables and roasting cobs of maize over fires in the kitchen room next door, and then it was December 12, the day of my departure for a visit to America.

"PASSENGERS MAY BEGIN BOARDING," I heard over the intercom at Moshoeshoe I International Airport, Lesotho's only commercial airport. It was called international because flights went to Johannesburg in the Republic of South Africa, 45 minutes away. There were two of those flights each day, and those were the only two flights in or out of Lesotho. Despite the call to board, I remained standing up on the balcony watching others walk across the tarmac and up the stairs into the South African Airways twin-prop airplane. In order to get to California, I was going to have to fly halfway around the globe, requiring me to spend the next 23 hours of my life sitting on planes and in airports—Lesotho to Johannesburg, to Cape Verde to Atlanta, and finally to Los Angeles—so I wanted to stand outside in the real air until the last minute.

Then I looked down and there were no more passengers ascending the stairs into the plane. I was the only one left. I rushed to grab my backpack from the table inside and went downstairs and saw Lerato, Lemeko, and another student named Selloane. They had said they would try to travel to the airport to see me off, but I hadn't expected them to actually make it. I told them I was glad they had made it. Now there was no time to chat.

There was no one at the check-in gate, no travelers or airport employees. The airport is tiny: one check-in counter, one gate. From the one hallway a woman walked up and scolded me: "You're late. Where have you been? We have closed everything." I gave her my boarding pass and passport. She stamped it. "Hurry. You will have to run. Everyone is already on the plane."

I turned and fled.

"Hurry!" The airport employee scolded again. She turned the security machine back on and the belt reeled my backpack up and through the black flaps as I walked under a metal detector. I grabbed my backpack and the woman ushered me out the doors and onto the tarmac. "You must run!"

I ran across the tarmac toward the plane, as well as I could carrying my backpack, and turning to look up at the balcony. Lerato, Lemeko, and Selloane were up there, and so were Principal Tsita and her daughter Lineo, who had driven me to the airport. We waved at one another.

"Run!" shouted the woman.

I ran. The black ground was hot, and my backpack was heavy, but I ran. Then in my right periphery I noticed something running at me: big black men in black suits. And they were shouting things at me. I veered left, away from them. I slowed down. They looked aimed for a tackle.

"He is OK!" yelled the woman. "He is OK!" She was waving her hands over her head. The men slowed and then conferred with the woman. I was OK.

I carefully went up the stairway and took seat 2A toward the front of the small cabin. As I caught my breath I noticed out of the window that the men in suits were now walking back to a group of black cars. Two of them were black Toyota Camrys with dark tinted windows and flashing lights mounted to the roof. In between the Camrys was a black Mercedes-Benz. The Mercedes' license plate was fancier than the usual Lesotho plates which had only red or blue block letters and numbers and the image of a straw Basotho hat. The Mercedes' plate bore Lesotho's coat of arms, which were two horses on their hind legs standing atop an image of Thaba Bosiu Mountain and facing a shield. The shield showed a crocodile, the royal Bakoena clan's totem animal. Also on the plate only two letters were printed: MK. I knew those letters. I looked across the aisle and there he was, his Majesty the King, David Mohato Bereng Seeiso, also known as Letsie III, the King of Lesotho, a middle-aged man of just over six feet tall and a tad overweight, wearing a dark suit and flipping through South African Airways' in-flight magazine.

I tried not to stare. It was funny to think that I had been fleetingly thought of as a danger to this important man, a potential royal assassin. Me. The plane took off, and I kept one eye on the king and the other out the window. I was briefly distracted by the new perspective on the land as we climbed higher in the air. From the ground in Lesotho you only saw peaks and valleys. "The mountains are always in the way," Principal Tsita had once complained. But from above Lesotho was flattened into a painting of simple colors: orange sandstone, peanut butter soil, green young maize fields, muddy streams, clusters of sparkling dots of tin roofs.

I stole glances at the king. Where else could this happen? This was what I found so endearing about Lesotho, and encouraging as a foreigner trying to understand it: Lesotho was small and unpretentious and accessible. It had only one language, one tribe, one mountainous climate. It was an intimate country, where you stood the chance of sitting down next to the king.

Through the 45 minute trip to Johannesburg I couldn't help but think of a number of ways to start a conversation with him. I didn't want to pass up this chance. We had a couple things in common. I knew he had been mostly educated in England, and I had attended some school there too. I knew that though there was a royal palace in Maseru, he preferred to live in his house in Matsieng, the quieter royal village, only a day's walk from my house in Tšoeneng. What else did I know about King Letsie? He had recently married and announced that he would break with tradition and only keep one wife. Previous kings had many. The first, Moshoeshoe, had more than 40. It was exciting to look at this man and know that here was a direct descendent of the legendary founder of the Basotho nation. Exactly, he was Moshoeshoe's great great great great grandson.

Ah! I should say something in Sesotho, which might please him coming from a foreigner. But what if my pronunciation was a little off and he had to ask me to repeat myself? I would feel silly. And anyway, speaking to him in Sesotho could look like a thinly disguised attempt to show off. His English is great, I'm sure. I should use English. Or, maybe I shouldn't bother him at all.

We touched down in Johannesburg, and then I felt a rush of pressure and I did it, I leaned over and asked, "Is this trip for business or pleasure?" As soon the words escaped my mouth I felt ridiculous.

In a deep voice with a slight British accent the king returned, "A bit of both actually." And at that this potential royal assassin pestered the king no further.

MY BROTHER MATT picked me up from the Los Angeles airport in his Ford Excursion, a hulk of a car that was bigger than the minibus taxis in Lesotho. The taxis in Lesotho got stuffed with upwards of 20 passengers, yet this was my brother's personal vehicle. It had DVD screens on the backs of seats and air conditioning vents throughout. The minibus taxis in Lesotho sometimes had cassette players, and never had air conditioning. We raced along the 105 freeway with only inches separating the Excursion's side mirrors from the side mirrors of other cars. It seemed precarious, and I felt tense. My brother changed into the carpool lane, and now on our left just inches from the side mirror was a concrete wall, and still on our right were the side mirrors of other cars. No roads in Lesotho were more than one lane each way. My mom was in the car, and so was my niece, and they asked me questions about my flight but I couldn't relax and stop watching the road long enough to carry on a conversation.

I had a hunch when I left for Lesotho that the experience would allow me to see America in a new light, or as my mom had put it, "You're going to be weird when you get back." But I could never have guessed what parts of American life would stand out to me. Soon after we arrived at my mom's house she offered to take me to the grocery store to get food for my stay. Her car was also an SUV, and we drove to Stater Bros. Upon entering we headed left toward the produce where I discovered pyramids of apples that outsized my fists. I wondered how anyone could eat that much apple in one sitting. The apples in Lesotho were half the size, and I did a quick price calculation: one rand for an apple in Lesotho; about one dollar for an apple here. A dollar is seven rand—big difference! I could get seven, albeit smaller, apples in Lesotho for the price of one in America. Next I noticed the stacks of bananas. They looked like bull horns and they were an unblemished yellow. The bananas in Lesotho were smaller, of course, but they were also always nicked and spotted brown, oozing sweetness into the air.

After marveling at the fruit, I marveled at the people in the store. They were tall and rotund, and compared to Basotho they were like a race from another planet, like the Boers from South Africa. That evening when for the first time I saw my other brother, Brian, he said to me, "Have you shrunk?" I had always been the runt of the family, but in Lesotho I was average size and I hadn't felt small since living there. In America I was short, skinny, my growth looked stunted.

In the checkout line at the grocery store I saw stacks of newspapers for sale, the San Gabriel Valley Tribune, the Los Angeles Times, New York Times, USA Today. The daily newspapers on offer in this city alone made a thicker stack than the whole country of Lesotho's newspapers for a week. America was so big and busy. It seemed unknowable, impenetrable. If America had a king, I would never happen to sit next to him on a plane.

We loaded the groceries into the car. And that was what everyone else in the parking lot was doing: they had also driven to the store. I hadn't driven to a store in a long time. I was used to walking to the village shop. Over the course of the few weeks that I stayed with my mom we drove everywhere. By car seemed to be the only way you could get places. I did see people on bikes, but they were never going anywhere. They were dressed in bright spandex and riding in a big circle, for fun. I saw people walking and running too, but they also had no destination and no purpose except exercise. The strangest thing I saw though was this one gym. There were a bunch of windows in the front and through them I saw people bouncing on treadmills, and I thought, not only are they not going anywhere but they are not even breathing fresh air, and they are paying the gym for this torture. I couldn't believe that people were paying in order to use a machine that allowed them to move their legs, which they had to do because all day they had been paying to use another machine, a car, to transport their body from place to place, from home to the grocery store to work, and even to the gym itself.

America was great. It was so rich a country that its people paid to move their legs on a special machine, and they also left food to rot on their driveways. Throughout town I saw fruit trees, avocado and orange mostly, and beneath them lay much fallen fruit decomposing. People just let the ripe fruit drop to the ground. In Lesotho, I had a peach tree beside my kitchen window. The hostelers began picking off it while the peaches were still green, and they cleaned it out before a single peach was mature enough to fall.

America was such a plentiful country that people also urinated into clean water. In Lesotho, people urinated on the ground. Basotho used buckets of clean water only for drinking and cooking. Yet here in America, people filled toilet bowls and peed in them. I couldn't do it, I couldn't urinate in a bowl of clean water. It was such a waste. I walked outside and peed on the compost pile in my mom's backyard. Fine, Mom, I was weird, but dirtying clean water by urinating in it was immoral.

I decided to take feeling weird as a compliment because it meant that I had adapted to Lesotho life, which meant that I had achieved my goal of really getting to know the place.

Still, when my grandparents drove me to the airport for my return flight in January I felt anxious. Even as I had stumbled my way through parts of American life, parts of my visit were delightful. I had felt a sort of social comfort being with my family and longtime friends that I hadn't been able to find in Lesotho. Using my first language with people and having known them for so many years probably accounted for this. I had reveled in every second I spent under a hot shower, which was so much easier and faster than the bucket baths I took in Lesotho. And I had gotten used to being able to turn on a light switch and keep the night at bay, extending the day as long as I wanted, to 10 p.m., even past midnight. As we pulled up to the drop-off zone at LAX I imagined my return to Tšoeneng being a return to a dark and lonely place. I was leaving my family and I was heading back to the land of strange Africans and poor food and no electricity. I didn't really want to go.

CHAPTER FIFTEEN

Tšoeneng the Rewarding

THE SOIL WAS DARK AND WET in Tšoeneng when I arrived. As I walked from the road through the fields to school after a taxi had dropped me off, I saw puddles in the hollows of the sandstone slabs beside the trail, which was pleasing because it meant that rain had fallen recently—good for my plants, good for every family who farmed, good for filling the water table and keeping the springs flowing.

School was closed for a few more weeks, and the campus was empty. I looked down over the fields below to the river valley and across the valley to Kolo Mountain, and the view was as expansive as when I'd arrived two years before. It could've been the same day I arrived. The scene was suspended in time. Nothing had moved. Fields, river, black ribbon of road, Kolo Mountain peak, dark mountain ridges behind.

The facade of my house had weathered though. Spider cracks were emerging from the cement underneath the yellow paint, like the first wrinkles on the face of a sunburned young man. I opened the door with my skeleton key. A patina of dust had formed over the orange paisley plastic floor covering in my house, and spiders had spun webs in the corners. I swept through with my hand broom. Just after the sun set there was a light rap on my door handle. Everyone else always knocked on the wood and said, *"Koko,"* but ntate Makoanyane always tapped my door handle with his *molamu*. And it always happened at dusk. I still asked who it was, just to make him say: *"Ke 'na."*—It's me.

I opened the door and before he was totally through he

asked, "Where's the meat?" He made the sign for meat, putting his finger on his front teeth and rubbing them. "I smell meat."

I had picked up some fried chicken at KFC on the way down from Maseru so that I didn't have to cook a dinner on my first night back. Ntate Makoanyane loved meat so much he would spend the entire day hanging around school whenever we slaughtered one of the school pigs, and he would eat any part given to him. I was pretty sure I saw him eating the penis once, but then again I was told that was something a lot of the old men did.

I gave him a drumstick. "It looks like it has rained," I said. As much as ntate Makoanyane loved to eat meat, he also loved to talk about the rain. He worked as the watchman by night, paid by Principal Tsita to guard the school, but he was a farmer and a herder by day. I encountered him in the countryside sometimes while I was running or climbing or exploring, and he was tending his donkeys. And he once brought me a sack full of ears of maize from his fields. Since ntate Makoanyane had no irrigation for his crops besides what fell from the sky in the form of rain, just like everyone else in Tšoeneng, and Lesotho as a whole, he obsessed over what the weather was doing. He liked to talk about how consistent the summer rains were. If things were normal, there was a thunderstorm every couple days, and a solid downpour once a week. In the spring he fretted over the season's storms beginning on time, and at any time he never admitted to being satisfied with the amount the sky provided.

But he said to me on this night, *"Hei! E nele haholo ntate!"*—It has rained a lot!

That meant it must have flooded. True enough, I later found out that a major bridge had been washed out up north. Lesotho's weather swung between extremes each year I was there, as weather tends to do. The year I arrived I was told the country was suffering a three-year drought. That summer the prime minister announced a state of emergency, saying 600,000 people were in danger of starving and asking for foreign donations. Now in the summer of 2006, the land was inundated, beyond saturated, and topsoil had eroded from December's abundant precipitation.

What was steady and certain was that Basotho saw rain from

a very different perspective than Americans. In America, we had the saying "Save money for a rainy day." In other words, rainy days were times when things went wrong. But it could rain any time in Lesotho—on a bride's wedding ceremony, on a funeral procession, on your head as you were walking to school—and it might be a little inconvenient, but it was still always considered a blessed thing. And that made sense to me now, now that I understood how ntate Makoanyane relied on the rain to grow his food and feed his family and to grow the pasture grasses that fed his donkeys, and now that I too benefited from good rains in not having to lug buckets of water from the pump to irrigate my vegetable plots. Rain feeds life.

"It's been boring with you gone," said ntate Makoanyane. That was nice of him. And then he asked as he did every evening, "I don't want to trouble you, but can you lend me some paper?"

I pulled an old newspaper from under my bookshelf and tore off a sheet for him. Under the poor light of my candle, under the hindrance of all the blankets he wore to keep him warm through the night, he took pinches from the yellow and red plastic pouch of BB tobacco and sprinkled it into the newspaper, rolled it up, licked the seam, sealed it.

"OK, ntate," he said as he left to smoke and make his rounds. I noticed that he had spilled some tobacco on the floor. He always did.

It was good to be home. And that's what it actually felt like, like I was home. Boarding my return flight with anxiety seemed to be part of a routine that would always occur whenever I left Lesotho. It had happened during my first winter break from school when I visited Durban in South Africa too. From the comfort of the hostel couch, in front of a television, eating fast food, hearing English all around me, returning to Lesotho was unappealing. It seemed a return to a spartan and solitary life where I only had a plastic chair and bland homemade meals and no Internet. But then as now, once I got to my house in Tšoeneng I quickly forgot about the first-world luxuries that had seemed so wonderful and necessary a few days before. They were out of sight and out of mind. And I slipped back into the Tšoeneng life.

IT WAS TRUE that it was dark after the sun set here. I only had the small globe of light from the candle, propped up on a blue metal holder, dripping white wax over the side. Beside the candle on my table I set my Sesotho memo book and flipped through it, where I had written some words and expressions learned just before leaving for America. *Sebapali sa hloahloa* means "good soccer player," a term I encountered while reading a Sesotho magazine called BONA, the only magazine in the world that's printed in Sesotho, albeit South African Sesotho, which has a slightly different orthography. *Ha re etse tjena* means "let's do this," a phrase I had been hearing the hostelers say often. *Hoja ke na le chelete, ke ne ke tla reka CD eo ea Mantša*, which means "If I only had some money, I would buy that Mantša CD." I had been getting confused while forming such conditional sentences. The difficulty was that the Sesotho literally translated, "If I only *have*," and I had trouble remembering to use that present tense instead of the past *had* as we use in such conditional sentences in English. As I sat at my table, I made up some more conditional sentences in my head to practice the construction: "If he *does* that to me, I would fight him. If it *is* winter, it would be cold."

It was nowhere near cold now. I kept my door and windows closed starting from dusk in order to keep mosquitoes out (my door and windows had no screens), and the tin-roofed, concrete-block house faced west and soaked up the late afternoon sun and heated up immensely through the evening. It was suffocatingly hot inside. I sweated even as I sat at my table. Still, that was preferable to letting the mosquitoes in.

I pushed my Sesotho memo book to the side and began reading an English book, *The Worst Journey in the World* by Apsley Cherry-Garrard, which describes the author's near-death experience while exploring Antarctica, and I practically got goosebumps. Despite the heat inside my house, I felt the cold of Antarctica. Only having a dim bubble illuminated around the book allowed that. Reading by candle light made me absorbed into the book's frigid antipodal world, despite my sitting in a stuffy room and sweating under an African summer.

Cherry-Garrard was part of the 1910-1913 expedition led by Robert Falcon Scott, in which crew members were dying as they tried to be the first men to reach the South Pole. They were cold. They were starving. "And I tell you," writes Cherry-Garrard, "if you have the desire for knowledge and the power to give it physical expression, go out and explore. If you are a brave man you will do nothing; if you are fearful you may do much, for none but cowards have need to prove their bravery."

There was nothing else around me but the ice and suffering of Cherry-Garrard, and the weight of his words. Was I a coward? Had I come to Africa to prove something? What was I afraid of? I was afraid that being raised in the comfort of America had rendered me incapable of surviving the more primitive lifestyle of a place like Tšoeneng.

I got up from the table, grabbed the candle and walked slowly so as not to blow out the flame, into my bedroom and fetched my toothbrush. After brushing, I opened my door and walked cautiously in the dark a few feet from my house, my feet crunching the gravel beneath my steps, and then I spit into the bushes. Before turning back, I heard the cry of a jackal out in the fields. It sounded like a baby crying. The cry had freaked me out the first time I heard it, but then the hostelers assured me that it wasn't an abandoned child out there, it was a *phokojoe*. It was a sound I knew well now. It was often the only sound at night during school breaks, when there were no hostelers around. In Tšoeneng, down on the school grounds in the middle of the fields, in my house, it was dark and I was alone, but I was not scared and I was not lonely, as I prophesied I would be from the Los Angeles airport. And I appreciated the way the evening invaded and blackened everything and focused my thoughts and prepared me for sleep.

I FELT IN TIME with the spinning of the globe. I slept when the sun did, and then the next morning I rose fresh when the sun rose. I grabbed my water buckets and headed up to the pump. I rinsed the dust off them and pumped them full of the cool underground water, and then I hauled them down to my garden plot. Even though there had just been a lot of rain, the sky was blue and hot again for the moment, the sun sucking the moisture back into the sky, and under that sun my plants could never seem to drink enough. I bent over to sprinkle cupfuls around the stocks of Swiss chard. I returned to the pump and the dirt path was warm under my bare feet. I stepped on a stone and it hurt a little, but I liked being barefoot. It was great to touch the earth again. I hadn't touched the earth much during my visit to America. There I had mostly worn shoes, or even if I hadn't been wearing shoes I walked on carpet in a house, or outside I stepped onto a concrete porch and then a sidewalk and then a driveway and then into a car and then a parking lot. Natural ground was never on the way to any place.

Back down the hill, the weight of the full water buckets strained my shoulders, but I didn't mind the burn. With my blue scooper cup I gently irrigated my onions. The sun heated the back of my neck as I watered my tomatoes and chili peppers. I was delighted to find that the chili pepper plants were now green and thriving and bushier than ever. Through the winter they had lost all their leaves and looked dead and dry as sticks, but then they came back to life in the spring and now they had so many flowers and baby peppers that I was never going to be able to consume them all. It was one of those problems that wasn't really a problem.

Having filled two more buckets with water at the pump, I hauled them back inside my house. I scooped out some to fill my kettle on the stove, and I struck a match to light the gas. While that water heated I laid out my wide blue basin in my bedroom beside my foam pad, washcloth, shampoo, towel, soap and radio. Once the water had boiled I scooped cold water into a small bucket and then poured hot water in until the temperature was just hotter than I wanted, as it would cool down fast. I set the radio to 97.2 FM. I knelt on the foam pad with my head over the basin and poured scoopfuls of water on my head as I worked through my hair with my free hand. I washed it and then rinsed it over the basin. Lastly, I rinsed the stray hair off my fingers. My hair never felt truly clean after washing it this way in the early days, but either I got used to the half-clean feeling or I got better at washing because I now felt comfortably cleansed. Then I stepped inside the basin, naked. This was the part that I dreaded in the winter. I felt so exposed to the elements, so rushed to get my warm clothes back on. I poured scoopfuls of water over my shoulders, rubbed some soap onto my washcloth, washed my shoulders to my waist, and then rinsed the washcloth a bit and rubbed more soap on it. I wet farther down my body and washed until I had gotten all the way to my toes. The water at my feet was gray by now. I rinsed by pouring scoopfuls of water over my body. The routine inevitably splashed water all over my floor. So after I leaned over and grabbed my towel and dried off, I wiped the water off the floor with my washcloth and then rinsed it out. After I dressed I took the leftover clean bathwater and poured it into the basin of gray water, and took it out to dump on my plants.

My month in America had been easy because machines did most of my daily tasks. Getting water had been effortless: I merely turned a knob. I pushed a button on the stove or microwave when I needed my food cooked. I switched on the vacuum and the dirt was sucked up off the floor—no sore lower back from bending down to sweep. But a light soreness in my lower back today meant a stronger lower back tomorrow. A pair of tired shoulders from hauling buckets of water now meant hardened and healthy arms later. Muscles were supposed to be used, broken down and built stronger each day. The work was good for me. I felt like here in Lesotho I was using my body as it was meant to be used.

I came to Lesotho expecting the lifestyle to be much more difficult than it was. I wondered if I could handle it, having grown up in the U.S. with so many machines doing my work, and I expected the daily tasks of living in Lesotho to be drudgery. They weren't. Partly they weren't because I knew they were good for the well-being of my body, but also they were engaging. I hadn't known how to do these things before I came to Lesotho. These weren't mindless efforts, but rather they were skills that required of me a period of learning. There was the training that I went through by watching the hostelers in order to figure out how to wash my clothes by hand. Now I could get a white shirt whiter than any washing machine. I was proud especially of how my white shirts had absolutely no ring around the collar or pit stains, because I scrubbed them so accurately in my handwashes. And I learned how to wash dishes efficiently without a sink and faucet, let alone a machine dishwasher. I used two plastic basins, one for washing and one for rinsing, and I got to where I didn't need to use much water for the job. I figured out how to shave well without a mirror, which involved heightening my proprioception. I learned to place the razor in just the right positions on my face and neck, and to start low on my jaw and then stroke higher and higher until I sensed the tug of the hair beside my ear. In that way I kept my sideburns short and of identical length without ever having to look at them. And now I even knew how to bake bread over my propane stove by kneading and then putting the dough in a pot and placing the pot on top of a piece of tin covered with rocks to diffuse the heat. This created an oven effect. The hostelers taught me that, just like they were the ones who taught me most things. That was how they cooked all their bread, and it took time and elbow grease but it filled my house with an amazing aroma. The bread was so fresh and flavorful that I ate it without accompaniment, in big chunks. No toast, no jelly, no sandwiches, just chunks of steaming fresh bread.

The tasks were tiring, but I came to appreciate that. Because I didn't just push buttons anymore, because I labored through the day just to keep things clean and keep myself fed, because if I needed to buy food I walked to the shop, sleep came easily as soon as I hit my pillow each night. And it felt right to be exhausted at the end of a day. While I rarely looked forward to doing the menial tasks that had to be done throughout the day—I would always rather have taken a hot shower than a bucket bath—when I was spent of energy at night and sleep came like a tidal wave, I was glad I had toiled. And I was glad I had spent my daylight in and out of the house doing meaningful acts instead of, say, walking on a treadmill going nowhere inside a stuffy artificially lit gym.

CHAPTER SIXTEEN

Mine Work

ALTHOUGH UPON MY RETURN TO TŠOENENG from America the mountains looked the same as on my first day, there was news among the people. Principal Tsita had gotten a new car. A few days before school opened, she came bumping down the dirt road in a blue Volkswagen. Her old Volkswagen had been white. She lived in Lesotho near Maseru, but this new car's license plate was from Gauteng province in South Africa, where she had bought it. We chatted near her office where she told me that Chief Thabo had a girlfriend. The whole village knew about it. His girlfriend was his neighbor, and he tried to hide the affair from no one, especially his wife. Principal Tsita told me that Chief Thabo defended his behavior by saying, "I'll stop visiting my girlfriend when 'me 'Malebusa stops drinking." Apparently, his wife had gotten particularly bad with the jugs of sorghum beer. She'd been drunk when I visited them before. One time, during the initiation of a new witchdoctor down at the river (where the new witchdoctor had supposedly walked into the water and entered a secret underworld for some time and then reemerged, thus proving her magic powers), 'me 'Malebusa was so inebriated that on our walk back to the village she collapsed in a ditch. She refused to even try to stand up again, and she looked up at me and my camera and commanded slurringly over and over, "Take my photo. Take my photo, abuti Thabang!"

There were still a couple days left until school opened for 2006 when 'Malefa knocked at my door. It was a privilege when 'Malefa visited. She was just a teenager, one of my students, but I had a lot of respect for her. She worked hard and she set a great example for the rest of her classmates. 'Malefa sat down and we chatted about last year's exam results, which had just been published. The government each year printed a newspaper insert that listed all of the grades on the national exams for all of the students in the whole country. 'Malefa and I agreed that we were both surprised that Sepheche, the bright boy I had first seen at the initiation ceremony on the day I arrived, hadn't gotten first class. He got second class. Then 'Malefa said, "I wanted to tell you that I won't be coming to school when it opens."

"Oh, when will you come?" I wondered if she was transferring to a better school like Khosi had done after my first year. I would miss her, but I would be proud of her.

"I won't be coming. There's no money."

"Money? Don't worry about money. There's money, just like last year. Unless you don't want to come to school?"

"I want to come badly," she said.

"Then come. I'll see you Monday."

Back in January of my second year, a few days before that school year started, 'Malefa had shown up at my door and said her father had lost his job in a South African mine and without his income the family could no longer pay her school fees. "I won't be there when school opens."

It was a story I'd heard before, of parents not being able to pay for school anymore. The government was starting to pay for primary school, but secondary and high school was still optional and private. I didn't mind letting go of some students who had trouble paying, but with 'Malefa it was different. She was the best student at Ngoana Jesu, far and away. She was a classmate of Lemeko the climber, and the first time I asked for a writing sample from their class, in those first days of my first year, a few students brought up unintelligible blobs of words; some successfully conveyed a message though not so correctly; and then 'Malefa put on my table a perfect paragraph. Perfect. I couldn't believe it, and for some reason I felt that as her teacher I shouldn't acknowledge it. With my red pen I placed a comma between two clauses in one of her sentences. "It's a good paragraph," I told her. "But you could put a comma here to make it clearer." 'Malefa squinted, as in, "Are you serious?" Her last name was Taunyane, "Little Lion," and I had been roared at.

"But do you *want* to attend school?" I asked her at my house that day back in January of my second year.

"Yes."

"Then I'll talk to Principal Tsita and we'll see if we can figure something out."

When Principal Tsita's white Volkswagen putted down the path to school the next afternoon, I walked up to her office and told her the situation. "'Malefa has to be in school," I said. "How can we teach the other students while she is sitting at home washing clothes and waiting for someone to marry her?" That was what happened to girls who weren't in school. Principal Tsita agreed to the sentiment, but she didn't have any solutions. The government of Lesotho offered help only to students in secondary school who were orphans. 'Malefa wasn't an orphan, so there were no scholarships available to her. Still, Principal Tsita said she would look for other scholarships for 'Malefa. I said I would also think of other ways to help.

I changed my clothes back at my house and I walked up to the kitchen storage room to get a spade because I wanted to turn my compost pit, and think through this 'Malefa thing. The way there were scholarships available only for orphans irritated me. I would rather call it quits and go home than teach in a system that only awarded students scholarships whose parents had died while allowing a cream-of-the-crop learner like 'Malefa to just fall by the wayside. Where's the future of Lesotho if students like 'Malefa are left to sit at home and waste their brains? This girl could run the country someday, really. I knew of students in my first year who had to stop attending school because they couldn't pay, but it had only seemed unfortunate then. Once money affected 'Malefa's education I could no longer ignore the issue. It was like a piano prodigy having her instrument taken away.

My compost pit was a square hole originally dug for me by male hostelers, including Tumelo, the one who grew vegetables so well, and who had once cut my hair. Now it was my duty to maintain, and the wetter stuff on bottom needed to be mixed with the rotting food scraps on top. I jabbed the spade in.

An easy and obvious possible solution was that I pay for 'Malefa's school. Scraping together the money would not be a big obstacle: I received about 1,400 rand ($250) per month to live on from Peace Corps and I usually had about 400 rand of that leftover at the end of each month. A student's school fees were only about 1,000 rand for the year at Ngoana Jesu. So I could save for 'Malefa's entire year of school fees in three months.

But I didn't want to give away money to anyone in Lesotho. I had set that rule for myself when I arrived. Besides paying for products like a normal consumer—taxi fares, eggs and milk from Motsie's shop, etc.—I didn't want to get involved with anyone or anything financially because that seemed like all that foreigners did in Lesotho. They flew in and dished out monies for aid projects (from as small as donating clothing to building huge infrastructure pieces like the bridge across the Tsoaing River). This wasn't the experience I wanted in Lesotho, and it wasn't the type of relationship I wanted with people in Lesotho. I didn't think it was ultimately good for either of us. I wanted, instead of the typical benefactor-receptor dynamic, genuine friendships. I wanted relationships that were on equal footings and based on working side by side toward common goals (like with the other Ngoana Jesu teachers and students), and based on just liking each other's company (like with Motsie and Chief Thabo and Witchdoctor Santu).

Was that possible, considering how different we were, considering the legacy of relationships between people who looked like me and Africans? I was determined to make an attempt.

As part of the students' agriculture classes they kept pigs at school. I walked over to the sties, which were between Principal Tsita's office and the boys' toilets, and picked up spadefuls of pig manure and walked them back to dump on my compost pit. I would mix that in too. This pit was going to transform my soil into something magical someday and grow tall and green plants all around my house.

There was even another reason I couldn't give 'Malefa money for her school fees. When the other students found out, they would come asking for the same. If I was going to pay for 'Malefa

she worked so hard in school, then I should pay for
rs who worked hard. Maybe I should start a scholarship
rogram based solely on merit.

After I mixed in the pig manure, I returned the spade to the storage room and went back into my house, sat at the table, and jotted down some notes and numbers. The top student in every class (there were five classes) could have their school fees paid for, and then maybe the second- and third-ranked students could get partial scholarships. If I did that for all the classes it might cost around $1,000 a year, total. I could ask friends and family back home to contribute, as I knew that they felt a connection to some of my students now through me and they would trust that the money was being spent well. And I especially liked the lesson a merit-based scholarship program would teach: Work hard, get rewarded.

But I wouldn't be in Tšoeneng forever, and what would happen to the program after I left? I could cut it off, but that might leave some students high and dry. I could continue to run it through Principal Tsita. However, as much as I trusted her, I couldn't accept the gap that would then exist between the source of the funds (America) and the beneficiaries (Lesotho). It would be a foreign aid program, essentially. There would be a huge disconnect, an unacceptably huge disconnect.

The next day Principal Tsita came to school again, this time to meet with parents to register their children for the new year and I walked up to her office. "I'll pay 'Malefa's school fees," I said. "If 'Malefa's not in class, then I don't want to be there."

"Oh," said Principal Tsita. She was lost for words.

Despite my deliberations the day before, I was also lost for a rational explanation, except to say that I had concluded that it would be unbearable for me to begin teaching her class that year without her. She would be at home and wishing she was at school, while another student sat at her desk but didn't care as much to study. I had to get 'Malefa into class in order to get myself in there. I knew in my gut that it was right for her to be there. And for that I was willing to break my rule of not getting financially involved. Sometimes in the face of reality abstract principles must be bent.

After an awkward moment where Principal Tsita conside
my announcement she said, "If you want to pay, I understand. But
you can't pay all. You know these parents, ntate, they need to pay
something or they don't appreciate it. You can pay the school fees,
but her parents should still find the money for her books." That
sounded fair, and that was something I had always liked about
Principal Tsita. She was loving but tough. I knew where she came
from. She had worked her own way out of a rural village in the
mountain district of Mokhotlong to attend the National University
of Lesotho, and now she was the principal of a school. She knew
that something for nothing could be insidious. Often the
sponsored orphaned students were the laziest in class, and they
failed their grade levels. They weren't paying their school fees, nor
were their families, and that seemed to reduce their motivation.
They knew that the government would even sponsor them to
repeat the grade level again the next year if necessary.

I met with 'Malefa's parents a few days later to inform them
that I wanted to help, and their reaction affirmed my decision. We
met in the morning beside the Form E classroom. The sun
bounced off the classroom's cinder block wall and into our eyes
with blinding brightness. 'Malefa's father looked frail. He wore a
blanket but I could tell he was thin underneath, probably with the
sinewy body of a man who had all his life earned his food through
physical labor. His jaw was strong, but his voice was weak, spotty
from inhaling dust in a mine for so many years, like every other
former miner in Tšoeneng. They were used up and spit out. They
never complained, but that's how they looked: used up. He said to
me, "I always taught 'Malefa to do well to other people and to
respect her teachers, and they would see it and do well to her. I
always taught her that."

I paid Principal Tsita 250 rand for 'Malefa's first quarter
school fees that day. 'Malefa excelled in class as usual throughout
the following weeks of the first quarter. By March it was time to
pay for the second quarter. I entered Principal Tsita's office and
inquired about when exactly the fees were due, but she said I
didn't need to pay. "I have found sponsorship," she said. That was
great news. But she didn't say who the sponsor was. I immediately
wondered if it wasn't Principal Tsita herself because I knew that

...eciated 'Malefa's drive and attitude as much as me.

At small schools like Ngoana Jesu, principals also teach ...sses. It was always hard for Principal Tsita to juggle teaching classes while performing all of her administrative tasks though, and one time Principal Tsita confided to me that she had not shown up to teach 'Malefa's mathematics class for a few weeks straight. She told me she feared her first day back in the Form B math class for one reason: "'Malefa is going to scold me with her eyes," she said. "I don't want to go in there and face her."

I never did ask who 'Malefa's new sponsor was. Later, I think I discovered it indirectly. Officers with the Ministry of Education showed up one day to register orphans for their sponsorships and Principal Tsita requested the roll books from all of us teachers. She would then hand the roll books over to the officers. When my roll book was returned a couple names had been added. The names were of students who had been at our school the previous year but didn't come back this year. And I knew that those students had been orphans receiving school fee sponsorship through the Ministry of Education. Aha! I wasn't about to speak up. As far as I was concerned, 'Malefa had earned the money the Ministry would send to the school in the name of some phantom orphans.

NOW IN MY THIRD YEAR, 'Malefa wasn't going to say it, but I knew why her family had even less money than the previous year after her father had lost his mine job. One of her classmates had come down to my house the day before and delivered the news. Maybe she wasn't bringing it up because she knew that I knew.

"I'm sorry about your father. How did he die?"

"We don't know," she said. "He was fine last week. He was working in the fields even, and then on Monday he got the hiccups. On Wednesday he was dead."

I remembered how frail 'Malefa's father had looked the year before. But dying from hiccups? Mysterious causes of death were not unusual in Tšoeneng. I had heard of people dying from hiccups before, or people dying from headaches, from curses, from being strangled in the night by a mythical creature called *thokolosi*, a small man who appeared to be an innocent boy walking through the village during the day only to turn into a murderous midget at night. There were numerous bizarre explanations for humans dying in Lesotho.

Tšoeneng people didn't seem to feel a need to investigate deaths like people might in other countries. There were no autopsies. Villagers died too often to spend a lot of time trying to get to the bottom of every passing. Statistics from governments and health organizations indicated that many of them had probably died of AIDS, Lesotho's infection rate being one of the world's highest at around 30 percent. But no one in Tšoeneng got tested for HIV, so who could really say?

'Malefa's father, having spent his working life in South African mines, might have succumbed to a number of diseases ultimately. Many miners returned to Lesotho infected with tuberculosis, for example, and I remembered 'Malefa's father sounding like his lungs were in bad shape. I never met a returned miner in Tšoeneng who appeared healthy, which was remarkable mostly because these men did not return old. They were still young, yet sickly. I came to be ambivalent about the mines of South Africa. On one hand, they offered Basotho men work. And there was really little other employment available to the majority of the men. General unemployment was estimated at 45 percent in Lesotho in 2006. In recent history, Basotho men found more work in the mines of South Africa than anywhere else. In the 1990's, the money they sent back to their families amounted to 67 percent of Lesotho's gross domestic product. But work in the mines was not ideal. The men essentially lived apart from their families, staying in dorms at the mines, returning home by bus for one weekend per month. That was why it was common for Basotho miners to have mistresses in South Africa, and to even start second families there. It was the toll on the miners' health that was hardest to watch for me though. These men entered the mines young and virile, without exception, as they were offered employment based on their performance in a physical examination, and then they were turned out a decade or two later looking three or four decades older. Their lungs were shot, sounding like they were breathing underwater, their bodies were creaky. They were not long for life when they retired back to the village. Before the passing of 'Malefa's father, I had already attended many funerals for the fathers of students who had been miners and were only in their forties when they died. To me that seemed so young, so truncated. The miners, however, expressed no resentment toward the work. I never heard the returned miners in Tšoeneng talk about their mining days with regret, and I had spoken with a number of them, particularly Chief Thabo, Witchdoctor Santu, and Motsie the shop owner. They acknowledged their health problems: Santu had much trouble breathing; Motsie walked with the aid of a cane. But they never complained. The mine work had allowed them to send their children to school, and to buy furniture for their houses in the village, and they seemed resigned to the fact that it had kept them away from their family for so long and that it would probably kill them off before their children were independent adults.

THE MINER who allowed me the closest look at his work life was Masopha's father, Masopha being the Form E student who loved to teach me Sesotho things. I first met the father when he was off work and visiting Tšoeneng to see Masopha one weekend. He introduced himself as Jasmine. That is a woman's name, I thought. Masopha later told me that his real name, his Sesotho name, was Lerata. Jasmine was his church name. Basotho often introduced themselves to me with their church names, I suppose because they thought the church names were more familiar to a foreigner, and easier to pronounce. But everyone called him Lerata, and so I did.

When he spoke he wheezed like the other miners I had met, and he limped. He still worked at the mines though. Masopha had told me that. But I knew right from the start that there was something different about ntate Lerata: he was chubby, and I'd never met a chubby miner.

I got the chance to visit ntate Lerata at the mine where he worked, outside the South African town of Welkom. It was called Beatrix 4 Shaft, and when we pulled up to it there was a desolation about the place. It was tall metal scaffolding surrounded by low buildings and a couple of artificial mountains made from the mine's innards, all of this alone in the middle of the Free State countryside. At the security gate the guard, an African man, said to me in English, "What are you here for? You can't take any photos. And no journalism." I was with Masopha and ntate Lerata in a car I had rented. "He's from far away," said ntate Lerata in Sesotho. "He wants to see the mine so he can tell people in America how it is. He's from America!" The guard took me into his office and made me sign some paperwork that said, among other things, that I wouldn't take pictures. Then he let me pass through the gate.

Ntate Lerata directed me to drive over and park near the scaffolding that surrounded the shaft. "You can get a good view here, and snap some pictures."

"But the security guard said I can't take pictures." Ntate Lerata didn't speak English.

"*Ach*, he's crazy. Take pictures. Take pictures now."

Ntate Lerata was about my height, but much thicker. And here at the mine he became very confident. He had worked at Beatrix 4 Shaft since 1992. So I followed his orders and got my camera from the car and looked around to see that I was out of sight of the security guard and took a couple shots.

"Yes, shoot!" said ntate Lerata.

Then I saw a white man in a neon orange jumpsuit and hardhat walking near the shaft and I hid behind a sign on the fence. Once he was out of sight, I shot a couple more pictures for ntate Lerata's sake, and then I got back into the car. I drove us over some train tracks where carts sat idle, marked on the side, *EXPLOSIVES*. Ntate Lerata said, "This is where I worked when I first arrived." There was also a sign that read in English: "If we can't mine safely, we won't be able to mine at all." Nearby was an equipment yard: large-diameter metal pipes, huge reels of wire.

Ntate Lerata directed me to pull up at a building signed "Hospital." Inside there was one hallway and a handful of rooms. He introduced me to the only people inside: a cook, a cleaning lady, and a nurse—all of them Basotho women. "He's seeing the place and taking photos," said ntate Lerata. I got nervous. "Show them your camera."

Before I even reached into my pocket, the cook, who was wearing an apron, gave a smile of gold-capped front teeth. (Would

I eat from a cook whose teeth had rotted?) And she said, "Shoot me!"

I shot her. And then immediately the cleaning lady wanted a picture. She was short, and she posed beneath a chart on the wall that read: "You can stop the spread of TB by covering your mouth when you cough." And a poster next to it displayed a different health message: "Life with HIV: family, recreation, healthy eating." I shot the cleaning lady.

And then the nurse called to me, "I'm going to do treatment. Come! Take my photo." She grabbed me by the wrist and led me down the hallway and into a room labeled "Ward." Ntate Lerata and Masopha followed. There were four rows of beds covered with maroon blankets that read "Oryx Mines," the former name of Beatrix 4 Shaft. I saw under one blanket the bulge of a body and the shiny pate of a brown head sticking out the top. I can't photograph her giving this ill miner medicine. I will not. This is too much. But she passed his bed and pulled a metal cabinet up to an empty bed.

She pulled out a clipboard and told ntate Lerata to lie on the bed. After he got on and settled onto his side, the nurse grabbed a plastic bottle and pretended to feed him medicine. "You see," she said. "I'm an actor. I'm acting. You see me? Shoot me!" I shot her.

The security guard had given me exactly two commands: no journalism and no photos. And all every worker on the mine grounds asked me to do was take photos. I knew I would break the first command, but they made me break the second.

Outside the hospital the mine grounds were quiet. I always imagined a mine to be loud with machinery, but there was virtually no sound. There was not even any motion. Masopha and I hiked up to the top of one of the artificial mountains of yellow earth dug out of the mine. From up there we saw other mines in the distance, identifiable by their similar flat-topped, artificial mountains. Otherwise, the land was perfectly flat. Some Boer farms were interspersed with the mines, this being the Free State, the South African province adjacent to Lesotho where the Dutch long ago trekked to from the Cape and booted off the Basotho. Directly below the Beatrix 4 Shaft mountain were some tanks and towers and machines that silently steamed. "That is where they cook the gold," Masopha said. "You can't see the gold when they take it from the mine. It looks like a seam of black. But then it gets cooked."

Masopha said he had a friend from his village who also worked at this mine, so we hiked back down the mountain and walked over to the dormitories to block A, number 67. Rubber boots were lined up on a rack outside the door. Inside there was a shared bathroom, and then we knocked on door B and Keletso eventually appeared. He had been napping. He looked as young as Masopha, even younger, maybe 20 years old. His room had a bunk bed, a single bed, and a closet, the whole room the size of a large closet. On the wall was a poster of a Sesotho music group: two guys dressed alike and holding hands. In the corner of the room was Keletso's *molamu* and on the floor was his mining gear: knee pads, a belt, a pouch carrying gloves, a safety manual, and a journal to record the mine's temperature. "The work is not so hard," Keletso said. "But the heat is brutal. It's even hotter down there than in other mines because this one is older, so it is deeper."

We spoke for just a minute. Since Keletso had been sleeping when we arrived, we let him resume his nap. As Masopha and I walked back toward the hospital to find his father I asked him if he wanted to be a miner someday. "Any shepherd can do that job. Go down in the hole. I'm clever. I like studying things." So that was a no.

I didn't say it, but I thought of warning him not to deride the mine work in front of his father. My own father had been a plumber. He never liked it. I didn't like it either. When I was young I was embarrassed about his job. I never said my dad was a plumber, I always told people my dad was a "plumbing contractor." And I thought of myself as being destined for better work than that. Later I understood more about work, about my father's work as a plumber, and about the fact that it helped pay for my education, providing me the opportunity to even imagine myself in other jobs.

"I want to be an engineer," said Masopha.

"You have to get good marks in mathematics to be an engineer." I knew that he struggled in Principal Tsita's math class.

We saw the wheels on the shaft begin to turn. "Someone is

going down or coming up," said Masopha. Soon we saw men in rubber boots, dirty jumpsuits and hardhats exiting the shaft and shuffling across the road toward a low building Masopha called the change room. This was where his father now worked. In ntate Lerata's earlier days at the mine he went down the shaft, but because of an accident which injured his leg his current job was to supervise the workers after they exited the mine and washed off and changed clothes to make sure they weren't trying to smuggle anything out.

But ntate Lerata was on his day off and still hanging out at the hospital where we had left him. When Masopha and I returned, there was an ambulance van and two drivers parked out front. But there was no emergency, no action, no movement. They were just there. And of course, they asked me to take pictures of them beside their ambulance. I shot them. And then I drove us back off the mine grounds. The security guard waved us out. I did so much journalism! I'm leaving with a million photos!

On the road I asked ntate Lerata how much money miners made. He said someone like Keletso started at about 2,000 rand per month, which is about $285, and which is more than a teacher's starting salary. And then a captain would make up to 9 or 10,000, which is something like $1,400 per month. I didn't ask about ntate Lerata's salary directly, but I guessed it was somewhere in the middle. So he had raised, or was still raising, six children on a salary of not more than $1,000 a month.

Ntate Lerata didn't live in a dormitory like Keletso anymore. He had his own place off the mine grounds now, which was where we were headed. We drove north toward the town of Welkom and on the edge of town is a township of simple houses called Thabong. Historically, this was where blacks lived, separate from whites, who lived in the town proper. To this day only blacks live in Thabong. But ntate Lerata didn't live in Thabong. Farther from town was Manny's, another township for blacks. But we didn't stop there either. Past Manny's was a weedy field of tin shacks on the side of the road. The shacks were spread across the empty flats and since it was winter there were many fires burning throughout. We motored past children warming themselves around piles of blazing trash, and my rental car barely cleared the ruts and holes in the dirt track. I had entered a jumble of smoke and tin and litter. In the South African media, these places were euphemistically called "informal settlements." Colloquially, they were known as "squatter camps." Or, by the people who lived there they were called a "location." This location was called Hani Park. We arrived at ntate Lerata's place: a tin shack, the exterior of which had been painted brown. He immediately asked me to take some pictures of the place. Masopha's mother came outside, as she was visiting from Lesotho, which she did often, and she wanted her photo taken, beside her plot of *moroho* between the shack and the dirt track. You can take a Mosotho out of Lesotho, but she will still grow a plot of *moroho*. I think if you sent a Mosotho to the moon she would immediately start sowing seeds of spinach and chard and mustard. Ntate Lerata then told me to take his picture as he stood next to his pit latrine around back. Finally, I took a picture of everyone in front of the shack: Lerata, his wife, Masopha, and Nteboheleng, who is one of Masopha's sister's daughters, who had accompanied Masopha's mother on the visit from Lesotho. They stood in front of the brown shack, between the plot of *moroho* and an old white truck that no longer worked and was up on blocks. Ntate Lerata used to drive that truck back and forth between Hani Park and Lesotho. The first time I'd met him he had been driving it. But the truck was now broken, and so were his eyes. "I'll kill someone if I drive these days," he said. He takes a taxi to the mine. I realized that I had noticed him strain to focus on seeing things. "I want Masopha to get a license so he can drive me around."

It was a chilly winter day, and the day was getting late, so when we went inside Masopha shoved some coal into a stove to warm us and smoke filled the room. But the smoky air didn't dim the glow around ntate Lerata's face as he opened a paper bag of French fries. On the way from the mine to Hani Park we had stopped by a store to pick up a special dinner that he had been talking excitedly about from the moment we left the mine. He tore the side of the bag open and the fries lay in a mound. I smelled garlic and salt. Ntate Lerata added more salt. Masopha's mother passed us each a white hot dog bun to go with the fries and we took turns grabbing handfuls of fries between bites of our buns.

GREG ALDER

Ntate Lerata made noises of enjoyment as he wolfed down the fries. After they were all gone Masopha's mother opened the quart bottle of Sprite that ntate Lerata had also bought, and she poured us cupfuls. I drank my cup, but afterward my tongue was still burning from the copious salt on the fries and so I also sipped on some water from my personal bottle. "Is that drink?" asked ntate Lerata.

"It's just water."

"Is it pure water?"

"Yes." I guess.

"I should drink pure water."

If the mine work didn't kill Lerata, his diet would. He was already taking medication for diabetes, which was probably related to his worsening vision. Yet he looked to the future.

"When you visit next time this will be a real house. I'm going to frame the walls. And they are bringing electricity here. We will buy a TV, so we can watch TV."

I had seen poles lying on the dirt track near some shacks down the way which looked like they were meant to be erected to carry electrical wires.

"The electricity comes next week," he said.

I couldn't believe that. Maybe electricity would come, but things didn't work that fast around here. I understood why the idea was so exciting for him though. Having electricity, or "power" as Basotho always translated it, was *the* sign that you lived in a better place than a village in Lesotho. Ha Motlokoa, where the family was from, just across the Tsoaing River from Tšoeneng, had no power just like Tšoeneng. So ntate Lerata felt he was moving up in the world. At the same time, he mentioned numerous times that evening how many criminals roamed Hani Park at night. "They will steal anything," he said. And he refused to let me spend the night in his shack and leave my KIA Picanto parked out front. He later made Masopha and me drive to another mineworker's house in a safer part of Welkom, where I could put the car behind the man's fence, surrounded by his guard dogs. Masopha and I would sleep there. I would much rather have lived in Ha Motlokoa, Lesotho, surrounded by mountains and rivers and pastures and stone huts than Hani Park. But for ntate Lerata

198

the mining job and the potential of life with electricity it brought, and the financial ability to send his children to school that it brought, was worth the separation from his family and being surrounded by criminals. Home still had ntate Lerata's heart though. He asked for one more photo before Masopha and I left that evening. He went into the shack's other room, the bedroom, and then a moment later he called me in. He had wrapped himself in his Basotho blanket, a blue one with yellow stripes and images of shields and crowns in black, and he was standing tall. I shot him.

AT THE FUNERAL for 'Malefa's father a cow was slaughtered, as custom required in Lesotho, and as a teacher I was one of the first to be served the beef, along with family members. I sat in 'Malefa's house beside ntate Lemphane, eating the funeral meal. I hoped 'Malefa would pull through this. Back at school, Principal Tsita told me that she found money for 'Malefa's school fees. Again, I didn't ask where she had found it. That 'Malefa was in school another year was right, and as if to prove it she continued to outperform everyone in her class.

CHAPTER SEVENTEEN

Grass Is Worth Dying For

MORE THAN A MONTH into the new 2006 school year now, one of the best male students hadn't started coming to classes. It was normal for returning students to miss the first week or two, and for new students to arrive even in the second semester. There were constantly new faces appearing in the classroom. Lefike, on the other hand, was a boy from the village who was more interested in school than most, and I was concerned about his absence. Did he not have money to pay school fees like 'Malefa? His father had died my first year, so he should be able to get an orphan sponsorship. Did he get the opportunity to switch to a better school? In the staffroom, I asked 'me 'Masamuel about it.

"Lefike can't get here," she said. "He's a Ha Mareka boy and he has to pass through Ha Mokhele to get here. The Ha Mokhele boys will fight him if he tries to pass through because the shepherds from both parts of the village are disputing over grazing areas."

I recalled a day the year before when all of a sudden there was a group of shepherds battling right outside the Form D classroom where I was teaching. The shepherds traded blows with their *molamus*, and then they struck the cattle they were fighting over, on the animals' heads and hinds, trying to drive the herd in opposite directions. The cattle were nearly busting the school's barbed wire fence down, kicking up clouds of dust, and somehow the violence had excited a bull and he began trying to mount the females. One shepherd, Boholo, whom I knew from the village, got cracked well on the head and blood began to glow on his dark hair. His sister, who was a student and who was watching the fight, started to wail and plead for them to stop.

So I imagined Lefike having to stick fight like this with other shepherds in order to get to school. It occurred to me that another boy who had also inexplicably not shown up for classes yet this year was also from Lefike's part of the village, Ha Mareka. His name was Lefu.

"But Molefe's here!" I blurted to 'me 'Masamuel as it occurred to me. He was a third boy from Ha Mareka. How had he come to school when Lefike and Lefu hadn't?

"Maybe Molefe wants to provoke the Ha Mokhele boys so he can avenge his father's death. They will just kill Molefe too." She said it matter-of-factly. 'Me 'Masamuel knew a lot about Tšoeneng village disputes because she had grown up here, in Ha Mareka to be exact, though she now lived with her husband closer to Maseru.

"How childish," I said.

"What is?"

"Dying over grass."

"Should they not take it seriously?"

"That's just it. They should take it very seriously, and therefore they shouldn't fight like children. They should solve the matter in a mature way." I was in a cantankerous mood, and also 'me 'Masamuel was fun to argue with. You didn't even have to prod her into conversation; all she ever wanted to do was talk. She was loud, she loved to discuss things, and that was part of the reason she was late getting out of her staffroom chair and getting to her classes on time. The bell always rang while 'me 'Masamuel was in the middle of a discussion.

"How?" she asked me. "What would you do if you found someone grazing his cattle on your land? Would you not try to drive them off?"

"Can't you go tell the chief?"

"Then the chief sends his men to drive them off, and a fight breaks out. It's the same thing."

That was what had happened on that day the year before. One group of shepherds had been sent by the chief to drive the cattle to the chief's corral to impound the animals for grazing in a reserved pasture. As the two groups of men fought over the herd of cattle, all of the students and teachers emptied the classrooms and lined up along the barbed-wire fence to watch. (Another canceled class. I had been teaching Shakespeare's *Twelfth Night* to the Form D's, and I couldn't blame them for wanting to trade reading about 16th century dandies pretending to fight for the live action of their brothers and neighbors bloodying one another.) "You're going to break my fence!" shouted Principal Tsita at the shepherds, but they paid her no attention. The men were shouting at one another. I stood next to ntate Lemphane, and he told me which group was the chief's men and that the other shepherds would be judged once the cattle were successfully impounded. The fight was evenly matched, but the chief's men were proving slightly more forceful and the groups and cattle slowly migrated down the path to the east toward the village and eventually out of sight.

"Can't you tell the police?" I asked 'me 'Masamuel in the staffroom, trying to think of an alternative to having a grazing dispute turn into a stick fight.

"Out here if you try to tell the police they never do anything. They always say, 'We don't have a vehicle to come way out there.'" Then she added with sadness, "They always just say they don't have enough vehicles for us."

I was experimenting at this life. I had grown up in a suburban neighborhood of a very rich country, and now I was spending a few years living like people in Tšoeneng, a rural village in a very poor country. Yet having a few years under my belt was really only having a slice of time, and there were still so many things that I didn't understand. I had seen the way the hostelers lived, I had been to Masopha's father's mine and his shack, I grew my own plot of *moroho* and I cooked *papa* every day. I knew some things, but many I didn't. My life wasn't theirs, it was an approximation of theirs.

But I wanted to understand, and I tried to analyze the conversation with 'me 'Masamuel. I wanted to really feel how grass could be worth dying for, so I traced the steps. If cattle didn't have enough grass to graze on, the animals would be too weak to plow the fields. If cattle couldn't plow, then you couldn't plant your fields. If you couldn't plant your fields, then you wouldn't have food. Many people in Tšoeneng didn't have employment beyond subsistence farming. They had no money coming in with which to buy food. They had to grow it. So it was very direct: if their cattle didn't have enough grass, then they didn't have enough food. No grass, no food. No food, no life. Life is worth dying for.

CHAPTER EIGHTEEN

Daughters

LEFIKE AND LEFU did eventually start coming to school again. The heat of the battle over grazing rights must have simmered down. Some new hostelers arrived too, with their trunks of clothing and foam mattresses and blankets and pots. Among them was a boy named Richard who was from Masopha's village. There was also Masopha's younger sister Mariti, plus a girl named Motšilisi who was from a village to the east called Thabana Tšoana—Little White Mountain—and two girls from near Maseru who quickly became best friends, Tholang and Makhala.

The shuffling in the cast of characters who lived in the hostel—because some graduated, some could no longer afford school, some got married, and some left for better schools—was good for my confidence. I actually felt more at home in Tšoeneng than the newcomers.

Tholang and Makhala started spending more time at my house than any of the other hostelers, even the ones who I'd known since the beginning like Tumelo and Nthabiseng. The girls were both in Form A, and they were attached at the hip. I started thinking of them as sisters. They came over my house together and left together. At first I helped them with their math homework or English compositions or religion assignments, then I handed them my Sesotho memo book and a red pen so they could correct things I had written in their language—typical interactions between me and hostelers. Students were strictly forbidden from having red pens at school, so that was thrilling for them to feel like a teacher and use a red pen to point out my errors. Then Tholang and Makhala stopped leaving. It would be dinner time and I was hungry, and I needed to go pick *moroho* and start cooking *papa*, but the sisters were still hanging about inside looking at my photo album, asking to listen to another song on the radio. "I need to go pick *moroho*."

"Give me your basin, sir. I will pick for you."

It was a kind offer, but I really just wanted them to go back to the hostel so I could get on with my evening routine. I needed down time from the students, when I could rejuvenate in the quiet of an empty room. But Makhala had already fetched my blue basin, and she was walking out the door toward my plot.

I shouldn't have been surprised. In Lesotho, students served their teachers. I had learned that. Every day at lunchtime we teachers sat in the staffroom and students came in to retrieve our plates, take them to the kitchen, and bring them back full of food. After we finished eating, students took our dirty plates, washed them at the pump, and returned them to the staffroom. Teachers were thirsty then. *"Hela, Puseletso! Tlo koano!"* 'me 'Masamuel shouted out the door. And when the girl arrived, "Bring me water." Puseletso picked up a jug from the table in the staffroom, filled it at the pump, and presented it with both hands to 'me 'Masamuel. It was no different than being waited on in a restaurant. We teachers never left our chairs during the lunch hour, except sometimes to move them outside to sit in the open air. Even then 'me 'Masamuel would walk outside and call a student to come get her chair from inside the staffroom and set it on the stoop for her.

Being served by the students made me very uncomfortable at first. I hadn't grown up serving the adults around me. Mostly in the U.S. it was the other way around, adults cater to their children. So while I went along with the other teachers during lunch, on my own I refused offers of help made by the students. They would try to take a stack of notebooks from my arms as I walked to class. "Let me carry for you, sir." A student would appear by my side at the chalkboard asking to erase for me. At the water pump, hostelers always offered to take over filling my buckets and haul them back down to my house. No thanks, no thanks, no thanks. In the beginning I didn't understand why they offered to help with everything. I thought they thought I was incompetent and in need of assistance. I wanted to show them that I was capable, strong enough, and not entitled. Later, I just wanted to be more respectful than the other teachers. Some of them treated the students like slaves. 'Me 'Masamuel never said thank you and she never said please, she just shouted orders from her chair in the staffroom. If she didn't like the portions a student had dished up for her at lunch, she let out her high-pitched shriek, "*Hey uena, Puseletso!* This is too much *papa.* Come take some off."

Over time though I learned that the students offered help not because they thought I couldn't help myself, but because that is how students in Lesotho are taught to treat their teachers. It was an extension of how children are taught to treat their elders in general. As Masopha had told me long ago, "Children are for sending." And 'me 'Masamuel didn't thank Puseletso for fetching her plate because it wasn't something supererogatory. In Lesotho, children serve their elders as a matter of duty. Thanking them for doing their duty would be as superfluous as thanking them for not stealing.

So this was the culture I was dropped into. You worked your way through youth, and once there were people younger than you it was time to start giving orders. 'Me 'Masamuel had fetched water, brought chairs, and erased chalkboards when she was young. Now she was on the other side. I just happened to enter the culture on the other side. I was a senior, a teacher, someone to be served from the beginning. It took me a little while to recognize my timing as lucky and not something to feel guilty or awkward about. Even after three years I was still adjusting to it.

As soon as Makhala left to gather *moroho* for my dinner, Tholang asked, "Sir, where is your maize meal?"

"In the cupboard there."

"Let me cook for you."

"It's OK. I can cook *papa.*"

She got the bag of maize meal from my cupboard anyway, and she poured water into a pot. Makhala returned from picking *moroho* and washing it at the pump, and she began chopping it. Once Tholang had the *papa* cooking, she asked for my broom. Before she stooped to sweep she asked, "May you play for us DJ

Bongs?" I put the CD into the radio and turned up the volume. I was losing some alone time, but how could I complain? The sisters danced as they cooked and cleaned. I eventually sat back down and flipped through my Sesotho memo book. Here I was, the teacher, in a leisure activity while my students worked. I was the senior, relaxing, while the youth were busy. For Lesotho, the scene was proper.

By April, there was a daily routine. Tholang and Makhala knocked on the door sometime after school, asked me to turn on the radio, and then swept, cooked, washed my dishes, my clothes, or whatever other chores were available. I ate well and lived in a very clean house, and the only effort required of me was allowing the local culture to proceed around me—that and keeping the batteries in the radio charged.

THOLANG AND MAKHALA never *had* to come over to my house in the first place. I guessed that they chose to because they liked me and they liked to listen to my radio. And I bought CDs that we all liked: DJ Bongs, Revolution, Bojo Mujo. (They didn't like Sesotho music so much; they liked this South African house music better.) Also, they liked my house. It had two chairs and a table. It had a shiny floor covering, painted walls, a ceiling, bright light because of its many unbroken windows, a slightly cementy but mostly neutral odor. Doesn't sound like much to ask for? Visit the girls' hostel.

One time I did in order to deliver some oranges. It was a Saturday, and I had gone to Maseru earlier that morning. While I was on my way from my house to the road, walking toward getting a taxi to the capital, dreaming of the KFC meal I would eat once I got there, Maleshoane Ramokone (the girl who had interrupted Mpatsi and me) shouted at me from the window of the girls' hostel, *"U tla ntlele le'ng?"*

"I'll bring you an orange. I'm going to the Home of the Oranges, right?"

"And for Likhapha. Thank you, ntate."

Oranges were special treats in Lesotho. It got too cold in the winter for citrus trees to survive there, so you could only buy imported ones. And for Tšoeneng people, the oranges were imported through Maseru, hence the nickname for the capital, *Habo Lilamunu*—Home of the Oranges.

When I returned from Maseru I knocked on the hostel door, *"Koko."*

"E, ntate," said Maleshoane from inside.

I walked into the dark room. Maleshoane lit a candle and I saw that she and Likhapha were lying on a mattress under blankets. It was dusk, but since the hostel only had one window it turned dark in there long before it was night outside. "Why are you in bed so early?"

"Likhapha is sick," said Maleshoane. But the hostelers were always saying they were sick, and it looked to me like they just hadn't felt like wasting a candle on this lonely night. It was the end of the month, and all of the other hostelers had gone home to visit their families for the weekend. I gave them both an orange.

I looked around. Even in the feeble candlelight I noticed the grime and dilapidation. There was only one window and it had broken panes and a sheet of tin leaned against it to cover the openings. The bare walls were dirty and damaged. Clothes hung from them on nails. The floor was concrete and cracked, on which metal trunks and foam mattresses, wash basins, blankets and stacks of books lay. Seven girls were housed in this one room. The place stunk of paraffin, even though no one was burning a stove at the moment. The hostel had a constant stench of paraffin. Overhead were torn ceiling boardsheets revealing the rafters that supported the tin roof. As I looked up Maleshoane said, "They scare us."

"Who?"

"The rats."

I imagined them scurrying across the rafters. Up above the ceiling in my house lived a colony of bats, but they didn't bother me. I heard rustling each evening as they took flight from the eaves, but that was it. I felt sorry for Maleshoane and Likhapha, and Tholang and Makhala, and all of the hostel girls for having to live there. At the same time, I knew that the hostel was a wreck partly because of them. Their walls were dented because they played a lot and broke things. I heard them. The place stunk like liquid gas because they carelessly spilled it when refilling their stoves. There was no longer a handle on their door because they had broken it when they slammed it too hard during a game of chase.

Nevertheless, when I returned to my house that night it seemed more luxurious than it ever had before. This very house seemed plain and lacking when I first moved in. It had no toilet or shower, no running water at all. It had no lights or outlets, no electricity at all. It had no couch, no TV, no computer, no heating system, and certainly no air conditioning. The windows didn't even have screens. I had just come from living in American houses built with every amenity imaginable. But over the years in Tšoeneng my frame of reference changed. I stopped comparing my house to the houses I had lived in in America, and I started comparing it to the abodes around me, like the girls' hostel, compared to which it shined.

Likewise, my general sense of wealth and contentment evolved. People in Tšoeneng often said to me, "Americans are rich." And in my early days I responded, "Actually, some Americans are rich, but some Americans are poor." But that wasn't true if Americans were compared to them. They were right. Americans were all rich. Even the poorest had light switches in their houses and could afford to buy an orange. Wealth is such a relative concept.

So even though my house was cruder than any I'd lived in before, and my diet was more limited than ever—as was my amount of material possessions—I felt secure and satisfied for the first time in my adult life. Maybe it was because for the first time in my adult life I was wealthier than some of my neighbors. I say some because even though I lived better than many of my students, I was the second-to-lowest paid teacher at Ngoana Jesu. Or maybe it was because having less material possessions meant that I had less to lose, and possessions could so easily become a burden like that, where you don't want to let friendly visitors in your house because you are so afraid of them seeing your camera and radio. You'll lose potential friends to keep things. Owning less somehow made me fear less. In addition to oranges, I had purchased a block of cheese in Maseru that day, and after I left the girls' hostel I sat in my plastic chair at my plywood table and nibbled on slices from the cheddar block. I wanted for nothing.

ONE DAY AFTER SCHOOL, Tholang and Makhala accompanied me rock climbing. I did most of the climbing, and the sisters stood by the boulders and chatted and watched. A shepherd came over to join us as often happened when I climbed, but this shepherd wasn't interested in my battles with the boulder. He spoke to the girls, in a low voice so I couldn't hear, and that I knew meant he was proposing. Soon, the sisters walked away from him. The shepherd followed them over to me and said, "Can I have one of your daughters, ntate Thabang?"

I was used to people referring to the hostelers as my children. We were like a family down there on the school compound, living together, helping one another, isolated from the rest of the village. In the beginning, I thought of Principal Tsita as the mother figure and ntate Lemphane as the father, since he was the only man at Ngoana Jesu. I thought of myself as a child, even less independent and less skilled at life than the hostelers. More recently, I started to think of the hostelers as my siblings. Despite my status as teacher, and the hostelers as students, I felt on an even level with them. I was a bit older and worldlier than them in some ways, but living in their homeland meant that they were more competent than me in most ways that mattered on a local, daily basis. However, on our way back down the mountain that day, I looked at Tholang and Makhala and thought that they actually could be my children. They were young, only in the eighth grade, and at this point in my third year I finally knew enough Sesotho and enough of the culture for others, any others, to be considered my junior. It had taken that long.

The sisters always called me sir or ntate—father—just as every student did. I learned that neither of them had a real father. Tholang's had died just the year before. She showed me a photo of him dressed in Xhosa attire. He had been from that tribe, the same as Nelson Mandela. Makhala's father had been Principal Tsita's brother. After his death, Principal Tsita took Makhala under her wing and brought her down to school at Ngoana Jesu.

Makhala had plump cheeks. She was also short like Principal Tsita. It was easy to see the relation. Tholang, on the other hand, was a little taller and thinner. She had a lower lip that stuck out a bit and made her look always innocent, and when her mother visited school one day I saw the similarities between those two. Tholang's mother looked too thin though; Basotho women are only thin if they're sick or poor. Tholang said that her mother sometimes found work cleaning houses of wealthy families in Maseru, which I knew couldn't alone sustain Tholang and her two siblings.

Tholang and Makhala were both unquestionably cute girls. And though students never made any public displays of affection, I was sure boys liked these two, and proposed to them often. I couldn't help but start to keep an eye on them. I knew what it felt like to have a missing father, and I imagined their fathers appreciating me standing in where they couldn't. Being poor, the girls were especially vulnerable to taxi drivers and conductors, who were infamous for giving girls free rides and then asking for sexual favors in return, as had happened with Mpatsi. The two were decent students, Tholang being slightly better in English, but they were teenage girls, and mischief was available everywhere. I was pleased to discover one day that their taste for trouble was vanilla, or chocolate.

At my house Tholang asked, "Sir, why are you throwing away the chocolates?"

"What? What chocolates?"

"The ones that look like money."

I recalled putting some chocolate coins that a friend had sent from the States in the trash because they had become old and spoiled and whitish. "How do you know?" I asked.

"We saw you," said Makhala.

"No you didn't."

I had thrown that trash out at night, when no one could have seen me. Then I also remembered that I hadn't burned it, a rare mistake. I was aware that hostelers and passing shepherds would poke through my trash pile if I didn't incinerate it immediately. The pile was particularly tempting to the hostel girls because it was near the path to their toilets.

"Yes sir. We saw you."

"No you didn't. Did you eat them?!"

"Nooo."

"Yes you did." I could tell by the look on their faces. "You're going to get sick," I said. "You're going to have to go to the clinic."

They confessed. They ate the chocolate coins. And then they implicated Masopha's sister, Mariti, because she had also put something from my trash pile in her mouth. "She is now using your toothbrush," said Tholang.

"Tell her she will have to go to the clinic too. I used that toothbrush to clean my toilet."

WE WERE IN THE SECOND QUARTER of the school year now, April of 2006, and the weather had started to fall toward winter. The rains were few and far between. The grasses were dying. During morning break between third and fourth period, Tholang came limping over to my house to give me some bread. She knew how much I loved the bread she baked. "Run, Tholang, Run!" I shouted. I took the gift of bread and I didn't ask why she was limping. After school I heard crying coming from the girls' hostel. Makhala came over, "My father, could you help Tholang to go to the clinic?" I hadn't realized Tholang's leg hurt that bad. I told Makhala to bring her over so I could look at it. Tholang came limping over with Makhala's shoulder bearing most of her weight. On her calf there was an open wound that was swollen. From my bookshelf, I grabbed *Where There's No Doctor* and read until I tentatively diagnosed her wound as an infection that needed antibiotics. She needed pills, which had to be paid for. Tholang sometimes didn't have enough money to pay for food.

I felt like I was in a familiar dilemma. This was like deciding how to help 'Malefa pay her school fees. It had to get done, but did I have to be the one to fork over the dough? Did I have to let money enter one of my relationships in Tšoeneng again? I only debated for seconds this time.

"Go to the clinic," I said. "And if they want money, tell me how much." Makhala gave her sister her shoulder and hauled her up the path to the village and the clinic.

They returned a half hour later, however, to say it was closed. I heard Tholang cry out in pain from time to time in the hostel that night, and in the morning she hobbled over to my house with Makhala's help and I took another look at her leg. She could barely put weight on it now. She was grimacing and teary-eyed. The wound was a mountain of pus. I gave her 50 rand and Makhala again gave her shoulder. I told Principal Tsita why Tholang and Makhala were missing class. When they returned from the clinic, Tholang had a white bandage wrapped around her brown leg. She said they cleaned it and gave her a bottle of pills. I referenced the antibiotic medicine's name in *Where There's No Doctor* just to see if the clinic had prescribed what the book suggested, and it did. Tholang was still in just as much pain, I could tell by the way she limped, but by having started the process to recovery her face belied a buoyed spirit.

People mattered. Money was a tool that I had been able to use to help a friend, a daughter, and I should have never even thought twice about it. At least it took me less deliberation than it had to help 'Malefa with her school fees. I was getting faster at knowing when to bend the rules and where to find the balance between witlessly dishing out money and miserly keeping it all tight and to myself. Still it wasn't yet intuitive when to help and how to help, and what was actually help and what was not.

Over the following days, Tholang's pain lessened as the wound healed. Soon her energy and smile returned. She was back to walking normally, and back to asking me to play a CD so she and Makhala could dance as they helped me with chores. Before she was fully cured she needed one more fill of pills from the clinic. The total I gave her was 70 rand, about $10.

IN EARLY MAY, I had just returned from rock climbing when I decided to rush up to Motsie's shop to buy a few things before the sun set. The hostel students were about the school grounds washing their uniforms and hanging them to dry. When I reached the school gate Lipolelo, a hosteler in Form E, came up to me and said, "They took Motšilisi. They're going to marry her."

I walked through the school gate and found a group of girls

standing on the path all staring to the north. I looked that way. In the distance, there was the long, flat top of Qeme Plateau, crowned in orange sandstone. But that was far off. The girls were looking into the nearby fields. Yellow and stiff as old men this time of year, the maize and sorghum stalks rustled in the breeze. Among them sprang a scene of flapping blankets, arms and sticks. I focused and figured it out to be two guys and a girl. The guys were yanking on the girl's arms. As the girl wriggled, one of the guys lifted up his *molamu* and hit her with it. I heard the snap of the thick wood stick on the girl's body. She yelped. It was true: Motšilisi was being kidnapped.

She was a hosteler who was in Tholang and Makhala's class. When I first met her she had been nervous around me because her English was poor, but once she saw that she could use Sesotho with me too she became more comfortable and talkative. I knew that she came from a village to the west called Thabana Tšoana, but I didn't know if she had a boyfriend. Of course, I didn't know if any of the hostel girls had a boyfriend.

I stepped onto a nearby anthill to get a better look. Motšilisi continued to scream. The guys continued to drag her away from school, deeper into the fields. She was writhing in their grasp. I didn't know what to make of it.

Two students from Ngoana Jesu had been kidnapped for marriage the year before. The practice was called *chobeliso*. I was vaguely familiar with it. Masopha had once explained to me how it worked. A boy likes a girl, so the boy proposes marriage to the girl. Then the girl says no. The girl always says no at first. But if the boy doesn't want to continue wooing her he sets up an abduction, usually with the help of a friend. The two guys kidnap the girl and hide her in a donga in the fields until it's dark, and then they take her to the boy's parents' house. The boy says to his father, "Here is the girl I want to marry." The father then sends a message to the girl's father explaining the situation, and if the girl's father approves of the boy and his family, and agrees to the bride price offered for his daughter, which is typically six head of cattle, then a sheep is slaughtered and the girl eats some of the sheep, and the marriage is a done deal. That's what Masopha told me.

Motšilisi was fighting hard, but I could see that she would

never escape these two strong men with sticks. I felt a call to action. These hostel girls were my daughters. But would interfering be helping? There was Mamphe, a Form C girl who'd reportedly been kidnapped for marriage during my first year. I saw her in the village often these days. She lived as a housewife and I passed her each time I went rock climbing. She greeted me, smiled, said life was good for her, asked me to bring her candy sometime.

One of the men then struck Motšilisi on the legs with his *molamu* to subdue her and her legs buckled. I was sure her resistance was real and I was sure that what they were doing to her was wrong. I needed to run them down. But then what? When the men saw me, my white face, would they have the curious reaction of the children in the village who seemed mesmerized by my appearance, or would they have the vengeful reaction of the shepherds who'd directed the dirt bike racer up a cliff? Would they drop Motšilisi and beat on me? Either way, could I stand there and watch Motšilisi disappear into the maize? Could I stand there until her calls for help faded out?

As if having heard my internal debate, one of the hostel girls on the path, Nthabiseng, looked up at me and said, "Those guys will shoot you."

I didn't want to be a meddler in Lesotho. I wanted to keep my nose out of others' business, especially cultural scenarios I didn't fully understand. It was possible that if I did go rescue Motšilisi, I might bring her back and everyone would say, "Why did you go and do that? *Chobeliso* is how things work here. Leave it alone. That's why we liked you, because you didn't tell us how to live. We thought you were a different kind of foreigner." I shouldn't presumptuously get involved in things like I had with the rental books and the newspapers and the Ministry of Education. Like my mom said, I should let them solve their problems. I figured I probably didn't understand the full picture, like I hadn't with the shepherds fighting over grazing lands. And really, this was another situation like I had when presented with the prospect of pursuing my attraction to Mpatsi. Was I American, or was I Mosotho? My American values told me with penetrating clarity that kidnapping someone for any reason was wrong. I had to try and stop it. But Sesotho values said differently. Frankly, they might have said just the opposite. Every year I spent in Lesotho its values made themselves felt within me more and the American values I grew up with were felt less. Whereas I once *felt* American values and *thought* about what Sesotho values were. (I *felt* so lazy when I didn't go teach during the rain in my first year, and I *thought* about why the teachers didn't go to class in the rain.) Now my thoughts and feelings were becoming conflated. Or at least now I was confused. Was I culturally an American? Or was I a Mosotho? And what in the world do I do right this moment because Motšilisi is getting hit again and again as I ruminate? She is getting dragged farther and farther away.

A hostel boy came running to the gate. It was Richard. He looked into the fields and then he yelled to the other boys back at the hostel, "They took Motšilisi. Let's go!" And then ntate Matlali showed up beside me. Ntate Lemphane also arrived at the gate. He had been pumping water, and when he reached where I was standing he put his bucket down and briefly looked off into the fields. Then he said, "Ntate Thabang, let's go!"

Like a pack of dogs in chase, we tramped through the fields and hopped over ditches for a quarter mile, never slowing, pumped with adrenalin, until Motšilisi appeared running toward us. The kidnappers hadn't been able to hold onto her as they ran from us. She ran by, back toward school, moaning incoherently and trying to refasten the blanket that had been torn from her waist.

The two kidnappers split up. One darted into a maize field, and the other jumped over a creek and ran up a hill. Ntate Lemphane, without slowing his pace, picked up a large rock and ran up the hill and hucked it at the closest kidnapper. He missed. Then the hostel boys followed ntate Lemphane's lead and picked up rocks and began throwing them too. "Hey, you! Hey, you!" they yelled as they chased. The kidnapper's run was slowed as he had faced us to try to dodge the rocks, and we all—about ten of us—eventually encircled him.

The kidnapper pleaded, "There's no problem!" His Basotho blanket had fallen off and now he was just wearing a black t-shirt. "There's no problem!" He turned round and round looking for an escape, but we had him surrounded and the hostel boys continued throwing rocks. They missed, or grazed him, until Tumelo, the fastidious hosteler who had cut my hair, heaved a football-sized rock with all his might and struck Black Shirt square in the back of the head. Black Shirt went limp and fell to the ground face first.

The school boys, always so docile in class, still didn't stop throwing rocks. They hit him a couple more times. I would witness a stoning. As he made an attempt to get onto all fours, I saw blood on Black Shirt's head. Then Tumelo stepped up to him, took Black Shirt's *molamu*, and whacked him across the back. This dropped the kidnapper prostrate once again. Maybe they wouldn't stone him.

I felt nothing. I wasn't scared or hungry for more blood. I was detached. I hadn't made a decision about whether to interfere and rescue Motšilisi. I had only followed the others' lead. And now I was like a piece of air caught up in a wind. The boys had become an animal mob, ripping their prey apart, truly vicious. But I was just floating with it all. I wasn't throwing rocks. I wasn't hitting Black Shirt. I wasn't speaking. I wasn't thinking. I was just there.

Tumelo grabbed Black Shirt by the arm and said, "We're going to the chief." The other boys helped drag the man to his feet. Black Shirt wobbled as Tumelo held onto his arm. "To the chief's!" Tumelo yelled.

I finally got a steady look at Black Shirt then. He was short, maybe 30 years old, and nowhere on his face did I read fear. Blood pumped from his head, coursing over his ear. He continued arguing, "It's nothing. There's no problem. It's nothing!"

The mob shouted back. "Hurry up!" And one of the boys, Teboho, hit Black Shirt again across the back with the *molamu* they had taken from him. "Shut up!" Another boy, Taelo, kicked him in the leg. The kidnapper hunt had awakened warriors in these hostel boys.

The farther we walked toward the village, the more each boy prodded and shouted at Black Shirt. And they started smiling as they did so. As we walked, they began to recount the capture and laugh. They took turns hitting Black Shirt and commanding "Stay on the trail!" or "Go faster!"

Then a boy named Majoro stopped the parade. "Put your hands there," he said to Black Shirt, indicating a large anthill. "We'll beat you now and you won't have to go to the chief for punishment." It was just Majoro's idea though, and the group debated. In the end, we decided to continue toward the village.

Night had fallen by the time we reached the chief's place. We all stood in front of his house in the dark, near some rocks where meetings were often held with the elder men of the village. As we told Chief Thabo who we had brought to him, Black Shirt went on, "There's no problem. There's no problem." For the first time I saw that the guy was drunk. His head swayed as he spoke. No wonder he hadn't looked afraid.

"Who's your mother?" asked someone from the crowd. A number of village men had heard the commotion and gathered around now.

"I already have a wife," said Black shirt. "There's no problem."

"Where are you from?!" someone else shouted.

"Ha Sello," he said finally.

Black Shirt wasn't from our village. No one knew him. But we knew that Ha Sello was part of Thabana Tšoana, the same village as Motšilisi, a few hours' walk away in the direction he had been dragging her. Chief Thabo then asked our group to tell him exactly what had happened. Ntate Lemphane told the hostel boy who first called the others to chase Black Shirt down, Richard, to speak. As they learned the details, the village men, who now numbered about fifty, began calling out, "Let me beat him!"

When the story was finished Chief Thabo went into his house. The crowd of men tightened around Black Shirt. "Give him to me. I'll beat him!" The crowd continued to ask questions—"Do you even have a job?"—and they grew angrier, their voices rising. There was no moon and the dense darkness seemed conducive to anonymous violence. It also was suitable for me to go unnoticed. Only one village guy arriving at the chief's place had greeted me, but otherwise no one paid me any attention. To make sure that continued, I pulled up the hood on my sweatshirt, and as the night proceeded I began to feel I was not only floating and watching but even invisible. No matter what the event in Lesotho, in the past the attention was always redirected to me, from the first day at the initiation ceremony when all of the women and children had set their eyes on me as I looked down the part in their crowd to watch the new men sing. But here I was disrupting nothing.

We were tightly bound around Black Shirt. As each threat followed another, I waited for the impending first blow, for words to be abandoned and for Black shirt to be devoured. Chief Thabo emerged from his house carrying a rope. He gave the rope to another older man who began tying Black Shirt's hands behind his back. He won't even be able to fight back. This is going to be brutal. The older man wound and wound and wound, and as he did he said, "You don't take a girl from school! From school! Do you see how you've troubled these teachers?!" He indicated ntate Lemphane, ntate Matlali, and me.

"Wait until a girl finishes school!" shouted someone.

Then when he'd used up all the rope, the old man led Black Shirt away, into Chief Thabo's house. The crowd then quickly disbursed. Quietly, like a meeting adjourned, the fifty men who had been threatening to mutilate a man only seconds earlier now walked off into the night.

"What's happening?" I whispered to ntate Lemphane.

"Maybe in the morning, when the guy's sober, he will be able to answer for himself better," he said. "There's nothing Chief Thabo can do now since the guy is from another village. Chief Thabo must consult the other chief." I walked with ntate Lemphane and ntate Matlali on the pitch black path back to school.

"Now you have a story to tell your friends in America," said ntate Matlali. That was true. That had been an adventurous evening. But storytelling was far from my mind. I was thinking about how tonight had been the first time I felt sure I had done the right thing in Lesotho. And it was the first time I hadn't influenced an event I was witness to in Lesotho. I hadn't meddled and the story hadn't changed course because of my presence. I was just another guy who was there through it all. That might seem like a very low goal to shoot for, but in fact it felt incredibly satisfying and it had taken almost three years to achieve.

The next morning, Lebusa, a Form B student and the chief's son, came to school with news that Black Shirt had vanished in the night. He'd been tied up to a chair in Chief Thabo's house, but sometime before morning he had freed himself from the ropes and slipped out the window.

CHAPTER NINETEEN

Snow

THROUGH THE WINTER BREAK from school, I went up to Maseru to help train a new group of Peace Corps volunteers. I was now the most seasoned volunteer in the country. I seemed very knowledgeable to the group of trainees. I knew the geography, the culture, the language. A girl asked how long it had taken me to become fluent in Sesotho. I didn't feel fluent in Sesotho, I told her. But to her ear for the language, after only some weeks in the country, I understood how I might sound so. I remembered having the same impression of older volunteers when I arrived. I envied how easily they seemed to converse and travel from place to place and read cultural cues. I told the group that I would have little left to teach them in only a short while. It was an honest prediction. It was amazing how much and how quickly you could learn when you were immersed, if you were open to it.

School reopened as we headed toward spring. On Monday, July 31, the wind blew and I seized the teaching moment and wrote the word "blustery" on the chalkboard in the Form C classroom and pointed the students to look out the window. The winds had arrived exactly one day early. August was the windy month, and I thought of it as the worst month in Lesotho. Every day the dead brown earth of winter was blown into a dust that turned the sky a fulvous haze. You had grit in your ears, dirt between your teeth, and cracked lips from the desiccation. The redemption of the August winds was that they eventually blew the winter away. When the calendar flipped to September, warm air filled in and, like clockwork, the grasses sprouted and the thunderstorms of summer would shortly follow.

Confusingly, on Tuesday, August 1, I woke up to find the morning air back to calm. There was barely a tickle on the eucalyptus leaves, and I feared the season was retreating. As much as I disliked August and its winds, I looked forward to their arrival as a sign that it was transitioning into summer, the best season in Lesotho. Later that morning a bank of charcoal clouds appeared on the western horizon, and slowly the dark wall marched toward Ngoana Jesu until the 10 o'clock break between classes when it started dumping rain upon our heads. Storms were infrequent in winter. This rain did not stop. It continued through the night and into Wednesday. I watched it from inside my house that morning as it puddled the already muddy ground. The students were up in their classrooms, but I had come down with a cold, having felt the first menacing scratch in my throat during the last class period on Tuesday afternoon. The illness had traveled up into my head overnight, and now I stood at my window staring dumbly at the drops crashing into the glass, hoping to distract myself from the discomfort. I had already called in sick, which meant calling over a hosteler from my door and asking her to tell Principal Tsita. Then the rain drops began acting funny. They appeared to bang into the window and stick. Was I that sick? I shook my head and lengthened my focus and saw that the rain now floated dizzily toward the ground. Everything was in slow motion. And white. The ground was turning white. It was snowing.

The peaks around Tšoeneng got capped with every winter storm, but the village, at about 5,000 feet in elevation, was sometimes too low and got cold rain instead of snow. I preferred the snow. There was something oxymoronic about it. Africa is the hot place. It's the searing sun of the Sahara and the savannah, or the humid heat of the jungle. It's not snow. I considered the juxtaposition of words—Africa; snow—and I forgot about the pounding in my stuffed-up head.

What about the poor students in class? They sat on wood benches wearing all the gloves and jackets and hats they owned but still couldn't stay warm with the drafts flowing in through the busted out windows. The teachers mercifully released them just before lunch. Some visited me to bring me some food from the kitchen and tell me how it had been at school that day before they went home and huddled around fires with their families as the land turned white.

Thursday was just like Wednesday, and those students who showed up in the snow were sent back home. Lemeko the climber stopped by and told me he had made a snowman, but I couldn't come see it because his little brother destroyed it with a fusillade of rocks.

Friday was still freezing, and I was still sick. I sat at my table wearing all of the jackets and gloves that I owned, plus a beanie, two pairs of socks and my Basotho blanket. I felt cold air coming from under the front door and through the cracks around the window frames. It chilled my bare face. My nose seeped constantly. I watched my breath condense.

This winter was the longest. It was very cold and it refused to quit.

Yet my first winter had hurt the most because it caught me by surprise. In early May of that year, the first frost hit and then I didn't stop shivering until I went to Durban. Having grown up in Southern California, I didn't own a jacket. I arrived in Lesotho with a hooded sweatshirt and my dad's old plumbing work coat. I brought both of those because Peace Corps told me that it got cold in Lesotho, but they also said I would be able to buy good winter clothing in South Africa if needed. When it got cold in May and I needed winter clothing I was stuck in Tšoeneng. A couple times I went up to Maseru intent on buying whatever I could find there, but the jackets I found were all so cheaply made that I couldn't get myself to spend the money. People in Tšoeneng wore blankets of course, but that was a Basotho thing. After Masopha taught me how, I wore my blanket in my house and around the school grounds and the hostelers never paid it any attention. But when I walked up into the village with it on once, a young guy I didn't know pointed me out to his friends and laughed. Wearing a Basotho blanket was like getting off a plane in Malaysia and putting on a sarong. It was ostentatiously trying to look native. I just wanted to be warm. I needed a jacket.

I went to the Peace Corps office in Maseru and got on a computer and ordered a down jacket from Patagonia, shipped to my brother's house in California. I emailed my brother and told him I was freezing over in Lesotho and could he please send that jacket to me as soon as he received it.

Back in Tšoeneng, the cold didn't abate. I survived by layering. I wore multiple shirts, then my hooded sweatshirt, then my father's coat. In the staffroom, my butt was cold on the chair and I didn't want to touch the surface of my desk. If the sun was out, I took my chair outside and set it up against the northeast-facing wall to get as much reflective heat as possible. I felt vulnerable to the air whenever it moved. I tried to keep moving myself.

At night I wished I could stop moving. In my bed I couldn't help curling up into a tighter and tighter ball all through the night, trying to get comfortable. Over me I had a sleeping blanket and my Basotho blanket (whether Masopha liked it or not), on top of which I draped my 20-degree sleeping bag, and I had all of my clothes on plus a beanie over my head. Still, on the coldest nights I woke up many times in the fetal position, unable to relax and dream.

In the morning, I dreaded leaving what protection the sleeping bag and blankets gave me. I kept my little mobile propane heater next to my bed, and I leaned over and opened the tank and clicked it lit. Once I felt that heat I was coaxed out from under the covers. I wheeled the heater around with me through the morning. I kept it right next to my plastic basin while I undressed to bathe, but the heater burned through its first propane tank quickly, and I saw that if I continued to use it like this I would run out of money. I started rationing propane by only heating water to bathe every other day. But I didn't feel good about that because my hair looked matted and felt greasy, and my feet began to stink badly. I wasn't washing them enough, and I also wasn't washing my socks since I had to use propane to heat water to comfortably wash clothes.

I never had any idea how many more cold nights there were to come, or how much colder it was going to get. I had no experience to draw from, neither in living through a Lesotho winter nor in living through a cold winter anywhere. Every day hit me like the lottery. I was stuck in Tšoeneng just dealing with each successive cold spell using whatever I had on hand, stupidly hoping it would warm up the next day.

Finally, in August, a package arrived for me containing the Patagonia down jacket. Unknowingly, I had already passed through the depth of winter at that point. At least I made it through. I was determined to handle my second winter more competently. I had a proper jacket now, and over the summer I found a third, thicker blanket to put on my bed: I was ready for the bitterness. The 2005 winter rolled in . . . and rolled right back out. It was short and relatively mild. I didn't complain, but I had kind of been looking forward to the challenge of remaining a hygienic and functioning human through a harsh season like my first winter.

I got my chance when this winter hit, my third. It was late to arrive in full force: May was chilly; June was cold; July was when I really needed to focus. Each morning I jumped out of bed slightly angry and did push-ups and sit-ups and up-downs. I ran in place and shadow boxed. It was a routine that I'd taken in part from Nelson Mandela's autobiography. He had talked about doing something similar while in prison on Robben Island. By the end of the exercise, I had built up an internal furnace of body heat, and I hadn't spent one loti on propane. I immediately undressed to bathe before I cooled down.

It worked, and midway through July I felt accomplished. I had been bathing daily and keeping my feet smelling good. With the help of my down jacket and my extra blanket I was fairly comfortable most days and nights. I even found the generosity of mood to celebrate a few things about winter in Lesotho. I appreciated that I could place a block of cheese on my cold concrete floor where it would stay as fresh as in a fridge. Also in winter, my pit latrine stopped smelling. Its contents got so cold that the odor vanished, and the flies did too. In the summer it was unnerving while I was seated over the hole and the flies buzzed up from the depths and banged into my buttocks.

The only failure of this third winter was that I quit shaving. The internal heat from my prison workout faded fast while I bathed. By the time I was finished, the water in my bucket had cooled and the water left on my skin chilled me and covered me with goosebumps. I just needed to put clothes back on and be warm again. I didn't want to spend another 10 minutes half undressed, wetting my face so I could shave. It was over the winter break from school that I let my face go, and the plan was to force myself to start shaving again once school resumed because I feared that Principal Tsita would think my beard looked lazy and unprofessional. Teachers were well-respected in Lesotho and I wanted to deserve the reputation. She showed up at school unexpectedly a few days before the opening of the third quarter and caught me with the winter harvest all over my face. I never wanted to disappoint Principal Tsita. It was like disappointing my mom. To my surprise, when she saw me she said, "Ntate Greg, you look like a man! The students will love your beard." I never shaved again.

By the end of July, I felt like I had faced the winter and mostly won. August winds would come and blow away the cold. I was done! Then August came and, instead of the spring winds, it brought the year's worst snowstorm. The season was dragging on too long for me to continue confronting it with energy. And since I was sick I felt extra weary. I would never live in a cold place again, I promised myself. Peace Corps volunteers who came from northern parts of the U.S. told me that winters there could be colder than Lesotho's in terms of temperature, but they were more bearable because you only spent brief moments outdoors: you mostly transitioned from a heated house to a heated car to a heated office or a heated store. In contrast, in Lesotho, you basically lived in the elements. No matter, I was sick of feeling so exposed to the frigid air, so afraid of my environment.

In my stuffy-headed daze I alternated between gawking at the snowflakes out the window and making coffee. In the winter, in Lesotho, it wasn't such a simple thing to turn out a hot cup since everything—the air, the water, the mug, the counter top—was so cold. Illness allowed me to reach a peculiar level of focus that day. I went through the steps with laser-point concentration: Boil water in the silver kettle. Heat mug by filling it with boiling water. Pour additional boiling water on counter under mug. Dump the water, which is now lukewarm, out of the mug, and place the strainer over it. Fill the strainer with coffee grounds. Slowly, drip hot water from the kettle over the grounds to brew through and fill the mug. Intermittently, dash the side of the mug with hot water. The process filled the room with a pleasant aroma. Eventually, I got to sit back down, my hands wrapped around a hot cup of coffee, a blanket wrapped around my shoulders, all surrounded by snow, in Africa.

CHAPTER TWENTY

Burning My *Mophato*

BY LATE AUGUST the afternoons were warm enough that I started back in the routine of climbing with Lemeko after school got out each day. It was a routine I relished, and one that I really missed during the cold of winter. It had always been about more than climbing. I got into the village, and on the way to the rocks Lemeko taught me the names of more plants. In addition to *tšoekere*, the sugar plant, he pointed out *motsukubere*, a small shrub that grew fruit inside a husk. It bore some resemblance to a tomatillo. Climbing also got me away from school and English speaking. Sometimes Lemeko and I clashed on that point. He wanted to improve his English while I wanted to speak Sesotho. It ended up that our conversations were bilingual, with Lemeko asking me a question in English, "Sir, where is Yosemite?" And me answering in Sesotho, "*E le* California."

Lemeko could, at last, make it through the entire Pacific Traverse. He was far and away better than any other student or shepherd who climbed with me. He had developed a fluid style that relied more on technique than muscle, which meant he no longer climbed like a novice. Climbing had certainly given him a confidence that he hadn't been able to find in other sports. Or that he hadn't been able to find in soccer, I should say. Soccer was really the only sport that boys played in Tšoeneng.

Whenever a friend sent me a rock climbing magazine from America, I passed it on to Lemeko and he studied it like a textbook. One day he came to me with a handwritten letter to the editor of *Climbing* magazine. In it he described himself as a young but dedicated climber from Africa, who had been introduced to the sport by his teacher from America, and he asked for help with equipment. He especially wished for shoes. I had a pair, and everyone he saw in the magazines wore special climbing shoes, so he felt like he needed them. But he climbed well barefoot. His feet were so tough that they probably had soles thicker than my shoes and the sharp surfaces of the rock didn't hurt him at all. Still, whenever I went barefoot, Lemeko put on my rock shoes and they flopped around like clown shoes on his small feet.

"Sir, will you please mail it for me?" I had to wonder where he had gotten the idea to write the letter. Had he remembered me asking his class to write letters to the Minister of Education about the rental books, and then the letter that I wrote to the editor of the *Public Eye* newspaper? I mailed it to the magazine's offices in Colorado, along with a photo I'd taken of Lemeko reaching for a hold as he moved along his favorite route, the Pacific Traverse. A few months later, a friend sent me a new issue of the magazine and an accompanying note: Did I know that one of my students' pictures was in there? The magazine had published Lemeko's letter and photo and said he could expect a little gift package of shoes and chalk and other gear in the mail. And with that Lemeko became undeniably the most equipped and famous rock climber in Lesotho.

Over the years Lemeko and I had gone all over Tšoeneng Mountain climbing every boulder and cliff face we could, and some that we couldn't, though luckily neither of us had yet taken a big fall. The most embarrassing falls were when we landed in dung, which happened to both of us from time to time. There were many mines that had been laid by both donkeys and cows, and even sheep and goats, right beneath the boulders. We climbed on the peak's summit a couple times, where we had discovered a few massive boulders, as well as a broad sloping face. We also found rock rabbits up there. They lived in the cracks of the rocks near the summit. Lemeko said some men from the village brought their dogs up there to help hunt down the rabbits. They were brown furry animals, but with smaller ears than pet bunnies.

NEVERTHELESS, OUR FAVORITE BOULDERS remained the first ones we ever climbed, where the Pacific Traverse was. Lemeko and I were there after school when he pointed to the fields in the distance down below and said, "Look at the boys. They look like a herd of animals." I saw a group of people, maybe thirty, marching toward the village. A single person on horseback raced off the front of the group and then doubled back to join the group again. Another guy on horseback took off and did the same, kicking up puffs of dust. "They are ntate Santu's men," said Lemeko. Then he pointed to another group marching through the fields toward Tšoeneng from the south, "Those ones are from Kolo."

"Ba ea kae?" I asked.

"They're going to ntate Santu's place. They're bringing the boys who will go to initiation school with him, and they're driving a bull to his place for a feast."

When we finished climbing I went down the hill to Witchdoctor Santu's house. It was the same cinder block house surrounded by thatch-roofed huts, with a stone corral nearby, with dirt paths lined by giant aloes, criss-crossed by grassy patches, where Principal Tsita had taken me on my first day in Tšoeneng, where I had seen the group of new men who'd just returned from months up the mountain and where I'd met Chief Thabo and been fed a goat leg covered in flies. Everything had seemed so enchanting on that day. I hadn't been allowed to see the initiates from the front. I had to sit with the women and watch them from the side. But I had visited Witchdoctor Santu often at his house since then and got to know him and during my second year another group of boys was initiated, and when they returned from the mountain Witchdoctor Santu allowed me to have a man from the village use my camera to photograph the faces of the new men while they sang. In the pictures their faces were expressionless, like they'd just been through something up on the mountain which they hadn't processed. And then, when a third group came down from the mountain at the beginning of 2006, Witchdoctor Santu allowed me to stand in front of the initiates and photograph and video their faces myself. I felt privileged. For some reason Witchdoctor Santu had taken a liking to me, and he allowed me to do things that uninitiated men, whether Basotho or foreign, were not supposed to do.

He came to Ngoana Jesu from time to time to visit me. He always came during classes, and he sometimes sent a student to find my classroom and call me out of the middle of a lesson so we could hang out. He had the authority that allowed him to do that. And then he sometimes invited me to ride his horse for a bit. And then sometimes he gave me a Sesotho music CD he wanted me to hear. Once he joined me and the other teachers in the staffroom and he said, "I'm going to take ntate Thabang up the mountain this year to teach him the secret things."

"No you won't!" said Principal Tsita. "I'll accuse you before the chief!"

They actually got along well, Principal Tsita and Witchdoctor Santu. Before Principal Tsita came to Tšoeneng, Ngoana Jesu had a rule forbidding the admission, or readmission, of students who went up the mountain with him for initiation. It was seen as antithetical to the education they were to receive at this Catholic secondary school, and boys who had been initiated had the reputation of being troublemakers, fighters. But Principal Tsita decided to allow initiates back in, students like Masopha and Ntheka and Sepheche and many others, and my experience with them was that they were some of the most studious and courteous pupils. Principal Tsita always said that she thought Santu ran an orderly initiation school where the boys learned respect, something that wasn't said about all initiation schools.

Witchdoctor Santu never took me up the mountain for initiation, but he was serious about teaching me certain things. I came home from a weekend away once and the hostelers told me that while I was gone one of Santu's men had come to school asking for me, looking to fetch me because Santu was teaching a new group of initiates to stick fight and he wanted me to join them. I always wished I hadn't missed that opportunity.

This day at Witchdoctor Santu's house was a new experience. It was not like the celebration for newly initiated men that I had attended on my first day in the village. Today Tšoeneng villagers—men and women, boys and girls—were wishing a group of boys farewell *before* they went up the mountain for initiation. *Bashemaneng*, "at the boys," it was called. They were called boys until they came back down from the mountain. "They ardently long for the hour when they shall be forever delivered from the detestable appellation of *bashemane*, which exposes them to incessant raillery, stigmatizes them as unfit for all the rational business of life, and renders them real pariahs," wrote Eugene Casalis in his memoir. Being considered a boy in Lesotho has always been shameful.

Initiated men from Tšoeneng and from Kolo and other nearby villages were sending off their sons and younger brothers to be taught by Witchdoctor Santu. Each group of men had arrived together from different directions to deliver boys from their village to the *bashemaneng* feast, and they wore distinct blankets and beanies so as to set them apart from other groups. The Kolo guys wore red blankets and argyle beanies, and I saw Masopha among them. In a dirt area in front of Witchdoctor Santu's corral the groups of men were taking turns dancing in unison and singing in front of one another. They held their *molamus* up, they marched toward another group, then backed away. A different group then marched and sang toward them, then backed away. It looked like taunting. I wasn't sure how friendly the different groups were or whether a fight might break out. Initiated men were united when they were around men who hadn't gone up the mountain, but among other initiated men they often formed smaller cliques with those who had been circumcised on the mountain the same season and lived in the same *mophato*— hut—with them. Sharing that experience had made them like brothers.

Masopha was stomping and singing and waving his stick with his brothers from Kolo. He stomped forward with his group, and as he passed he called out to me, "Come sing with us, sir!" I was surprised. An invitation to join the initiated men? Listening to the deeply pitched songs always entranced me. And I had practiced singing with my voice really deep for years now. Here was my chance. But I shook my head. I didn't know all the words to the song. Worse than being a boy and standing on the sidelines watching the men sing would be to try to join them prematurely and have everyone see that you didn't know the words and look foolish. It was like the day I refused the invitation to play *morabaraba* with the men on the rocks. Better to be patient and hide your inadequacies.

The women and girls around me shrieked. They scattered in different directions. I saw a bull. It had jumped over the stone wall of Witchdoctor Santu's corral. It faced my way. It pivoted left, then back at me, confused. Then initiated men ran toward it with their *molamus*. The bull ran from them and they chased it down a path away from me.

As soon as my shoulders slackened and I started breathing again, the men and the bull appeared coming back toward me. Dozens of men surrounded the bull, striking it with their *molamus* over and over again, stopping it in its tracks. They may have been trying to subdue the beast, or play with it, or make it angry. The way they hit it, I couldn't tell. They eventually drove it around the corral to the opening and secured the gate once it was inside.

The crowd of women and girls and boys reassembled into a circle and the men resumed their singing and dancing in the center. A couple of village girls came up to me and asked why I hadn't run with them when the bull faced our way. I had remained standing in place. "Do you not fear it?"

I had been lost in my thoughts of being a man or not being a man. "No," I said. "I don't fear it."

"What if it charges you?"

"I'll ride it."

Actually, beside me was a wall of giant aloes, and after the girls shrieked and fled I thought not to follow them but rather to just slip into a pocket between the big plants and hide there and hopefully the bull would run past. Maybe I wasn't ready to join the initiated men and sing, but neither was I going to join the girls and run screaming.

The bull leapt over the stone wall again, and this time it came rocking straight my way, no hesitation. It rammed horns first into the very pocket between the aloes that I'd planned on hiding in. The bull couldn't back up: it had stuck itself into the tangle of spiky green tongues. Men beat the bull, driving it deeper into the aloes. The beast was wedged in, snorting, stamping. I imagined myself under its hoofs, mangled. But I hadn't stepped into the pocket. When the bull ran my way, although I hadn't screamed, I had run with the girls.

And I just kept running, south, all the way through the fields to school and home.

I thought about why I'd fled and who I was in Tšoeneng. I was no longer a boy, and I was different from the girls, but I wasn't quite a man and I never would be. I sensed I had reached a limit with my growing up in Africa.

The following day I spoke to Lerato, my former student, about how the feast had ended. He said that the men eventually killed the bull and ate it together with the boys who would soon be heading up the mountain for circumcision. It was a traditional meal to bid the boys farewell before they spent six secluded months becoming men.

MASOPHA WAS ALREADY A MAN, in the sense that he had been circumcised and gone through initiation school. And he had also graduated from Ngoana Jesu and earned his COSC, the high school certificate. So he had gotten his Sesotho and his Western educations. He was a complete adult. Yet he didn't know what to do with himself next.

After boys came down from the mountain they were considered ready to marry, and many of them did marry soon after initiation. But Masopha had no one in his sights. After students finished high school they sometimes tried to get into one of the few colleges in the country. But Masopha hadn't passed his high school exams very well. He was a responsible young man with a decent work ethic, but he wasn't gifted academically. He didn't have the grades he needed to get into Lerotholi Polytechnic in order to pursue his stubborn dream of becoming an engineer. He seemed to be acknowledging that when he came to my house one day and said, "I am not satisfied, sir. I have Form E, but I am just looking after my father's cattle. What can be your advice?"

I related too well to Masopha's feeling of floating. Young adulthood had been hard for me to navigate too. Like Masopha finishing high school, when I graduated from college I became the most educated member of my family, and I felt expected to parlay that education into a solid job. I was making surfboards. I wasn't satisfied by that, and in my time off I stressed about finding a better career to pursue. And also like Masopha, I had no one in my sights to marry. I did join Peace Corps in order to experience living in a strange culture and to try to learn a second language, but there was truth in saying that Peace Corps was also an escape.

I forgot all about my future when I came to Tšoeneng. Here my mind was so focused on getting something to eat in the next hour, or learning some new Sesotho words before I visited the chief, that there was no consideration beyond tomorrow. It was what I needed. Listening to Masopha worry about his direction into adult life reminded me of the escape that living in Tšoeneng provided. I was so grateful for it.

Masopha came some days later and told me he had applied for a job with the Lesotho Mounted Police. (In the not too distant past, the police had no vehicles and all rode horseback.) Did he see the destiny? Masopha, who had been head of the school's discipline committee and nicknamed Officer Mokhele, was applying to be a cop. I was eager to help. I wanted so badly for Masopha to find a job and direction and satisfaction. The police recruiter had given him a sheet of questions to drill for an upcoming interview, and we talked them through. "Why do you want to be a police officer? What are the duties of a police officer? What are the challenges for police officers in a democratic state?" He said he would visit the following week and tell me how the interview went.

IT WAS SEPTEMBER NOW and soon this year's Form E class would be taking those same exams Masopha hadn't passed well. And the Form C class—Lemeko and 'Malefa's class—too, would take their own national exams. The second half of the year revolved around these tests—the students studying for them and the teachers neglecting other classes in order to spend maximum time with the C's and E's.

Even though I wouldn't be leaving until December, a meeting between the teachers and the parents was held where it was decided they would throw me a farewell feast before the exams started in early October. In the weeks before the feast, little teaching of any classes was going on. Students spent most of their time in groups in various corners of the school yard practicing dances and songs and dramas for my farewell. Women had started brewing sorghum beer in the kitchen. I was bored in the staffroom, so I wandered over to watch a group of students, but 'me 'Malimpho caught me and scolded me, "Hey, ntate. What do you want here? You'll see it on the feast day." The next morning Principal Tsita shuffled over to my desk in the staffroom and gently asked, "Ntate Greg, can I expel you from school?"

I went up to Maseru and spent the next two days at the Peace Corps Transit House. I knew the feast they were preparing was big, and I knew that at every feast there were speeches, so I spent most of each day at the T-House reflecting on my time in Tšoeneng and honing some Sesotho words I could offer if called upon.

Throughout the years Tšoeneng people had been so good to me. All my safety worries were unnecessary in the end. No one ever stole from me. No one ever murdered me.

I wanted my speech to prove my appreciation for that. I knew how seriously they took speeches. Every morning a handful of students was required to give a short speech during the school's morning assembly, and every Thursday after school there was a formal debate. The students who held their own on those stages were praised. But many of the students didn't understand English well, and barely anyone in Tšoeneng did, so my speech would have to be in Sesotho.

With this speech I would be representing myself and my whole three years. Beyond that, I had a sense that the speech would represent Peace Corps volunteers. I wanted to bolster the reputation of Peace Corps as best I could.

I also felt that I represented America in this little corner of the world. I knew I was the first American that people in Tšoeneng had gotten to know. I might be the last, but if someone from Tšoeneng did meet another American down the road I wanted to be sure I had laid a positive foundation for that meeting.

And like it or not, my skin's being white meant that I affected Tšoeneng people's impression of others who looked like me. They would probably treat any whites who came through Tšoeneng based largely on their experiences with me. More generally, I was a foreigner. Foreigners could be mercenary, like the Chinese, or condescending, like the Western aid workers and expatriates who rarely left the capital. I tried to be an interested and respectful and assimilating foreigner. Was it going too far to think that the tracks I laid in Tšoeneng would influence the reception of every foreigner who came through this village after me?

With so much riding on my speech, if I was asked to give one, I could have cheated and asked for help, but I never considered it. I wanted the speech to deserve whatever reception it got because they were genuinely my words, just as I wanted to have earned the relationships I developed because they were not influenced by money or donations. I worked through some drafts and finally decided to keep the quantity down, so I wouldn't lose my place while I was speaking in front of so many people, in my second language. I couldn't use notes. That was taboo. Basotho see notes as a sign of an immature mind. Notes are a memory aid for children. With the speech on the short side then, I would focus on keeping the quality high.

I worked out some thoughts that were my own, and that were genuine, but were also targeted at my audience. I felt I had gained over the years a sense of the elements that Basotho desired to hear in a speech. Before I concluded, as a back up, I asked the T-House housekeeper, a Mosotho woman named 'me Eunicia, to proofread the text for grammar errors. She said it was fine, and I hoped she wasn't trying to protect my feelings.

I ARRIVED BACK AT SCHOOL the morning of October 14. As I walked on the path to school a group of parents and teachers and students ran circles around me holding a banner that read: *"Tsela tšoeu, Ngoana Jesu ha e hole"*—White road, Child Jesus is not far. A road being white meant a road of good luck in Sesotho.

Sheep had been slaughtered, lots of sorghum beer had been brewed, and a big tent had been put up in the middle of the school yard. We all gathered under and around the tent. In the chairs under the tent were the VIPs: teachers, the chief, a few parents, some Peace Corps volunteer friends.

A group of eight female students started things off with Mokopu, the pumpkin dance. They formed a circle and shuffled clockwise and tapped thin white sticks on the ground and spun around their sticks as they sang together. It was the first of many dances performed by girls. In the next one some other girls got onto their knees and waved around *machoba*, cow tails, like the one Chief Thabo had given me. But the main move of this dance, called Mokhibo, was a jerking of the shoulders back and forth so that the girls' breasts shook. They shook for ten minutes straight.

Then it was the boys' turn. They started with Ntlamu, where a group of four, including Masopha, wore orange reflective mineworkers' vests and loincloths and lifted their bare feet high and stomped them in unison on the dirt. They did so in a complex rhythm that was directed by one of the boys blowing a whistle. It was the most popular male dance and I had spent many evenings up at the hostel, out in the fields and on the road trying to do Ntlamu with the boys, though the more difficult moves eluded me. To accentuate the stomping, the dancers wore tassels around their calves and shakers made of small tin cans or cow scrotums filled with beans fastened to their ankles, so that each stomp was flying ribbons of color and rattles slamming down on the ground. It was hue, motion, and music. Billows of dust rose with each landing. A large group of boys kneeled nearby and clapped for rhythm and sang in very deep voices (What else?) to support the dancers. I knew their song, so under my breath I sang along: *"Khotsong, bo-ntate. Rea le lumelisa"*—Hello, men. We greet you.

Following Ntlamu, another group of boys did a modern sort of hip hop dance imported from the urban townships of South Africa. It was like break dancing, and these boys were called Mapantsula.

There were group dances too, one with twenty boys and girls in a mock wedding celebration. For this there was not singing but music played on an accordion, backed by a drummer. The drum set was a large red and blue tin can on which was printed "USA, Not to be sold or exchanged." In its first life, the can had been a donation of cooking oil from the United States Agency for International Development. Animal skin was stretched over the top of the can, and for a cymbal there were two upright sticks fastened to the can holding a wire between them on which bottle caps had been strung. The bottle caps clinked each time the drummer tapped them with his sticks made from tire tread. Resourceful.

In between acts, Witchdoctor Santu provided music for the crowd, using his stereo powered by Motsie the shop owner's generator. Ntate Lemphane was the master of ceremonies. "It is time for gifts," he said. Principal Tsita put a chair from one of the classrooms in the dirt, facing the VIP tent, encircled by the crowd and told me to sit. "Form A, bring your gift for ntate Greg," said ntate Lemphane. A girl came forward and presented me with a box wrapped in red paper. I received it with two hands and then tore it open and pulled out a cassette tape of Le Lumme Ha Leponesa, a Sesotho music group. Though I bought CDs of Sesotho music, most Basotho still bought tapes.

"Hold it up so everyone can see," said Principal Tsita. I held up the tape and the crowd cheered. "Form B, bring your gift." Richard, the boy who led the chase for Motšilisi's kidnappers, came up with another box wrapped in red paper. I tore it open to find a pair of slippers made from the hide of an antelope. After I held them up and the crowd applauded, Principal Tsita whispered that I should put them on. I squeezed my feet in: they were a little too small. The straps over my big toes were sprouting with tan and white fur now.

"Maform C!" From them I was given a DVD of Sesotho music videos by a singer named Chakela. I hadn't even known they made such a thing. I knew no one in Lesotho who owned a DVD player, but I was glad they had found a DVD for me. I could play it back in America. As for the cassette tape of Le Lumme Ha Leponesa, I guess I would have to buy a used player at a thrift store. Did they sell new ones in America anymore? I held the DVD up and the crowd yelled its approval, then Principal Tsita took it and held it up higher and pirouetted so all could see. Everyone oohed and aahed some more. The Form D's gave me a t-shirt that said "Lesotho" on the front. The Form E's gave me a CD of more Sesotho music—the students knew how much I'd grown to like Mantša and the other Sesotho singers. I was always

asking them to help me understand the idiomatic lyrics. Each class had collected money and bought the gifts on their own.

A teacher from St. Peter Claver primary school gave me a gift, and so did a teacher from the primary school in Ha Letsie, on the other side of Tšoeneng Mountain. Chief Thabo gave me a gift, as did ntate Khiba, a man from Tšoeneng who owned a taxi and sometimes let me drive it. The Ngoana Jesu teachers presented me with a yellow Basotho blanket that had maize cobs printed on it. I had long ago mentioned that the design was my favorite, and they remembered. Principal Tsita and 'me 'Malimpho asked me to put the blanket on for people to see. "Where is a pin?" 'me 'Malimpho asked into the crowd. "Who has a pin we can use to put on the blanket?" No one was coming up with one, so I draped the blanket over my shoulders and put the opening on the side and tucked the ends into a bulky knot just like Masopha had taught me way back when. And the crowd started cheering. "Like a shepherd!" said 'me 'Malimpho.

The table beside me was covered with boxes and wrapping paper and gifts. People had spent so much, and I knew very well that they didn't have so much to spend. Parents had a hard time buying their children books, let alone gifts for me.

Ntate Lemphane announced that it was time for speeches. Chief Thabo stood before everyone and said nice words, as did a teacher from the primary school, and ntate Khiba the taxi driver, and then Lerato, my former Form E student spoke. Eight students from his class, last year's Form E's, had come for the feast and stood beside him, including Mpatsi. It was the first time I had seen her since she disappeared from school after her supposed beating by a taxi conductor during exams the previous year. I had trouble paying attention to Lerato's words, and I had trouble paying attention to the words of the next speech by Lefa, a current Form C boy, but more than thinking of Mpatsi it was mostly because I was feeling overwhelmed by all the gifts and now the words of appreciation. They were saying I had helped the village, and that I liked people, and that I had an open spirit. Principal Tsita took the stage on behalf of the school staff. "You left your home and lived with us for three years. Thank your mother for lending you to us." She looked to the crowd. "When he came he had nothing here," she said pointing at her cheeks. "But now look at his beard everyone. We are sending him home as a man!"

And then Ntate Lemphane called to me. "Perhaps now we can have a word from ntate Greg, and maybe in Sesotho."

The crowd affirmed: *"Eh"*—Yes. I was glad I had prepared something. All got quiet as I walked out from under the VIP tent to the middle of the circle and turned around. Students and villagers surrounded me on all sides, probably four or five hundred of them. There were Ngoana Jesu students in blue uniforms and St. Peter Claver Primary students in maroon. This speech was my most important moment. It was my chance to show everyone at once my gratitude for their hospitality, and that it was true, they were "sending me home as a man." In my new antelope fur slippers and with my hands clasped in front of me I said with as deft a tongue as I could, *"Leha ke sa tsebe Sesotho hantle, ke tla leka"*—Even though I don't know Sesotho well, I'll try.

The crowd: *"Eh."*

I remembered to speak slowly too, so that I could keep my voice low, manly.

"Ach, ha ke tsebe na nka re'ng. Lilemo tsena tse tharo tse fetileng li ne li le monate haholo-holo. Batho ba Tšoeneng ba ne ba ntšoere hantle, le matichere, le bana ba sekolo ba ntšoere hantle. Ka 'nete, lilemo tsena ke ne ke thabile ho feta bophelong ba ka. Ke tla re, ke lebohile. Kea leboha. Kea leboha."—

"Well, I don't know what I can say. These past three years have been wonderful. I've been treated so well by everyone at Ngoana Jesu, the teachers and the students, and by everyone in Tšoeneng. And truthfully, I've been happier over these three years than at any other time in my life. Thank you, thank you, thank you."

I heard a woman say, *"Eh, ntate."* But everyone else remained silent. Even the children kept surprisingly quiet for me, quieter than they had for Chief Thabo's speech. For some of them whom I didn't interact with often, it was still such a curious thing to hear a foreigner speak Sesotho.

"Nke ke ka le lebala,"—I won't forget you guys, I continued. I wanted to say more than just thank you.

"Ho hang. Kea le tšepisa. Hobane ntho eo ke tsebang ke ena: Ho ea ka

makhoro ha se ho lahlana."—

"It can't happen. Because the one thing I know is this: To go off on different paths is not to abandon each other."

"Hele! Ululululululululuh!" The crowd exploded. The ululation and applause startled me. Some women waved their hands. I noticed a shepherd in his blanket toward the back with a wide smile.

I had quoted a well-known proverb. That must have been the spark. To use a proverb like that one was to use "deep Sesotho"— *Sesotho sa 'Mankhothe.* If you could do that, then you knew the language. And of course, if you knew Sesotho, then you knew the place, and the people. And you have done what you were supposed to do.

The crowd of Tšoeneng people and teachers and students cheered so loudly for my proverb that I felt a little guilty. I had lifted it from a Mantša song. So many times while cooking *papa* and *moroho* I had listened to my Mantša CD and sung along. And then while hiking to the boulders to climb, while working in my *moroho* plot, while walking to my toilet, I had sung those lyrics. They rolled off my tongue without effort. I couldn't even help but finish my speech with the song's next line, which was in essence an interpretation of the proverb: *"Re tla kopana hape"*—We will meet again, I said.

With that last part, in my heart I felt I was also making a promise. I wasn't just a visitor that would leave in a month never to be seen again.

People disbursed and food was served. I ate mutton stew and then sat down with a group of old men. Usually this group was gathered at the bar next to Motsie's shop, but today the men were passing their jugs of sorghum beer around at Ngoana Jesu Secondary School, at my farewell feast, right next to the staffroom. I felt I could at last capitulate and drink with them. I had always wanted to do so, but I knew it wouldn't be good for students to see me do so. I was passed a half-full makeshift cup, a plastic jug with the top cut off. The beer looked like cream of wheat. It went down smooth, as there was no carbonation, though it was grainy and tasted much more like a meal than a beverage. I passed it on and it came around again. The old men asked when I was leaving

Tšoeneng and *why* I was leaving Tšoeneng, if I enjoyed the place so much. "It's not because I don't like you guys, it's just that my family misses me, and my teaching contract is finished."

'Me 'Makopano then called me into the kitchen. She was one of the ladies who cooked our school lunches, and she directed me through the kitchen into the attached store room. Inside were three women in their underwear. This was one last going-away present.

Remember that the path I usually took down the mountain from rock climbing each evening passed by a stone hut near 'me 'Makopano's house, and from that hut I often heard women's voices chanting and drum beats and metal rattling. The hut had no windows, but I slowed when I passed it so I could listen for a bit. Sometimes the women caught me dragging my heels as I walked by and shooed me away.

This was their gift: to let me see what the ladies did in the hut. It was hot and sticky inside the store room. There were three women in white underwear and white bras. One woman had a whistle, which she blew, and the group began dancing. 'Me 'Masechaba, the other school lunch cook, beat on a drum and a few other old women chanted to support the movements of the dancing ladies. There was really only one movement, though: the lifting of the buttocks. The women put their legs together, straightened their knees and kicked up their rear ends at the same time over and over again. To accentuate the movement they wore many bottle caps strung together and tied around their waists so that the rump thrusts also made a rattle. Fluffy tutus made from nylon grain sacks hung over the bottle caps and those tutus flew up to reveal the women's brown bottoms. I wasn't sure what to do with my eyes, but I thought that if I didn't stare at the tutus and the rattles and the bottoms I would seem unattracted or ungrateful. They wanted me to watch, right? But how aggressively should I watch? They danced for me for a full thirty minutes.

THE SCHOOL YEAR ENDED in a whisper. The feast had happened, and then the exams started, and so the Form C's and E's disappeared. Then the rest of the students finished their internal final exams, and we teachers were left marking and writing up grades on an empty November campus.

I spent much of that marking time in the fresh air in a chair in front of the staffroom, and in between check marks with the red pen I chatted with the other teachers, particularly ntate Lemphane. He was a quiet guy, not just compared to the women. He stayed inside his house after school, except when he played soccer with the boys or when he was watering his vegetable plot. His wife came to live with him, and she had their first child this year, and they brought him onto their porch to play but still they spent most of the evenings after school indoors. But after chasing the kidnappers down with ntate Lemphane, I started to feel like I got an insight into his character. He had been the first to attack, to throw a rock at Black Shirt. And I wanted to know more. I asked him about his youth. He grew up about a day's walk south of Tšoeneng, close to the Mohokare River, which formed the border between Lesotho and the Free State province of South Africa. "When the Mohokare was low, my agemates and I drove our cattle across it to graze on the Boer farms," he said. Across the Mohokare were large tracts of land owned by whites. On the Lesotho side of the Mohokare the pastures for grazing were communal and governed by the local chief, and picked over by way too many animals—cattle, sheep, goats.

"The Boers would be so angry when they saw us," he said. "They would chase us in their vehicles and sometimes even with helicopters and they would shoot at us. If they caught us they would beat! But they were so stupid—we could see them from far and we could cross the river before they reached us."

Doing what he had to, especially in winter when the grass was barely growing, in order to keep his cattle alive, he didn't see anything wrong with grazing on Boer land, land that had once been part of the Basotho kingdom. I imagined the white farmers being so frustrated with these little African shepherds who wouldn't stop sneaking over to steal their grass, who wouldn't stop trespassing and breaking the law. It was a strange circle of history. The Boers had forced Basotho off land they'd been using for centuries, but Basotho still outnumbered them and continued to get little bits of revenge.

Ntate Lemphane loved the news. I gave him the *Newsweek* magazines that Peace Corps sent me, and he sometimes asked me geographical or political questions related to the articles. At that time in Lesotho, there was an act before parliament that interested us both. It was called the Marriage Act. By tradition, when a man died his possessions were inherited by his oldest son, not his wife. (The oldest son was so significant in fact that it was said that a wife was not truly a wife until she bore her first son.) But the act would deem that a husband's assets go to his wife instead. The act would affect other areas of life as well. In Lesotho, if a woman wanted to open a bank account she needed her husband's authorizing signature. The act would change this too. It proposed to generally make things more equal between a husband and wife.

"This is a thing for the white people," said ntate Lemphane. "The United Nations tells our parliament to do these kinds of things. Then they bring them to black people in the rural areas and these people don't even understand what they mean. A man and a woman are equal? Tšoeneng people will laugh!"

I liked that ntate Lemphane had become more expressive around me, and I thought of it as being because after three years we knew and trusted each other. But highs were always followed by lows, even to the end of my time in Lesotho. I took a taxi ride that month that reminded me that people outside Tšoeneng and Ngoana Jesu, my little home corner of the country, didn't know me and didn't necessarily like or trust me.

I was riding in the back, heading home to Tšoeneng from Maseru when the taxi pulled over at a junction called Masianokeng and the conductor opened the sliding door but the prospective rider defied the conductor's invitation to sit in the back and instead opened the front passenger door himself. He hopped in next to the driver. Then he turned around to scan the load of passengers behind him. He noticed me and shouted, "Hey Daniel!" I didn't respond. I had known he was trouble from the minute I saw his hair. He had cornrows, which was something only women did in Lesotho.

He shouted again, "Hey Daniel! Hey you man! *Lekhooa!*— White guy!"

I looked out the window. Sometimes that word *lekhooa* was

just a word of description, and people spoke it as I walked by in a place where they didn't know my name, like they were identifying me, like they would if they saw an unusual bird fly by, "Parrot!" Sometimes, however, people did use the word *lekhooa* in an offensive way. It became clear through context when someone was just identifying me and when someone was name calling.

Since I didn't react to the guy's provocation he asked the taxi driver about me. "Do you know this *lekhooa*? Does he know Sesotho?" The driver said I did, and so then Cornrows asked me why I wouldn't talk to him. I stayed quiet and continued to stare out the window. He shouted at me, *"Ua ipoza!"*

That was not Sesotho. It was Setsotsi, a conglomeration of slang used by thugs from Johannesburg and other South African cities, crafted by mixing together Sesotho with Zulu, Afrikaans, English and other languages, even Spanish. Young men in Lesotho sometimes threw around Setsotsi words in an effort to sound urban and cool, and I had heard *"Ua ipoza"* before. It just meant, "You're ignoring me," as in the question, "You think you're better than me?"

I *was* ignoring Cornrows, but not because I thought I was better than him. I ignored him because there could never be a valuable conversation with a Mosotho who didn't greet you. Basotho took greetings very seriously, and for someone to disregard greeting you was a blatant sign of disrespect. Nonetheless, Cornrows only became more determined to get my attention. He turned all the way around in his seat and started hurling insults. I didn't understand a lot of his Setsotsi slang, but among the words that jumped out at me were "white" and "Boer" and "love money." I tried my best to feign deafness and boredom.

After a few minutes of insults Cornrows ran out of breath, and when he did I rotated my head to stare out the other window and I caught a glimpse of his eyes. They were bloodshot. It was the last weekend of the month. Everyone in Lesotho got paid at the end of the month and bank lines in Maseru stacked up for blocks. Miners and others who worked in South Africa made their visits home. People shopped and spent most of their money that very weekend. Men filled the bars, buying quart after quart of beer.

Cornrows caught his breath and resumed his rant, looking straight at me, and this round I heard "Chinese" and the English word "fuck." Not one of the dozen taxi passengers told Cornrows to shut up. I couldn't imagine riding in a bus in America with the whole busload allowing a drunk to berate a lone foreigner. This realization just after gushing about how hospitable and protective people in Tšoeneng had been to me.

Cornrows shouted at my face for twenty minutes until he was dropped off at Ha Mantšebo. When I got off at the school junction in Tšoeneng the driver finally spoke. "Hey Thabang, everything's OK, yeah?" A late and feeble response. It was a driver I didn't know as well as other drivers, but I was still terribly disappointed that he had tolerated Cornrows. I stepped out the sliding door. "We'll beat that guy up next time," he said.

I walked away from the taxi on the path to school and I felt abandoned like I had way back when I was mugged. But I didn't let the feeling linger. Who cares if a drunk from Maseru insults you? And who cares if people you don't really know let it happen? Ntate Lemphane wouldn't have sat by and let Cornrows boil all over me like that. Chief Thabo wouldn't have, Witchdoctor Santu wouldn't have, Principal Tsita wouldn't have, my students wouldn't have. Right?

PEACE CORPS CALLED ME up to Maseru one more time for exit administrative tasks at the very beginning of December. I took a medical exam there, and though I was given a clean bill of health—no HIV, no TB, nothing—the nurse still handed me a form: *Authorization for Payment of Medical Services*. She explained to me that the U.S. government was offering a voucher that would pay a psychologist or psychiatrist of my choosing for "three one-hour sessions" once I returned to America.

Skimming the voucher, I also noticed a box that described my "Problems/Symptoms." There the nurse had written, "Lived in Africa for 3 years as a Peace Corps Volunteer."

Did she know what I'd been going through or what? It was a mountain and then a valley, it was confidence and then bewilderment. Whatever it was, it was engrossing. I had gone all in. And now I was to start extracting myself. Maybe that's what the "Problems/Symptoms" referred to. I had been brought to tears getting settled into Tšoeneng. If adapting to life back in America was going to be anything like adapting to Tšoeneng had been, then the nurse was right, counseling could help.

I got off the taxi from that final trip to the capital and crossed the road to walk the dirt path to Ngoana Jesu. I looked over the timeless scene below. The volcanic Kolo Mountain loomed across the river. The Tsoaing crept westward without a sound, through the expansive valley it had carved. The fields were budding with the traditional crops of maize and sorghum. Ngoana Jesu Secondary School was just a cluster of tin-roofed buildings baking in the sun. In my life I could never live in a more stunning setting. Nothing had seemed to change out here among the mountain schools. I walked through the school gate. I passed the water pump and the girls' hostel and approached my front door. But my *moroho* … it was gone! Only white stems poked out of the soil. Upon a closer look I saw that it was the work of animals. I guessed cattle. Now what was I going to eat over my last couple days?

I was peeved, but quickly I settled down and recalibrated to decide that I liked the fact that my cabbage and Swiss chard and *sepaile* and turnip greens had been devoured by grazing cattle.

In 2004 I had arrived to no garden at all. I cultivated the land and learned to grow *moroho* pretty well, but now I was leaving and I would depart with the land being as wild as it was three years before. I never aimed to leave a mark on this place.

Since marking tests and giving grades were now finished, the teachers had all gone home too, and I was alone again on the school grounds with a few days left to move out of my house—save ntate Makoanyane, who still showed up in the evening to watch the school through the night. He rolled a cigarette with my newspaper and spilled tobacco on my floor. And he said to me, "Do you have *mofao*—provisions for the road?" Whenever a Mosotho travels, he takes food for the trip: there are no mini-marts or fast-food restaurants along the way in Lesotho. Ntate Makoanyane knew that I would be returning to America by airplane, and I had told him the airplane people would feed me, but he insisted on sending me with the best *mofao* he knew. "My hen just had chicks. They're still small now, but if they're big enough by the time you fly away I will give you one. You will slaughter it and cook it and take it with you." I imagined being served an airline meal, and then pulling from my own bag a supplementary couple pieces of ntate Makoanyane's chicken.

The next day at my trash pit I was burning my few leftover belongings. I had already given away some things. I gave a pair of pants to Lefike, a blanket to Lemeko's grandmother, a shirt to Moraba, my winter jacket to Principal Tsita, a pair of shoes to ntate Lemphane. And I had packed some other things to take back to America: my wall map of Lesotho that had sunflower cooking oil splattered on it from years of cooking *moroho*, my Basotho blankets, Chief Thabo's *lechoba*, the little green Sesotho book. While I stood next to the fire turning my English lesson planning notebooks to ash and incinerating expired medicine that Peace Corps had given me in a medical kit way back in 2004, Masopha showed up followed by his dog, China. At first I thought Masopha had named his dog China as a slight to the Chinese. But he said the sheepdog mutt with wiry hair was named so simply because of its color. The dog was white, just like the color of Chinese skin, according to him.

His interview with the police had gone OK, but he had yet to be notified about being hired. He had been looking after his father's animals and lounging at home again, dreaming of where he'd like to take the rest of his life.

I asked him about my garden. Only his father's cattle and those of Chief Thabo were allowed by Principal Tsita to graze on the school grounds. "Did your cattle eat my *moroho*?"

"Sir?"

"You see my *moroho* plot? It's been eaten by animals. I know it was your cattle!" I really didn't care.

"I haven't been looking after the cattle. Ramphume has."

"Ooh. Then tell your brother I'm going to make him pay."

Masopha looked at the fire where some threadbare clothes of mine were now being consumed and said, "You're burning your *mophato*."

"Yeah," I thought. "I am." When boys had finished with

initiation up on the mountain, they stripped off their clothes and lay them in the hut which they had built and lived in. There they had entered as boys, and now they were exiting as men. They torched the *mophato* as a sign of being done with their youth. It was the end of an era in their lives.

Masopha was right: I was ready at last to come down from the mountains of Lesotho. When I had arrived three years prior I was like a child, not knowing how to talk, or wash my clothes, or cook *papa*. But I learned how to live in this world. I grew up. I didn't know what kind of man I had now become—not exactly a Mosotho man—though I did now have a poise, a calmness, a confidence when my feet were on the ground in this country.

Masopha helped stoke the fire, the burning of my *mophato*. My things turned to flame and smoke and rose into the sky, disappearing essentially. Someday soon I would be in America, that other of my dual worlds, and I would be swept up by the pace and worries there, where I would struggle to even picture Masopha and his dog China, his rubber boots and his *molamu* and his cattle.

In the fire some photographs were now feeling the heat, curling and melting into one another, and Masopha moved them away from the flames. "Are you losing these photos?" he asked. "Can I have them?" They were doubles that I didn't need, of me with American friends and relatives. I told Masopha he could take whatever he wanted from the fire. Maybe I didn't mind leaving a trace in Lesotho, for a warmth came to my chest when I thought of Masopha later showing people those photos and talking of our times.

ACKNOWLEDGEMENTS

I AM GRATEFUL to the generous folks who read parts of this book and gave useful feedback: Erik Johnson, Jeff Williams, Nate Denver, Tim Pfau, Keith Jackson, Dean Nelson, Kate Johnson, Jamie Karnik, and Rethabile Masilo.

Thanks to Julie Rubtchinsky for help with the cover. I look forward to paying her back with crates of avocados.

My family never quit writing me letters and drawing me pictures to put on my walls while I was in Tšoeneng. They also never quit asking when the book was going to be finished. I needed the harassment. My brother Matt, in particular, helped me keep a website and blog, and I'm so grateful for his never ending assistance with all things technological.

Peace Corps brought 24 of us education volunteers into Lesotho in 2003, and I formed many lasting friendships out of that group. I also found volunteers from other groups to hike off the map with, make tortillas with, speak natural English with, share stories with, and get teaching advice from. I couldn't imagine experiencing Lesotho alongside cooler people.

I appreciate the friends and family who took the time and money to visit me in Tšoeneng. My mom and Aunt Lisa came in 2004, and friends Drew Card, Katie Card, and John Ormond came in 2006. Listening to their observations taught me a lot.

Since moving out of my house in Tšoeneng I've visited Lesotho and South Africa a number of times, for periods of a few weeks up to many months. I would like to thank some of the many people who were especially hospitable during those visits: Lemeko Molefi, 'Matšepo Tsita, 'Malimpho Ramosoeu, Becky Banton, Clement Lephoto, Masopha Mokhele, Lerato Thaki, 'Mapoloko Ramatseka, Garth and Yvonne Robinson, Ben Marsh and Sara Latrielle.

Not long after I left, three of the most important people in Tšoeneng passed away: Chief Thabo, Witchdoctor Santu, and the shop owner, ntate Motsie. They had all worked in the mines in South Africa, and they were all middle-aged. I felt their absence the next time I visited. Then again, there were still so many friendly and wonderful people in the village that I continued to feel at home, and I appreciate that. I hope Tšoeneng people find many things in this book to laugh at, but more importantly I hope that they feel like through it the wider world can gain an accurate glimpse into their part of Africa.

A handful of my students from Ngoana Jesu Secondary School have been accepted into the National University of Lesotho. They are studying tourism and public administration, environmental science and political science, and some are majoring in education. I'm proud of them, and I'm thankful to all of my students for patiently teaching me so many things, especially Sesotho. I pray that when the education majors become teachers they won't have to do as much learning on the job as I did.

Upon leaving Tšoeneng in December of 2006, I returned to the U.S. but could only stand it for a couple months. In part, I felt out of step, but more compelling was my need to get back to Ursula. She was a Peace Corps volunteer whom I'd met during my third year—her first—and she was living in the very rondavel where Nate had resided in Qacha's Nek. I decided to write an account of my time in Tšoeneng in book form, and Ursula and the Ramatseka family with whom she lived said I was welcome to return to Lesotho and stay with them to do my writing. Throughout 2007, Ursula left to teach school early each morning and I sat down to work at a table in her thatch-roofed hut. It made sense to be back and working in Qacha's Nek—still in Lesotho, yet somewhat removed from Tšoeneng. It also felt right to be working on a mature relationship with a girl; in a sense I was continuing the growing up I had done in Tšoeneng. Ursula and I came back to the U.S. together at the end of that year, and in 2010 we got married.

Developing our relationship's early days in Lesotho, while we were both volunteers and she was in Qacha's Nek and I was on the other side of the mountains in Tšoeneng, had its romantic side as well as its share of obstacles. Communication was a challenge. We couldn't speak by telephone, and the mail service was so unpredictable that letters between us sometimes took only three weeks to arrive, but a couple times arrived months after being sent. Because of that, every time we met we had to set a precise time and place for a subsequent meeting. Otherwise, we had lost touch. But I knew when I began to write *The Mountain School* that our relationship was another story; it didn't fit within the parameters I had set for the book, despite the fact that it began during the period of Part IV. Yet Ursula deserves much credit for the book ever coming to life. Beyond giving me that first place to write in Qacha's Nek, over the years she was my first editor, she put up with my incessant note-taking—even at the dinner table— and she cheered me to follow through with the publication. I thank her most of all.

PRONUNCIATION GUIDE

SOME SESOTHO WORDS are easy to sound out; others are not. Here are some words and names that are used often in the text, and that I thought might be challenging to pronounce. You'll notice that Sesotho almost always stresses the penultimate syllable. These renditions of the sounds aren't perfect—some sounds that Sesotho uses simply can't be represented with a group of Roman letters—but if you follow them you'll be close.

Khosi (KHOH-see) [*Kh* is the sound you make when you're clearing your throat.]

Lesotho (leh-SOO-too)

Maseru (mah-SEH-roo)

Masopha (mah-SOO-pah)

'Me (mmeh) [To pronounce the double *m*, just hang on the *m* sound for an extra millisecond.]

'Malimpho (mmah-DIM-poh) [When an *l* comes before an *i* or *o*, it is pronounced like a *d*. No one knows why the missionaries didn't just use *d's.*]

Mophato (moh-PAH-doh) [In Sesotho, the *t* has a sound between that of an English *t* and *d*. It's harder than an English *d* but softer than an English *t*. For a sound as hard as an English *t*, Sesotho uses *th*.]

Moshoeshoe (moh-SHWAY-shway)

Motsie (moh-TSEE-ay)

Ngoana Jesu (NGWAH-nah JAY-soo)

Ntate (n-DAH-day)

Thabang (tah-BAHNG)

Tšoeneng (tsh-way-NENG)

Pere (?)

Made in the USA
San Bernardino, CA
11 December 2017